Pagoda Dreamer

for Marlis

– all the best!

Judy Davis

Pagoda Dreamer

Judith March Davis

LANGDON STREET PRESS

Langdon Street Press
212 3rd Avenue North, Suite 290
Minneapolis, MN 55401
612.455.2293
www.langdonstreetpress.com

ISBN - 978-1-934938-90-4
ISBN - 1-934938-90-4
LCCN - 2009936438

Front cover image: Dorothy Rowe in Beihai Park, Beijing -- May, 1925. It is one of many photographs that Ben March took of his wife during their years together.
Back cover author photo credit: R. W. Barker and E. Taylor-Richards
Cover Design by Peter Honsberger
Typeset by Peggy LeTrent

Printed in the United States of America

Langdon
Street
Press

CONTENTS

PROLOGUE

幸运

"Writing letters is, for me, second best to seeing people. I can be quite happy writing. It is romantic and perhaps unreal, but I have found it a good game for times of loneliness, and a means of sharing high moments when no one is near to hear my words. Even though it is more difficult for you to write to me, because your domestic situation allows so little peace and quiet, you know I shall go on writing to you always, Precious, rambling on, raving about things that excite me, grumbling about small woes"

— Dorothy Rowe 1944

The box is large and flat — the sort that, years ago, department stores gave to customers who purchased coats. Pulling it out from under Lurry's bed, I see that it holds an overflowing jumble of letters. Excited, I call out to my cousin Bob.

As we freshly mourn the death of our unmarried aunt Louise Rowe (*nicknamed Lurry in the family*), he is helping to clear out her apartment. Bob, his brother and I are heirs to whatever she left behind.

"Look," I urge, "These letters are from my mother. I recognize her handwriting and the stationery of the typed ones. Lurry told me that she'd saved every letter her sister wrote to her — starting in 1920, when Lurry left China to come to college over here. Doré was back there, teaching. They must cover nearly 50 years."

"Wow — what a treasure," Bob says. "You may learn lots of family history…"

I assume so. My American mother, Dorothy Rowe (*who went by Doré after marriage*), was indelibly marked by living nearly 30 years in China. She was a writer — author of four books, scores of other stories and published poems. Her letters must contain more than mundane minutiae. But, as her only child, I feel both curiosity and dread.

I take the coat box home to New Jersey and shove it unopened under our bed. It is September, 1986.

Now, it's 1999. Standing in our Arizona garage on my 70th birthday, I feel ready to open that box. I should be old enough to face anything I might learn about my mother.

"If not now, when?" I ask myself.

Reading the letters turns out to be the first challenge. Lurry had admittedly "shifted them from place to place" so they are no longer in any chronological sequence. Envelopes had been discarded and more than half of the letters are undated, simply headed "Sunday afternoon" or "Tuesday night."

For weeks I organize them, surmising from content when they were written. They are as intriguing as a novel one can't put down. My husband quips that they are pages of "a loose-leaf novel that someone dropped."

Feeling as if I were traveling in a time warp, I become totally absorbed in my mother's descriptions of her life as she lived it, not just the life I had constructed from what she chose to tell me.

"What shall I do with them?" I keep muttering. The letters are so beautifully written that they are impossible to ignore — and impossible to burn. "Maybe I should write a book..."

I stash the box back on the garage shelf.

But it is never far from my mind.

...

It's 2003. I discover a slim manuscript that my mother intended to expand into a book about her father's experiences as a missionary in China. Eight typed sheets are all she managed to complete, but they include family stories that she had heard and quite a few details about her childhood in Nanking. I also have a brief sketch of her early life that she provided to the publishers of The Junior Book of Authors (*The H.W. Wilson Company 1934*). These pages evoke my own memories and I drift into renewed speculation.

"Maybe if I combined everything I know with excerpts from the priceless letters Lurry saved in that old coat box, I really could write the story of her life."

Eagerly I begin. Gradually I continue. Eventually I succeed.

Now at last, I invite you to meet an exceptional woman best known as Doré.

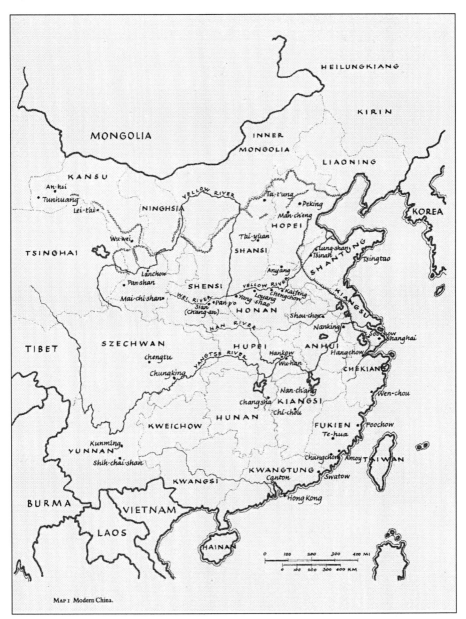

CHINA in the early 20th Century
(The Arts of China by Michael Sullivan, U. of CA Press 1984)

幸运　　**PART ONE**

"The past is never dead. It's not even past. All of us labor in webs spun long before we were born— webs of heredity and environment, desire and consequence, of history and eternity. Haunted by wrong turns and roads not taken, we pursue images perceived as new, but whose provenance dates to the dim dramas of childhood, which are themselves but ripples of consequence echoing down the generations. The quotidian demands of life distract from this resonance of events, but some of us feel it always."

—William Faulkner in <u>Requiem for a Nun</u> (Random House, Inc.)

CROSSING THE PACIFIC

Cuddling her nine-week-old baby, the young mother glanced down over the edge of the ship's lower bunk, grateful for the reassuring sight of a little metal pan provided for seasickness. Despite her weakness and the ship's continual pitching and rolling, Margaret Nelson Rowe had so far been able to fight her nausea and respond to the needs of her daughter.

The year was 1898. Margaret was the wife of a young Methodist minister, Harry Fleming Rowe. Pronounced *"Rau,"* the name was Anglicized when his German forefathers arrived in America. Harry had answered a calling to bring the light of his Lord Jesus Christ to the heathen in a foreign land and save them from what he saw as dark, empty lives without His Gospel. Soon after the birth of their daughter in upstate New York they embarked on a six-week journey aboard a Canadian Pacific steamship headed for China.

<u>China!</u> The image of smoky opium dens, fierce armored swordsmen, dusty poverty, acrid odors, inedible foods and unintelligible language, filled Margaret's mind with dread. But her duty was to accompany and support her idealistic husband, who was as excited as she was fearful.

"If you'll be all right my dear, I think I'll just go up and take a turn around the deck," said the Rev. Rowe.

"Of course, Harry," Margaret answered softly, as he stepped out through the cabin door. "You go right ahead. The baby will be wanting to eat soon."

Brave and silent, she unbuttoned her high-necked, starched Victorian shirtwaist, nursed the infant Dorothy. And prayed.

Harry was never seasick, nor was his daughter as she grew. Although she later rejected his religion, their shared love of far flung travels was central to the lifelong bond between them.

...

Margaret never learned to appreciate the ancient culture and beauty of China. She furnished the rooms of her large Nanchang home with American horsehair sofas, long lace table cloths, heavy white curtains stenciled with Grecian designs, an Axminster rug rampant with cabbage roses, and a small oak organ – all of which she'd had shipped from New York. She planned to make a home in China as nearly like the beloved Utica farmhouse where she was born, and she did it with staunch determination, treading her feet on the small organ as she taught her children old Protestant hymns.

Lips set in characteristic firmness, she learned only enough Chinese to communicate with the servants. Throughout 38 years in "The Celestial Kingdom," she never stopped longing for Pennsylvania.

For her daughter, on the other hand, China was home. As she grew, Dorothy spoke Chinese first, because most of the people who cared for her spoke that language.

Her father found it daunting that just a slight variation in tone would completely change a word's meaning, but he studied hard to make himself understood in his sermons. Marveling at his child, he wrote to American relatives, "Dorothy is thriving here: talks all day long, always understood as she switches fluidly from English to Chinese as called for."

Dorothy adored her Chinese amah, a nursemaid named Chang Ma who was called 'Missy" by the family. Whenever she could, the child chose to toddle around after Missy or the other servants, rather than sit with her stiff and proper mother. In fact, according to the tale later told by her father, the tiny child's love for the Chinese people saved her life and that of her parents.

"CARRY ME"

During the 1800's, Western countries had increasingly interfered with China's way of life. Great Britain established an opium trade and fought to maintain it. After China lost the 1839-1842 Opium Wars, it was forced to give many more privileges to the West. The year the Rowe family arrived, China leased the port of Hong Kong to Britain for 99 years.

By 1900, the country was torn with the chaos created by a life-and-death struggle known as the Boxer Rebellion. A contingent of anti-foreign, anti-imperialist Chinese belonged to The Society of Right and Harmonious Fists. These rebels were called "Boxers" by the Western press due to the martial arts and calisthenics they practiced.

The dominant leader of the Qing Dynasty court, Empress Dowager Cixi, regent to the ineffectual Guangxu Emperor, had few modern armies for protection from Western guns. Conservative court factions won her favor by pretending that they had a secret magic to rid the land of all infidels, especially the missionaries who had come to replace native beliefs with Christianity. She was persuaded to issue an edict ordering the rebels to kill all foreigners on sight.

When the Boxers invaded Peking, the United States consul ordered all missionaries to move to Kiukiang, near the river, where a government gun boat would take them to Shanghai. The men and their families could carry only a few items of clothing and personal necessities.

Margaret Rowe was so sure death was near that she put on her best American clothes and dressed two-year-old Dorothy in a long white silk coat and ruffled embroidered bonnet, suitable to meet her Maker. Carried in a sedan chair by two native bearers, the mother held her child tightly on her lap, with Father walking alongside. As the day grew hotter and the journey long, the little girl grew restless at the slow measured pace of the bearers and squirmed for release.

When they entered the unnaturally quiet, boarded-up city of Kiukiang, suddenly ten Boxers sprang up. Bare to the waist, bronzed and hairless, they wore bright green pantaloons with wide red cummerbunds and carried great shining curved swords. Faces flushed with rage, the rebels yelled at the party to stop. Terrified, Margaret understood that her husband would be powerless to prevent a bloody death at the hands of these heathen devils. She prayed silently to her Lord.

A tall leader pushed the chair bearers aside and stood between the poles, facing the woman and the small American child. His sword, held threateningly over his head, shone brightly in the sun. The colors of his clothing delighted Dorothy, and she had no reason to fear any Chinese. Tired of the endless restrictions of sitting, she reached out her chubby arms and called out in Chinese, "Bao bao! Bao bao wo!" — "Up up! Carry me!"

At this sound, the other rebels rushed forward, ready to do their duty and kill the foreigners.

"Stop!" shouted the leader. "This little blue-eyed one speaks our language. Some mistake has been made. Surely our Empress did not desire the death of this small one who speaks our language and asks us to carry her. Let us consider this. We will decide this for ourselves and I say let us escort them to the river's edge where the boat of their government waits and they may go in peace."

And so they did, with the residents of Kiukiang aghast at the sight. The American Marines hung over the railings of the boat, watching as the mother stepped down, her baby in her arms. The great bronzed Boxer put his hand on the child's head and said, "Go now Small One, and do not come again until there is peace in our land. But do not forget our language, and forgive that I could not carry you when you were tired."

Thus saved, the family fled on this last gunboat to Shanghai and from there by steamer to Japan, where they stayed for several months, continuing to marvel at their miraculous escape. On their return, they learned that, while none of the other Methodists had been killed, several were wounded, many robbed, and seven missionary homes and chapels destroyed before a multinational coalition rushed troops to their rescue.

Reforms implemented by China after the crisis of 1900 led to the end of the Qing Dynasty and the later establishment of the modern Chinese Republic. Twice more, in his lifetime, Dorothy's father would have his home and all his possessions burned by rebels.

THE FAMILY GROWS

For four years after The Boxer Rebellion, the Rowe family was stationed in Wuhu. There, on May 30, 1902, a second daughter, Louise, was born, three weeks before Dorothy's 4th birthday on June 20th. Father managed to soothe his older daughter's disappointment in finding that the tiny infant couldn't play with her red ball, and persuaded her to wait a while for her new sister to grow.

In 1905, the Methodists sent the family to Nanking, seven miles from the Yangtze River. In those days, English-speaking people spelled Mandarin words according to the Wade-Giles system: e.g. Nanking, Peking and Chungking. In 1958, the People's Republic of China introduced a new standard of Romanization called Pinyin, which was adopted by the United Nations in 1977. The spelling for those city names became Nanjing, Beijing, and Chongqing. In this book, however, I will use the old spelling found in my mother's letters.

In Nanking, a brother was born, named David Nelson after Mother's eldest brother. Three younger children, Caroline, Harry, and John, came along in ordered succession. Dorothy had wanted her baby sister to be named Barbara, and stubbornly nicknamed her "Barbie" the rest of their years.

The servants called Dorothy Da Mei Mei, meaning eldest sister. Louise was Er Mei Mei, second sister.

Gradually, as he mastered the difficult new language, her Father's missionary work expanded over a wide district. He called it "itinerating," and wrote to American friends about the frustrations. "There are apt to be insincerities cropping out on the part of the pagans. It is our duty to try as much as in us lies to put them on the right road and keep them there. The great danger lies in their being so oppressed that they seek our help in temporal things and entirely overlook the spiritual salvation we seek to bring."

NANKING

Once the capital of the rich Ming Dynasty, Nanking was protected by a 25-mile long city wall, one of the finest in China, made of large bricks and so wide at the top that several chariots could ride abreast. Within the wall the city of many trees and parks was designed centuries ago with sufficient space for its populace to survive any long siege. Winding cobble stone streets were lined with little shops, each selling its own distinct wares.

The Rowe family was assigned a square, grey brick house which stood in a wide garden. Inside the wall, it was an American home, where the children were educated by their parents, practiced the piano and ate with knives and forks. Thanksgiving and Christmas were exciting celebrations.

"Outside the compound wall," as my mother later described it to her Western readers, "there were no American children and no sounds, smells, nor sights like any in the cities of America. Whenever possible, I slipped out through the great gray gate that led from our garden to the noisy yellow street. There I spoke only Chinese and behaved as my Chinese friends did. Sometimes we walked together up to the low hills and the end of Yellow-Mud Alley and flew great paper kites in the March winds. Sometimes we followed enticing street vendors. We knew the sounds of each peddler: the candyman who blew magic shapes from warm barley taffy covered with sesame seeds and molded perfect dancing dolls from sugar-moistened rice flour; the man who had trained mice and would make them do tricks for a few pennies; and the vendor who came at sunset selling chrysanthemum-flavored rice balls, warm and fragrant in a thin, white sauce. T'ang hulers—sticky syrup-covered fruits on skewers—were my favorite treats, whenever I had a big copper coin to spend."

Sometimes, the Chinese children came inside the wall with Da Mei Mei to romp in the grass under the apricot trees or sniff the fragrant purple wisteria on the trellis by the front door. Other times Da Mei Mei went to the homes of her Chinese friends and ate with chopsticks as easily as they did. She smiled when their mothers said, "Goodness, your hair is nice and black and straight, but I never saw round, blue eyes before."

One of Dorothy's dearest friends was Kwei Xian, her amah's daughter. The two girls were just the same age. Dorothy could hardly tell the difference in her love for her own mother and for the Chinese nurse, so tender and gentle and fair was Missy, who had been with the family ever since they came to China and now lived two turns away on Big Horse Street. She was never too busy to help Da Mei Mei and Kwei Xian build a cave from the dining room chairs and two steamer rugs, or to fix them special Chinese food for supper when Father and Mother were to be out for the evening. And always, her amah told stories at bedtime, sometimes fairy stories of old China, sometimes songs her mother had taught her about the Rabbit in the Moon, or the fairies who guard the flowers, and always, for the last of all, a song the ended softly, when the children were almost asleep, "Mother of all Dreams, send them the rest dreams now.

KULING

Despite the charm of Dorothy's home in Nanking, the city was steamy hot in summer. Luckily, her family was able to spend July and August in Kuling, a place that Mother Rowe called "a blessed retreat."

Kuling was more than a summer resort. It was a lifesaving station in those days of so many deaths from malaria, carried by mosquitos swarming over the flooded rice fields, and cholera borne by flies. Deaths of children compelled Westerners to find some place where families could go for the worst months of tropically hot summers. Men such as the Rev. Silden, Pearl S. Buck's father, explored the site of ancient temples atop Mount Lushan in the heart of the Li mountains, where they found air of fresh cold purity and clear running brooks. On plots acquired from Chinese on long-term lease, white missionaries and businessmen built small stone houses and a church, surrounded by pines, dwarf chestnut trees and oaks. The pretty enclave became a perfect sanctuary.

The trip took two days: one day by steam boat up the Yangtze River to Kiukiang and a night spent with friends in that city; then six hours carried by chair across plains and up hills and steep winding paths into the mountains. Four bearers carried each chair, suspended by ropes from poles across their shoulders. As they raced up the stone steps with light rhythmic stride, their passengers avoided downward glances that could be terrifying. Beneath the winding path churning rivers filled the gorges.

In Kuling the children thrived, running about freely while their mothers chatted about problems with the servants and details of their winters. Years later my mother remembered hearing "the rushing of waterfalls over the sounds of the portable organ during services."

The mention of picnics always evoked for her "salmon salad, the water jar, wide smiles, a piqué hat, and singing 'Sailing, sailing, over the bounding main.'"

FURLOUGH

Every eight years, the missionaries were allowed a "furlough" in America. There, Father Rowe would speak before church and community groups, telling of his work in China and asking for money to further his efforts. Mother Rowe would thrill to be with her brother Dave and his family on his farm in Meadville, Pennsylvania.

Before the first trip, all the young had been told repeatedly of the wide streets and tall houses they would see in America. Dorothy talked about it so much that her amah sought a way to bind the child to her so she would never forget China. She led her down a long quiet street, and turning a corner, brought her to the open bazaar that blazed with holiday decorations.

Above their heads, swinging out over the street, and at their feet on low boxes or on their own comic wheels, were paper lanterns in the shape of ducks and flowers and even a rabbit.

"O, Missy look!" cried Dorothy.

Missy answered softly, "In America, are there New Year lanterns to be bought on the corners of those wide, wide streets among those tall, tall buildings?"

Dorothy was afraid there might not be, and felt, for the first time, a longing for China that for the rest of her life was with her when she was away from that beloved land.

They bought a rabbit-shaped lantern, fuzzy white, with great red eyes and a tail that danced on a hidden spring. Dorothy carried him home and planned to take him with her to America. Alas, not even in the hat trunk was there room for a paper lantern that was rather battered by June. But he stayed in her heart until years later when she put him into her first book titled The Rabbit Lantern.

The voyage across the ocean on a steamship was thrilling for the eight-old-girl. Dorothy discovered a love for the sea and ocean liners that also stayed in her heart forever. No details of that early trip still exist, but in her adult letters, she wrote often of the joy such travel gave her.

Once they landed in America and traveled by train to Pennsylvania, Dorothy and her siblings were warmly welcomed by their American relatives. They were, however, also treated as something of a curiosity. The strange, loving aunts repeatedly begged the two small girls to speak Chinese and to sing "Jesus Loves Me, this I know" in the strange foreign tongue. At their mother's urging, they obliged, their shrill soprano voices pealing out "Yesu ai wo, wo jeh dao," over and over.

Dorothy couldn't help noticing that more fuss was made over her sister and little brother. She later wrote of feeling that, "It was my disgrace to have been born in Rome, NY, when Louise and David were considered so special because they were China-born."

The Rowe family on furlough in Meadville, PA, 1907. In front: Harry F. Rowe, son David, and Margaret N. Rowe. In back: Louise and Dorothy.

Before that first furlough the girls had been told of the delights of fresh milk, cold crisp apples, butter that didn't come in tins from Australia, and water that didn't have to be boiled. But those things were very strange to them. Dorothy acutely embarrassed her mother by turning up her nose at foaming cow's milk. "Don't they have any Carnation in a can?" she asked.

The family rented a house in Meadville that winter and Dorothy went to a public school, loving the excitement of being with many other children. Her mother drew praise from relatives for the delicious Christmas dinner she prepared and served, after eight years of having servants. Margaret Rowe never confessed what a joy it was to be in control of her own kitchen, instead of merely going over accounts with a hired cook and ordering meals in her hesitant Chinese. Despite taking new American furniture and a piano back to China, she wept bitterly when she left America.

HIGH SCHOOL AND COLLEGE

In 1910, one of the Americans visiting missionaries was the Rev. John Franklin

Goucher, a visionary educator who had established mission schools in Japan and Korea as well as China. He was also a founder and president of the Women's College of Baltimore, Maryland. Earlier that year the respected liberal arts and sciences school had been renamed to honor him – Goucher College.

According to family legend, as Dr. Goucher was leaving the Rowe home, twelve-year-old Dorothy was standing a step above him on the staircase. As he bid her farewell, he put his hand on her head and declared, "This must be a Goucher girl!" From that day, she told me, her destiny was never at question.

To prepare for an American education, she was sent at age 14 to spend two years at Miss Jewel's School in Shanghai. I don't know how boarding school life affected her. I imagine she missed her home, but she may have enjoyed learning from teachers other than her mother, and she had a talent for making friends. One of her classmates was Pearl Buck's sister Grace Silden. Through Grace, Dorothy came to know the older girl who would become the celebrated author of <u>The Good Earth</u>. As daughters of Presbyterian missionaries, Pearl and Grace lived through many experiences which paralleled those of Dorothy's family.

I do know that because of her lovely singing voice, my mother was often called upon to perform for boarding school assemblies, prayer meetings and church socials.

When she was 16, her whole family came to the states for a second summer furlough. In September, when her parents and siblings returned to China, Dorothy stayed on in Meadville with her mother's relatives so that she could graduate from an American high school.

"It seemed very strange and lonely," she later wrote, "especially since no one knew anything about China. When I told them a little, they laughed and said, 'How funny,' until I stopped talking about my cherished home."

Goucher College was a welcome surprise. There, she found that her exotic background could draw others into her orbit. This was a discovery that Dorothy used to full advantage most of her life.

Although not conventionally "pretty," she was strikingly attractive, with thick dark hair, a long straight nose, high forehead and a pointed chin that she sometimes quivered in mock sorrow while the twinkle in her deep-set blue eyes gave away the pretense. All her life that "Rowe chin" was a symbol of her stubborn resolve. Never, she often asserted, would anyone see it tremble in public.

When she was a little girl, a playmate kidded her about her ears, saying they stuck out like an elephant's. This cruel exaggeration lingered in the back of her mind. From college on, she chose hair styles that covered her ears.

While she still missed China, she didn't mind being nicknamed "Dot" and plunged wholeheartedly into campus activities. In addition to enjoying her studies and excelling in classes, she began to have the kind of fun she'd never known at missionary schools – learning the latest popular dances and performing in school plays and musicals.

Dorothy had always expressed her dreamy, pensive, romantic side in poetry and prose. Encouraged by the Goucher English faculty, she started writing seriously – winning awards and prizes for her work, which often appeared in college publications. During summer vacations, she earned money by working as a live-in nanny or governess for children of wealthy New England families.

Was she aware of the vivid intellectual and political turmoil in China during those years? I feel sure that her father wrote to her about it, but no letters survive to describe it.

HOME TO CHINA

In June, 1919, Dorothy graduated from Goucher at 3 p.m. and boarded a ship back to China at 8:00 that evening. I picture a heartwarming homecoming after five years – with her younger siblings rushing to hug their Da Mei Mei. Her mother was particularly relieved to have her back. She could use her help. By then, Father Rowe was president of the Nanking Theological School and traveled quite a bit to other regions, often as a translator for visiting bishops.

For the next four years, Dorothy spent her weekdays teaching English to Chinese students at the Methodist Girls High School, a boarding school run by the Women's Foreign Missionary Society. She was also expected to direct and stage school plays. For extra spending money she worked in the school office, keeping "the books" and typing.

Starting in September, 1920, she began writing letters to "Er Mei Mei" [second sister] Louise, who had, in turn, traveled to Baltimore to enter Goucher College. The usual salutation was "Puss Dear" or "Precious Puss" and she signed as Dot or Dorritz.

In addition to complaints about the restrictions imposed by living at home with "the fam," the letters were full of news of mutual friends, with expressions such as "Clem is such a peach of a girl" or about another who was "a good scout." She wrote long passages about clothes—about the patterns and fabrics of "duds" made to order by a talented Chinese tailor who only needed to see sketches before working his wonders. One day she joked, "I feel dandy today. For why; I ain't wored a corset for a week."

Nearly every letter included a description of long walks in picturesque settings. From the top of Nanking's wide city wall, one could look across the countryside to nearby mountains. Dorothy's favorite mountain, standing high and clear against the sky, was Tze-ch'ing Shan or Purple Mountain. Stone-flagged paths beneath tall pines led to ancient temples that promised hidden repose.

Typically, she reported, "I woke at five and couldn't resist the world so I hiked for three hours by myself. It is such a joy to roam again the beloved hills where I cherished sunsets over Purple Mountain and was refreshed in the shady quiet of the Temple of Everlasting Greenness. I wandered on the wall and saw peat fires over the canal, resting my eyes on all the spaces of childhood."

"Saturday I went over to Clem's at four after a busy day fussing around in the house. We took a bite of lunch and went out the road by Kuloe to Kulingan. We never got to the Temple because we were stopped by a sunset of wondrous gold and American beauty rose. We sat down on a hill under ancient gnarled cedars and watched until the darkness came and a tiny crescent moon appeared. We ate our food by feel and headed home. I thought the moon rather vain for so young a girl, for when we passed a rice field, I saw her looking at her lovely self in the water."

"Sunday we got up at four and watched the sun rise – feeling very intimate with him. Then we went out to that wooded hill just before the foreign cemetery. The day was dreamy and half asleep… from the very top of the hill it was lovely to look out over the city and the canal outside the wall to the far horizon where the lazy Yangtze wounds like a yellow ribbon binding some old picture album."

"After my last class in the morning, armed with a sandwich and a book (Anatole France's The Aspirations of Jean Servien, which I like), I went out over the hills back of the University in the direction of Lia Tsi An and lay on my back under a tree and read and loafed and dreamed until the ten of one bell at the Middle School rang. It was so restful. I was absolutely alone except for the voices of a man yelling at his water buffalo and a woman talking to her neighbor as she washed rice. Nothing like getting down with nature to cure the troubles of the human soul."

When Louise's first letters from America arrived, Dorothy described the family's excitement: "Puss dear we are just too wild for words. Dave has the first sheet and is standing up by the door reading. Barbie and Mother are on the bed trying to read the same place. Dad has sheet three and is on the shirt waist trunk simply splitting the air with his amusement. Mother is positively choking over some parts. I'm so hap I got to read them all first. Honestly, how can you ever, ever write such cracker jack letters? Your fib regarding your promise to Father not to dance is clever. I hope, Honey, that you are learning to dance at Goucher with all those blessed girls. I simply adore dancing and get half my exercise that way. I daydream of the two of us going to the Baltimore Country Club with two god-like men."

"Don't take rushing too hard," she advised when Goucher sorority rituals came up. "It's very little and silly and time wasting, but has to be. I know the feeling of revulsion, but I hope you get peachy girls…Write me as you develop feels."

…

In December, Dorothy and her pal Clementine – called "Clem" - took the train from Nanking to Shanghai for Christmas shopping.

"You can judge by my hen tracks that the train jazzes and shimmies all over the place," she wrote. "When we just handed the conductor our tickets, he looked surprised, grieved, hurt to find us happy in second class.
'Dis blong first class'
'Oh?' we feigned, continuing to write our letters
'Other car have got plenty seat'
'Oh?' we sigh, not looking at him.

'Can go that side.'

He waits, we write, he shifts to left foot, we write, he shifts again then gives up and goes. Just when we had settled down for the night, he reappears.

'You no move?'

We feigned sleep

'I take you ticky you no can get out station,' he threatened.

Thrilling as a dime novel, eh wot?"

Apparently the girls held onto their "tickies" and encountered no problem disembarking in the morning, for the rest of Dorothy's letter simply describes the gifts they bought for family and friends: jewelry, picture frames, stationery, fabric for curtains and skirts, ribbons, books, a box of American apples, chocolate mints, gingersnaps and books. "I bought myself poor on modern verse and sheet music, three wonderful collections," she reported. "I wish, O wish you were here to play and practice them with me."

Thanking her sister for the Christmas present sent from Baltimore, Dorothy wrote, "You know I'd rather have hope chest junk than any thing else, and this little my-blue breakfast set is so precious! You were extravagant, you dear!"

Mother Rowe gave her eldest daughter a dozen silver teaspoons – clearly another hope chest item, but no wedding date had been set.

Dorothy had accepted a marriage proposal from Hosmer Johnson, a distant cousin who was "very keen on" her. The round-faced, sandy-haired, bespectacled young man had given her an engagement ring before leaving to study in America. During the next two years, he rarely wrote which both annoyed and disappointed her. Longing for romance, she began to have serious doubts about marrying the uptight, straight-laced young man – doubts she confided only in Louise.

In the spring of 1921 Dorothy's whole household was quarantined for two months when youngest sister Caroline came down with scarlet fever. Mother Rowe stayed confined to the delirious patient's room during the whole frightening period. After her fever broke, the child had to continue to be kept flat in bed for an extra eleven days – "to make sure that her heart will keep right."

That summer, Dorothy, her cousin Paula Simmons and their friend Clem took a cottage together near Tientsin at Peitaiho Beach, a northeastern summer resort. Freedom from the family, swimming in the ocean, eating whatever and whenever they felt like asking the faithful Chinese servants to provide, loafing in cool sea breezes, dancing to jazz records on "the Vick," constituted what she characterized as "marvelously lazy life-gorgeous doings of busy nothings." By adding excursions such as exploring a remote Confucian temple, she had "the most perfect summer of my life."

Dorothy was furious when a letter from Louise addressed to her was delivered to her parents by mistake. "Damn the luck!" she told her sister. "The family, dear and trusting, opened it. Only the dinner dance they ought not to know of, but it makes it hard to ask you things. I perish for your comments about Hos, but don't mention anything you don't want the folks to read.

"I love writing to you," she said. "In a way I make you a safety valve for all my feels. You and I are lots nearer than we ever were before. Someday we will be inseparable old maid sisters known as the Rowe Girls. Dost have longings to travel? I'd give my neck to meet you somewhere and then embark together as stewardesses or whatever to get to Europe and India and Africa and Penang. Gosh! I can't settle down yet!"

In another letter she reports: "We have gotten into a bunch of books this week. I read Henry James' <u>Daisy Miller</u> and I re-read aloud <u>The Light That Failed</u>. How we laughed when, on the evening we planned to finish it our lamp ran out of oil!"

Knitting became Dorothy's new passion. "Clem reads to me the while, so I have many lovely thoughts knitted into the garment. Have you read <u>Main Street</u> by Sinclair Lewis? It is worthy of all the talk it has aroused I think."

She wrote that after attending the summer's only obligatory "tea," at a neighbor's, "I got into my worst old rags and made for the country and hiked until dark. The sunset was a glorious mantle of flame over the western mountains, and the sea, ever adaptable, took all the rose and gold of the sky and beautified it in the mirror of its breast."

Before going back to work, the three girls spent a week in Peking, visiting all the celebrated sites popular with tourists then and now. As Dorothy described it to Louise: "From the wall of the Tartar City, it fascinates and allures as the gold dust of sunset and the grey smoke of chimney fires combine to form a gauze above the yellow and green tiles of imperial roofs and the weird cosmopolitan buildings of legation quarter."

"The next day we got some rolls and olives and a thermos of ice water and went by ricky for two hours to the Summer Palace. It is a place of desolate beauty. The succession of palaces stretches along the border of a lotus-grown lake at the foot of the Western hills. Each building is perfect, and within is dust-covered furniture of lacquer and walnut, cloisonné inlaid. The most beautiful view is from a little artificial island connected to the mainland by a marble bridge of seventeen arches. Against a background of green forest and grey rock the imperial artists splashed all the colors of the painter's pallet framing it in yellow tile and white marble paving. In the water it looks as if the artist, weary, had thrown his paint box among the lotus pads."

On a train ride through wild and rugged Nankou Pass, she thought of the many ancient battles between Chinese and Tartar hordes at this northern gateway to China. "All along the Pass the Great Wall crawls over impossible slopes, standing out against the sky at marvelous heights and squirming over the roughest ridges. We walked up a stoney gorge, climbed onto the Wall and hiked up until we stood on a distant watch tower perched precariously…It seemed as if the Wall had been poured indiscriminately from each summit and had trickled down, so coiling, winding and purposeless it seems…the most daring, careless, bold feat I ever saw. Never does its huge dragon-like body writhe <u>around</u> a mountain or try to take any easy way…always over the highest peaks and the roughest way. It seems a superhuman task, but it was done, as all China does its tasks, by masses of men."

…

Back in Nanking, Dorothy lamented the "fearful narrowness of missionary life."

"They seem to have no tolerance for any ideas but their own. Their concepts of religion, of duty, of friendship and most everything else are utterly repugnant to me. I sang a solo at prayer meeting, but my soul rebelled every minute. I felt so sorry for the folks who had to find their God in the hot stuffy fullness of that room instead of out in the moonlight adoring sleeping ponds and the silver ecstasy of leaves in the wind."

Throughout her life Dorothy resented the whole thrust of missionary work. She could never understand why Westerners thought they had the right to come into "foreign" lands and strive to convert the inhabitants to Christianity. She felt strongly that all people have the right to follow their own beliefs and that it was the height of arrogance for missionaries to exhort the people of other countries to give up their ancient accepted faiths.

During the summer of '21, she also found family expectations hard to take. She adored her brother David ("Davey") and little sister Caroline ("Barbie") but she loathed the antics of the youngest boys, Harry and John. Moreover, every time house guests were expected, which was frequently, she would have to give up her bedroom to the visiting dignitaries, sometimes for extended periods.

She told Louise, "I have to fight self pity all the time. There is no more despicable trait and none so easy for me to fall into. I have a very hot little ego that is always burning me and I have to fight her all the time. But the teaching is my refuge, so I think I will stay here and go through the daily death that is supposed to be me happy home."

Her days were soon enriched by a new friendship with a young woman named Eleanor Holgate. "Her father is dean of Northwestern," Dorothy wrote Louise. "He is taking his sabbatical year here in the university and Eleanor, her mother and sister came along. The kid sister is in Ginling and Eleanor teaches half a day in the middle school. She has been out of college six years and is alive, interesting, seems to be adventurous and loves beauty.

"Last Saturday we hiked to Hsia Kwan and went to the ferry landing. There, pretending we were going to Egypt; we boarded a boat and rode back and forth on that old, shining yellow river six times. The water was embroidered with sails, orange and white and brown, stiffened with bamboo which glistened in the clear light. We saw the sunset over Pukow and the moon rise over Purple Mountain. It was a perfect spree."

"Yesterday we met in a cold drizzle and hiked off out the gate to Lotus Lake. We explored Pink Temple and Eleanor stood quiet before its age-old mystery. I like her heaps. We can talk our dreams to each other. It's strange the new way I look at people and what I expect from a friend. Is there anything as miraculous and thrilling as personality? Oh, Puss, it's good to be growing up a little."

In October she wrote, "On the envelope you will find one of the new

Chinese stamps commemorating the tenth year of the Republic of China. It is a rare issue and David is buying them up to take to America and sell. The men pictured are supposed to be the three greatest presidents of China."

...

When Dorothy learned that her fiancé Hosmer Johnson was in Japan, en route home to China, she told Louise that she felt "frightened by the absolute lack of excitement it gave me. I wrote to tell him how his long silences seemed to kill something for me, and how much I have changed. He will have changed, too."

When Hos replied to her letter, she said, "His words proved his love, and he made clear what he expected of me someday. Isn't there something unjust about the fact that when a man and a woman marry, it is always the man who decides what the life work shall be and where they shall live? I feel as if I'd suffocate if I have to be a missionary's wife.

"All marriage is compromise, I think, but how I long for a man with keen understanding of me, with fine sympathy and a gentleness that knows a woman's psychology. Not much to ask! You asked if I love Hos. Honey, I don't know him at all after two years and so few letters. Nothing to do but wait and see him, I guess."

She was persuaded to spend Christmas with his family at Tsinanfu – as a surprise for Hos's homecoming. "I am rather thrilled over the thought of the trip, but I fear that when he comes in on the midnight train and finds me there, he will think that I mean by coming that everything is all right between us. And I want to ask him to let us have that week as if we had never been engaged, so that we can learn to know each other again."

As it turned out, Hos was "a perfect sport" when she had a chance to tell him of her uncertainty about her "feels."

"Thank heaven he likes hiking," she wrote, "for I felt much happier out in the open. Monday we hiked to the Temple of a Thousand Buddhas, a fascinating monastery on Chien Buh Shan. At the top of the world we sat on a windswept rock and talked. I like Hos but I do not love him anymore. It's been rotten hard to hurt him as I had to. I would much rather have broken off entirely, but considering our two families, the notoriety of it, we decided not to end it formally. I wore my ring all the time there and no one knew what was in my heart, but it is entirely bluff for me now. I am so glad I came, for, before, I was uncertain and now I am very sure, and happy to be free…Hos isn't happy, but he will be very busy…"

In January, 1922, she told Louise, "Dad and Mother both think I am an idiot to have busted up with Hos. They rave on about how I will never find anyone so pure and good…and ugh! I say I may be sorry and lonely when I'm thirty, but I did what I felt was right."

Near the end of the school semester, she wrote, "Today I had no exams, so I went meandering the length of Hwa Pai Lou, poking into little stores and talking to people on the street. I watched an old carver of chops [personal seals] at his work; fingers callused where he had held his knife for years. I saw half naked men carrying baskets of newly picked goldy-red apricots on their shoulders. Inquisitive women asked me why I did not ride in a ricky on so hot a day, and one old fat one laughed out loud when I answered, 'It would bore me to death.' I found a Japanese 'hidden picture' store and bought two to use with my students as memory sharpeners. I bought a bowl of chow from a street peddler. The crowd around me as I ate was as dense as the gang around the bulletin board when exam grades are posted. A policeman showed me a black dog with six wee blind pups asleep on a bit of straw in an alley. He promised to see that no kids pester them. I came home by Da Tsang Yue with keen remembers."

…

During the first week of school after the New Year Dorothy wrote to Louise, "My teaching is going wonderfully. I can stay on top of it and live so satisfyingly in my writing. I really get such joy from that. It is the most exquisite pleasure to get my reactions to China down on paper. I keep thinking that I must write up this and that before I go to America. No telling if any of it will come to anything or not, but I have planned a book, with wild dreams of publishing it on stunning Chinese paper which should make a hit with the editors. If it comes to nothing it doesn't matter. I'm expressing me and that is what most humans try to do in some way. There are so many things I want to write about…"

Eleanor Holgate's family decided to return to America in March. "She has been an entirely new kind of friend and I am going to miss her muchly." Dorothy told Louise. "There is no joy like someone who gets you and loves you in spite of it; someone to whom you can talk your real self's thoughts." Despite this enforced separation, she maintained a long, close friendship with Eleanor (later nicknamed "Denny") and many shared adventures lay ahead.

In May Dorothy described "a miv of a day, cool and blowy. The great trees were so excited over the weather that they talked almost shrilly of it all day. The city is all abuzz about preparations for war. The machine guns at the arsenal play at practice war every day."

Ever since rebels overthrew the last emperor Pu Yi in 1911, ending China's centuries-old dynasty system, rival factions contended for control, keeping Mother Rowe in a perpetual state of fear. But this is how Dorothy described it:

"Two generals up north fight under the shadow of the Imperial city. We grab the papers to see if Chang So Lin or Wu Pei Fu is victorious today. One of the teachers at Hillcrest has all the kids upset about it and leads long sobby chapels about 'Lo I am with you even unto the end.' I think it will not come anywhere near Nanking." She was right, later describing "the very funny week-long war" as "perfectly Chinese."

...

Confiding, as usual, in Louise, Dorothy wrote, "It has been darn hard living at home of late. What a queer unbalanced world it is, where such things as not going to church and walking alone at night are greater sins than self deception and the attempt to control another human's religion and morals by rules and conventions.

"Last night Dad said that one of the jazz songs we were dancing to was *immoral*. Davey [16] is a perfectly marvelous dancer now. He swings you around like a full grown man and has such rhythm and smoothness. I hope he'll have some place to dance in America out of Dad's view. I shall be glad to get free of the fam and this time it will be forever. No more of this living in the bosom again."

The freedom she longed for would begin in June, when her parents sailed for "home." Her father had been invited to teach at the Princeton Theological Seminary and Dave and Caroline (still "Barbie" to Dorothy) could follow the model set by their older sisters by finishing high school in America.

Initially, Dorothy had been expected to accompany the family and live with them in New Jersey, but she decided that by staying on in China, in a familiar job, she could concentrate on the writing that had become so important to her.

"There is no place else where I can have as much time to myself and where I will be able to get the exact local color I want in my writing," she explained. "To get things published, it will be vastly better to send it from China. You know editors and their susceptibility to the exotic. I began to realize that I could never finish it before June.

"So, I am going to stay in Nanking for another year – in a suite of rooms in the school dormitory, with old precious, faithful "Missy" [Chang Ma, her amah,] to take care of my food and duds and washing and ironing. I expect to be bored at times and lonesome and hate the missionary atmosphere, and I may think that it was not worth it. But at present I feel it is worth the risk…I want so much to succeed in this writing.

"I expect to come home in June 1923, spend a month with the family, wherever they are, and then begin to live in some new fashion that I do not now know at all. I'm sorry it means so long a wait before the sight of you, but if I could then bring you something more of me that would be great, would you be glad?"

Reluctantly, Mother and Father Rowe accepted Dorothy's "declaration of independence." After singing "O' Promise Me" at a wedding and some equally inspirational solo for the Hillcrest commencement, she went to Shanghai with her family to see them off.

Before their sailing, she had a chance to go out to the ship and have dinner on board. As she described it to Louise, "The tender with serious, worried mishes, gorgeous French women with adoring black-eyed men, tall helmeted Brits with their frightfully attired wives, Japanese amahs with plenty small babies, all this and the blueness growing from the great, endless ocean, the ship and the lights, the boat smells and white-clad officers – enticed me as always. I wanted to go just to go. The lure is eternal to me."

Staying on in Shanghai with family friends, she enjoyed a tea dance at the posh Spanish-style Columbia Country Club where there were 15 men to five girls. "Some were frightful bores and some were drunks," she told Louise, "but two were really marvelous dancers. Gee, my soul spread its wings and flew. I was hap and free.

"How relative freedom really is. Is one ever really free? Is the anticipation of freedom the supreme satisfaction? At least I can say that I have a me that is much better company than ever before. That is a necessity if one is to be happy while free."

"Yesterday, because it rained so hard, I did the shops – the world-famous fan shop where some cost ten cents and some a hundred dollars; ham shops, tea shops, silk shops. The most curious place was the medicine store. I told them I had come from distant Nanking to see this store whose fame I had heard afar, etc. As a result, they took me proudly around the place, where I saw them make medicine of frogs and lizards, peppers and bark, deer horns and tiger eyes, herbs pungent and bitter, red clay and dried seeds, tallow and paper."

Exploring new places with alluring names, such as "The Temple of Secluded Light" and "The Monastery of Pure Compassion," inspired her to write several stories and poems during the week.

A Confucian Temple

I have gone with a friend to a temple
High on a grave grown hill,
And we found there no priest nor idols
Found but the magic thrill
Of great loveliness held in deep silence,
Watched by dark cypress trees;
And the swift, soundless passing of ricebirds
Swayed by a southward breeze.

She also received mail.

"You will turn up your toes and order flowers," she told Louise, "when you hear that I have had six letters from Hos in the last six days. I admit I need smelling salts myself. He is a dear, but so childishly transparent."

The sweltering July heat in Nanking finally persuaded Dorothy to accept a standing invitation from Hosmer Johnson and his parents to spend August with them, his brother and two sisters on the ocean shore at Chefoo. She described it all to Louise.

"Their summer cottage is on the top of a wee hill, surrounded by water on three sides and lawn right down to the sea. At night ships dip red and green fingers in the Bay. The 18 gunboats in the outer harbor are like so many dropped stars. Coffee is served out on the lawn. I like the luxury of everything. It's so wonderfully cool and the sea is perfect. Hos and I go for a dip each morning before breakfast and that peps me up for the day. We loaf a lot and read a good bit. Hos likes to read out loud while Margaret and I knit or sew.

"Yesterday we went out in the motor boat with a crowd of nice young fellows and then went swimming again, all of us, into the sunset. Usually after tea the others play bridge and I escape to write. I love the world from this window. Corrine [pet name for her Corona portable typewriter] sits on my lap like a well-behaved child and I pat her little fingers which makes her send love thoughts out to you."

"The white duck knickers I had made have been a perfect riding suit, and I found a little shop in Chefoo where they make real sailor middies for the Navy. I got them to make me a white one all regulation with stripes and symbols. It's a beauty and I will wear it with a pleated blue serge skirt. Wish I had a fringed skirt. Eleanor writes that they are the rage in New York – along with Eskimo Pies. Eat one for me. And is it true that in place of the word 'spooning,' they now say 'petting'?"

Sometimes Hos's sister Ruth got on Dot's nerves "with her eternal bossing and grouching. But I would just escape to the hills by myself until I had my hot little ego squelched. Nothing will quiet it like limitless space and immensity. It gives perspective which, after all, is absolutely necessary. We are only small white pebbles on the beach or thin blades of grass clinging against the cliff. Why is it so hard to remember this down among humans and hotness?"

"This has been a long, lazy, ideal and happy vacation. I hate the ends of things. But now that the summer is over, I am quite ready to get back to work. I had fun, but part of me simply faded away. I am much surer of what it would mean to marry Hos. He would adore me and spoil me and satisfy that feeble desire most of us have for being loved. But my spirit would go on alone. The comfortable calmness with him is not at all the thrill I need to feel for the man I marry. Hos says, 'There is no point in breaking windows, Dolly, for you always have to pay for the glass.' I live on busts, you see."

"The Nunnery"

That was Dorothy's nickname for Lawrence Hall, which was the "ladies house" of the mission boarding school. With a comfortable bed on a sleeping porch, wicker furniture and a few beloved possessions purloined from the family home, she found her rooms "entirely satisfactory." Her old amah, Missy, came every day to take care of her "bodily needs," and the Rowe family cat Sonny easily transferred his loyalties to the dormitory.

"The Chinese teachers and girls are in my rooms a great deal," she reported. "I think they may like Sonny and the Saturday Evening Post as well as Dear Teacher, but they are cute and keep me supplied with fruit and candy."

New to Dorothy that year was responsibility as "school doctor." Supervising the infirmary meant treating malaria as well as colds, fevers and tummy aches – one of which turned out to be appendicitis. A physician was called for a child with a "weak heart." He said, "Two drops of digitalis three times a day." A typhoid suspect was given 18 grams of quinine each day "in hopes."

"I must rave to you about the medical work," Dorothy wrote. "I love everything from swabbing out boils and painting throats to taking temperatures and dispensing medications. I get more kick from it than any unselfish occupation I have ever known. I keep fresh flowers in there. I had Missy wash the medicine cupboard and scour the pans, basins and jars. I wash off the thermometer with alcohol every time and keep meticulous charts…"

The typhoid suspect was announced to be a real case. "Her folks refused to let her go to the hospital so I had to get her ready to be taken home to a Chinese doctor. Then Missy and I had to clean the room and wash all the things in Lysol. I hate Lysol smell."

"You would be amazed at Missy. She simply runs me. She decided my breakfast was too meager so she went out and bought coffee and has it hot and ready for me each morning. My hose are all mended and clean and my rooms immaculate. I love coming in and finding the old dear and Sonny sitting about."

"Mostly I like it here. I never worked so hard and all the people I appreciate and I am never bored. Hikes are as refreshing as ever. But the part of me that is used to being in a loving family is lonesome. This aloneness is good for my character, but at times I get 'a whooping cough in my tummick' from it."

One Friday night she invited a group of women and girls to her family home [still un-rented] for "supper-round-the-fire" the way her mother always prepared it, with hot cocoa and candlelight. "I had a wonderful time doing all those domestic things such as fixing the tables and making the big chairs in a cozy circle near the open fire. I read out loud to them all for an hour and they unloosed and sank into soft comfy sighs and were happy. I was too. And once more I am assured that out of a void, atmosphere may be created, and from cheerlessness, cheer may come."

Mary Tang, a fellow teacher, invited Dorothy to have breakfast in her room one Saturday. "After a huge Chinese feast of pork/cabbage rolls, preserved long beans, sweet rice cakes and the like, I took a blanket, pillow, books and pen to Lotus Lake, hired a little boat and spent the afternoon at will (not my will but the boatman's) floating through the plants. When the sun set and the moon rose, the rosy blossoms closed, but their sweet fragrance lingered while I lay in the boat completely warm and comfy and happy. Then I hiked to Buh Gih Goh and took a ricky back to school. It was 7:30 by then so I missed supper, but so what. I do dislike supper at six o'clock. It affects me like a black hat worn with a brown dress or bad grammar from an educated person."

In addition to a full infirmary and two serious infections to dress twice a day, she ran an eye clinic every afternoon. A Dr. Peterson taught her how to put drops in the eyes of trachoma patients and rub their eyes with boric acid crystals twice a week.

"I began to suspect that some of the little girls were infested with head lice. So this morning I marched 40 of them out from chapel. They were simply speechless as Missy and I inspected each head, unloosed their braids and let most of them go off to re-comb their hair. We found ten darlings with buggies and buggy eggs so we kerosened the bunch, tied them up in old cloth and put them in the large room to wait. Now all the little heads are washed and out in the sun to dry. More fun."

Despite her discomfort with church, Dorothy gave in to expectations and attended weekly services and prayer meetings. Reporting to Louise she wrote, "Isn't it funny how piety or the preparation for piety affects a face? A wee bit melancholy about the mouth, the eyes either lowered or raised up high, never the normal level of vision, and the head tipped to one side while the entire collection of features are corroded with the worm-in-the-dust look of 'I am a sinner.'"

She accepted an invitation to spend Christmas break with the Wilmots, who were among the few "mishes" that she didn't see as narrow snobs. She enjoyed "the glee of kiddies" excited by gifts and treats, and feasted on traditional English fare.

After the holidays, at the urging of her special friend Eleanor Holgate, Dorothy sent a sheaf of her writings to "Poetry, the Magazine of Verse" in New York, claiming to care not whether they saw print. She also coaxed Missy to re-tell old folk tales that became the basis for some of the stories in the book she hoped to publish.

...

Winter brought "ten coat weather and frozen minds as well as hands and feet."

"You know the Chinese twelfth month," Dorothy reminded Louise. "It is hard work teaching. I have all my padded clothes on and go about looking like a disjointed elephant." But after she arranged to have a small stove delivered from the family home to her dormitory rooms, she was snug there. "Missy builds a fire nobly," she wrote, "and a nice school coolie carries coal up for us. The cheery warmth makes such a difference."

In late January she told her family, "All day yesterday and all night it snowed. It was dry, blowy, un-Chinese snow. My down comforter which was over me while I slept was white with snow this morning. Missy came out on my sleeping porch and shoveled a path for me and found my slippers, which were buried."

Predictably, illness among the students increased. "We have had two cases of diphtheria, which had to be quarantined for two weeks, and forty cases of Flu this week. Caring for the patients is exhausting, I'll tell the world. I now have a good Chinese woman to do the cleaning and carry their food, so that helps."

In another letter, Dorothy reported that "The event of my week was a tea party for four of the mish ladies who have been so kind to me. I wanted to entertain them in my own wee spot. Missy and I fussed as if it was a huge reception — cleaned, put flowers about, made nut and raisin sandwiches and fudge. I used the family tea set to serve coffee, tea, and chocolate cake which I bribed the cook to make. The guests enjoyed it all, admired my rooms and each took a book of mine home to read. It <u>was</u> fun."

By March, she could finally sense the promise of spring and was moved to write:

Willow Mists
I seemed to see the far off willow trees
With vague green mists for veils.
I thrilled to spring.
But, near, those willow trees
Looked bare and winter-gray.
And then I heard them laugh at me.
The willows by the pond
Had only thought of pale green veils.
Can I see thoughts?

She was also happy to be able to ride her bicycle again. One afternoon, Missy shrieked with distress when she saw her young mistress dragging herself up the stairs soaked through to the skin.

"Ah no, ah no!" she wailed. "Wah hoppen? Wah hoppen? You hurt?"

"No, no." Choking with laughter, Dorothy explained in Chinese. She had been riding her bike along a narrow concrete wall dividing sections of a city moat. It was an accepted way of getting from one side of the moat to the other. That day, as she was about half way across, a boy peddling furiously from the other side rode head-down in the middle of the limited space.

"Ah no...bad boy!" Missy interrupted, anticipating the outcome.

To avoid a collision, Dorothy told her, still laughing, she'd had no choice but to ride down the incline into the dirty water!

"Oh! Bad boy, no good!" Missy scolded as the two women wrung out her dripping garments. The old amah certainly saw nothing funny about it. At her insistence, Dorothy agreed to a hot bath and gargled with "Dobell's Solution" to ward off any ailments that might be caused by her foul immersion.

...

In contrast, on a Sunday afternoon, Dorothy "fled for the Ho Gardens in South City, that unbelievably quiet, restful old Chinese estate, where for seven coppers you can spend a day in fairyland. I explored all the luring paths, climbed in the rockeries and pagodas, read in little pavilions by lotus ponds, lay on my back in a bamboo wood and saw only three people all day... Life is very good."

...

The April wedding of a close friend drew Dorothy to Soochow, where "canals like gray ribbons reflected the moon." The streets, she said, "are so Chinese – narrow, winding and so like the careless leisure of this country to have bridges so high you can't ride over them, but get out and walk while the ricky boy puffs along behind."

"The wedding was adorable, with candles and lilies and a pipe organ and a real bishop in robes but with a damned-if-I-care Episcopal voice. The bridesmaids wore yellow taffeta with silver lace and carried lavender sweet peas. Agnes wore a graceful gown of heavy Chinese brocaded satin with puff sleeves, real lace and star-shine in her eyes."

In Nanking again she was cheered by "jasmine and willow boughs in my yellow vase, apricot blossoms in a tall green vase and droopy magnolia in Mother's blue pen holder. All the windows wide, no fire for a week, and birds – you know how thrilled they are as spring dawns. I was thrilled to get up to hear them. Imagine being thrilled on a Monday! The fruit trees that have been so tired all winter are flushed with life and joyfulness again. The willow trees are thinking of the new styles in leaves.

"Is there anywhere so shrill a green as Chinese gardens in spring?" she asked Louise.

"I suppose spring is always spring anywhere. But I hang onto this spring in China as if there were to be no more. What restless contradictions we humans are – wanting the new and different feverishly, clutching wildly to the familiar."

...

Meanwhile, her friend Eleanor Holgate went to spend a weekend in Princeton with the Rowe family, including Louise who was on spring vacation from Goucher. Dorothy was glad to hear about it because, as she confided to Louise, "I haven't told the folks yet, but I plan to live with Eleanor in New York next winter. She is miles ahead of me in brains and freedom, but I'm quite crazy about her. I want to take some courses at Columbia, but I must have a job, too, and write. I don't care how poverty-struck we are… but I dream of selling so many stories and poems that I shall have plenty of cash to go to Europe after a year in Manhattan. Keep this under your hat. As usual, my looker-ahead works rapturously. We must have illusions or die."

Dorothy's mother and sister often sent her American patterns to have clever old Tailor Dong create suits and gowns out of beautiful Asian fabrics. She began to ask Louise for ideas about the latest fashions that she could have made for her return to America.

In response to repeated questions from her parents, she finally admitted that she and Hosmer Johnson had formally ended their engagement. "I returned his ring and pin and gifts and am absolutely a new woman, free to seek adventure in New York next winter."

Apparently her mother wasn't surprised or angry, because a month later Dorothy told her, "You can't know how anxiously I waited for your letter…I wanted you to care just as little as I did and I feared you'd care so much more. You took it so marvelously, seeing that it just had to be and I am infinitely happier. As for not telling, I am not standing on Purple Mountain yelling, but I am, at last, being sincere when anyone asks. By the time you get back it will all be blown over and you won't have to be embarrassed by my mess. As for whether it feels like a funeral, NO. I feel as if I had been to a borning, for now I can act real and not pretend to be what I'm not."

As she counted down the final weeks of teaching, Dorothy and her pupils countered the restlessness of spring by throwing themselves into planning the annual May Day Festival. "Again, and for the last time, I have charge of the costumes," she wrote. "It is to be a cantata, The Hours, and there are a hundred girls in it. I have made many pilgrimages to South City for cloth and to the dyeing place. It rained for ten days, but the nice old Dye Man smiled at my fears and said, "Of course. I promise, so are ready.""

After the celebration, she wrote, "May Day? Nightmare! But worth everything to have the director say she'd never forget what all I did. We had 1500 guests and an alumnae program as well as the play. The kids looked adorable, tons of flowers in their hair and the stunning costumes...the drills so pretty...the soloist perfect with rosy wings. The young stags from the boys' schools were very excited. I suppose we'll be deluged with slushy epistles..."

...

Whatever free time she could manage Dorothy spent researching and writing a paper on "Temples of Nanking" which she read to The Literary Club on May 8th. Of her preparation she told Louise, "It is fascinating and means much hunting and work because no one has written about it except in Chinese. Mary Tang is helping by translating for me, and I spent two hours with the classics teacher at Ginling. He knew so much and I took copious notes."

After visiting four Buddhist temples, she wrote, "At Pei Loo Si, five thousand small gold idols sit in glass cases and look longingly out at the sunshine and new willows. At Hsiang Ling Si, tucked under the shelter of the Wall, and at Taiping Men, everything is so old and dusty that the maple leaves in the courtyard looked very young and nervous. Then I saw the sunset from Peh Gih Goh, where the characters over the tower say 'Hills Rivers superbly seen.' Love it?"

At one of two Taoist temples in South City, she found a soul mass being read "at the order of two wealthy women who, with numerous children and servants, sat in the open court chattering while the priests in red robes read and chanted their mysterious prayers."

Fellow teachers began planning a farewell luncheon for Dorothy, and the students begged to throw a party too. "If people are going to have goodbye parties for me, I must really be going," she wrote to her family. "I'm violently restless to go – anywhere, somewhere — at once. How do people live who never can go hopping about? I ought to be so grateful for that one thing that I never would crab…Missy and I have cleaned out all the drawers and cupboards and have really begun to pack."

It was a relief to turn over "the books" of the school to another teacher. "I won't have to spend my last day in Nanking hunting for some wayward ten cents in the pass book bank balance. Of course I'll likely get so hard up some day in New York that I'll put an ad in a newspaper reading: Experienced bookkeeper, middle aged, reliable, seeks immediate position. A1 references from Methodist Girls Boarding School, Nanking, China."

In her last letter from China, she wrote of plans for "a farewell trip on a Flower Boat and a hike on The Wall" and let her parents know that she would arrive in New York on June 23rd and come straight from there to Princeton for a grand family reunion.

Caroline, Louise and Dorothy in 1923

幸运 # PART TWO

"How sorry we are for all the folk that have not had the wonderful joy of being brought up in China! But the lack can be partly made up for those who will take Dorothy Rowe as guide. She has seen and felt, but more than that, she has the gift of charmingly vivid writing that will make you see and truly feel it all.... Without knowing it, you will have come into a new relationship of sympathy with an alien people and (their) ancient culture."
—Lucius Chapin Porter – Introduction to The Rabbit Lantern 1925

NEW YORK

In the next letter saved by Louise, dated October 13, 1923, Dorothy wrote of "the thrill of our bus top rides to work." She was sharing an apartment in Greenwich Village with her old friend Eleanor Holgate, who had somehow acquired the nickname "Denny."

Dorothy landed a well-paying half time job at Rankin Circulating Library on West 49th Street – checking out books and shelving returns. She also tutored immigrants in English at an uptown place called the Blue Bowl Cafeteria. Her pupils Manuel, José, Guinevere, Ingeborg, Vicente, Alvarez and Petri, offered "delightfully diverse views on subjects from washing clothes to being the boss."

Additionally, she made extra money selling Chinese goods in a department store. "My days are rushed," she wrote to Louise at Goucher College. "But life is joyful and I am writing four or five sketches a week."

Mary Tang, Dorothy's Nanking mission school colleague, was in New York for the Thanksgiving weekend. "We had a good time," she wrote, "but difficulty remembering to say 'grace' at each meal. Once Denny burst out giggling at my piously hypocritical bowed head. We went to the Waldorf for the holiday dinner and danced until five. Much fun."

At Christmas, both her sister and their brother Davey crowded in with Dorothy and Denny in what they called their "stable." No description of that holiday exists, but Dorothy expected it to be "lovely."

She later wrote Louise, "It's feeble to love any two like I love you and

Davey, but I *do* and I'm glad. I wish I could take every single bump for you both. Write me about the real you, Dearest. I love you so much."

Dorothy took up smoking that year. Forbidden in "The Nunnery" back home, cigarettes were popular with Americans of her "flapper" generation, and she smoked with daily enjoyment the rest of her life. Reporting on her social life, she confided, "The married beau grew strenuous. Turning him down twice seems to have quieted him. I miss the dancing!"

Meanwhile, she remained committed to her writing. She sold poetry to Century Magazine and stories to the John Martin Book, a children's magazine. "Prestige comes from this," she told Louise, "and cash and courage. I'm planning to deluge the market with juvenile stuff and become famous."

Soon, she focused all her energies on pulling together a full-length book of tales describing the Chinese way of life as she knew it, so that Western children might imagine it. When it was accepted for publication by the Macmillan Company, Dorothy raved to her sister, "It's some thrill, to have the editor talk about who will illustrate the stories, and so forth."

Her editor was Louise Seaman, director of Macmillan's Department of Books for Boys and Girls, established in 1919 as the first editorial division in publishing devoted exclusively to children's books. She was among the first in a number of women to gain prominence in what had been considered a man's world. Apparently editing children's books was considered a "mothering" profession to which women were supposedly uniquely suited. Louise Seaman considered Dorothy Rowe a significant "discovery" and was a friend and supporter of the young author for many years.

When Dorothy's book came out in 1925, The Rabbit Lantern charmed readers with stories of Little Golden Daughter and her parasol, Little Quite Poor who led the Blind Music Maker to the tea house, and, of course, the New Year lanterns.

Lucius Chapin Porter, for many years an American missionary educator in China, offered an introduction to the book. Dean and professor of philosophy at Yenching University of Peking, he was visiting lecturer at Columbia University when he wrote: "Part of the charm of (Dorothy Rowe's) stories is that they are all true. I speak with authority because I was fortunate enough to be born in China. Boys with pet birds on sticks, ragamuffins who go with cheerfulness to rake for fire grass, girls with gaily figured umbrellas, boats…

with rakish upturned sterns and strange eyes,…beggars who chant in a haunting drone as they follow you to the Summer Palace, the schoolroom with shouting boys and tea-drinking (teacher) *and* the fascinating candy man… all these were a part of my experience and are still a part of me. There is not a stroke in Miss Rowe's tales that is not vividly true."

JAUNTING WITH DENNY

In June 1924, with an advance on her royalties, Dorothy traveled again – this time accompanied by Eleanor "Denny" Holgate. After crossing the Atlantic on the Svenska Amerika line to Sweden, they took a "thrilling" train ride to Norway, where they hiked for miles above fjords and boated below. From Stockholm they went by ship on the Baltic Sea to Estonia and Russia, and then on the Trans-Siberian Railway to China. The journey included 44 nights on the train from Moscow across the Ural Mountains to Manchuria and on to Beijing.

In letters home, Dorothy described a stopover in Estonia, where the two American girls stayed the night with villagers. "The family pushed a big double bed, complete with bright blue quilts and red-bordered sheets, into the astonished parlor." Over tea, dried fish and bread with strawberry jam, the man of the house went on about how much he hated the "Bolsheviki."

Dorothy and Denny could see for themselves the changes wrought by the Revolution. In Narova-Joesuu on the Gulf of Finland, an area of beautiful white sand beaches and tall pine trees, they saw great summer dachas turned into pensions offering room and board, or abandoned to overgrowth – "shells of days so full of gaiety." The girls stayed a week in a tiny apartment over a grocery store where they could buy fresh eggs, milk, bread and meat, which they sometimes cooked over a beach fire.

One day they joined a procession to the Monastery of Petchory, "a bit of the Middle Ages untouched by the rush of modern life." When they stopped at a thatched roof cottage to ask for food, they were cordially ushered into a low pink-walled room. "One corner was hung with icons, the floor covered with bright woven rugs, and a crude bench ran along three sides of the room. The barefoot hostess wearing a flowered kerchief set thick pottery plates, large lacquered spoons, a pitcher of fresh milk, hunks of black bread, new butter and honey on the wooden table. Two small blonde boys stood in one corner and watched with wonder and amusement. One by one, the rest of the family came in to gaze at us. We gladly accepted their offer of a loft full of hay to sleep on for the night."

Dorothy's "sketch" of Narova-Joesuu was published in The Monitor magazine, which brought her "some needed dough."

In Moscow, they spent three days in the 6th floor walk-up apartment of Dr. and Mrs. Ward, pacifists from Union Theological School, studying the changes in Russia. Dorothy found the city skyline the most beautiful she'd ever seen, and remarked on the 497 churches on seven hills.

"The government is not against religion," she wrote home, "as long as the religion is not against the revolution. But there is a strong campaign against religion by those who believe the church is used to keep people ignorant, superstitious and oppressed. In front of churches, worshippers continue to cross themselves under posters declaring religion to be the opiate of the masses."

On the Trans-Siberian Railway train, Dorothy and Denny rode in a "hard" compartment [third class]. The calendar said August, but they were so cold they wore "woolen hose and riding suits and bundled in blankets at night."

In their car, long sleeping benches were occupied by 50 people plus several children. Luckily, the American girls were in a section with six upper and lower bunks. Their companions were an elderly couple and two "soldier boys." One tiny lamp served everyone, so all travelers went to sleep at dusk.

The train burned wood and spewed smoke, but was kept very clean. The conductor swept every day, and white-kerchiefed women mopped behind him. At the station stops, passengers could dash to buy bread, cheese and cucumbers and fill their teapots with boiling water at brass spigots. Once, the girls splurged 40 cents on a delicious hot roasted chicken. At Ural Mountain stations, vendors offered trays of lovely stones—aquamarine, green and rose—and monstrous brass candlesticks.

In Tyumen, where between 1823 and 1898 all exiles and convicts passed on their way to Siberia, Dorothy and Denny met a Russian who spoke some English. He asked about their American clothes, apparently offended by seeing young women in pants. When they explained that their jodhpurs were simply for comfort while traveling, he seemed relieved and passed the information on to his comrades.

"Manchuria was an endless grassy treeless steppe, like a great yellow sea with blue shadows across the waves," she wrote. "It is thrillingly big." But the weather was now broiling. "I wear the thinnest blouse I own and drink quarts of cool tea."

When they reached Harbin, Dorothy was so happy to hear and speak Chinese again instead of struggling to be understood and hearing "Nyet! Nyet!" from officials. "My heart is so gay," she wrote, "that the Chinese words come bubbling up."

On September 6, 1924, she wrote of, "The sweet rest of Chinese twilight on a summer evening – the world is wide and green – blue hills with spicy grey smoke rising through low hanging mist from tiny, walled villages."

PEKING

In Peking at last, both girls soon found jobs. Denny worked for the English Department at Yenching University, and Dorothy combined teaching in the government's Girls Normal School with private tutoring, which paid the best.

Setting out to find a house to rent, they rode in rickshaws along the warrens of alleyways, called hutongs, through traditional neighborhoods of provincial guilds, opera houses, bordellos, hot pot restaurants and courtyard homes. Dorothy wrote her sister about "the familiar smells of incense, frying food and hair oil perfumes, little children running naked and brown, men sitting fanning themselves while women's shrill voices call back and forth. The winding, narrow passages are so luring. The high walls hold mystery. The trees drooping over the walls fling moon shadows, and the calling of night vendors and ricky boys give such a sense of security."

The wee house they found to rent was on the "Street of the Crystal Canal's Beginning." A pomegranate tree grew in the tiny courtyard and ivy covered the high outer walls. Their "three sweet rooms" had latticed windows and arched ceilings. They even had the luxury of electric lights and indoor plumbing. A kitchen, servants' room and storeroom completed the small compound. The girls had fun bargaining on the streets for furniture – "two black carved desks, funny old red lacquer chairs, a table and some wicker things."

In addition to their cook, they employed a coolie boy to polish silver, sweep floors and pull the rickshaw to take them to their far-off jobs. "It is such a silly life," Dorothy wrote, "to have two servants after a year alone in New York. But one must do it here, and they are keen about working for the two strange girls who dare to set up a house without a man."

CRAVING ADVENTURE

In February, 1925, she told her sister, "Having stayed in one place for four months and being crazy for adventure I set out for Nanking to see the fam. The boys in the American legation said I was a fool to try the trip because the trains have been so uncertain. Dr. Ferguson (a friend of the family) wrote me a note about the danger of the trip. The newspaper men in Peking who heard I was going called up to say it was a risky thing to do. Dad wired me 'advise delay.' So, with all that to tell me it would be a real adventure, I set out."

After a two-day wait at the Tientsin station, a train finally arrived. "One other foreigner and his wife ran with me to see what kinds of cars were available before we bought tickets." she wrote. "The officials will sell you first or second class with alacrity although there be only third class coaches on the train. We found five box cars and three third class coaches. You never saw anything like the rush for those three, which were soon bulging. We pushed and shoved and yelled our way in the dark and at last found seats.

"It was freezing cold that night. I wore two fur coats and three pairs of wool hose, wrapped the ensemble in two steamer rugs and slept well, as is my wont, on the wooden bench. All the next day we waited hours at each station and the old engine crawled and had the heebies.

"About seven the second night I found that the heat was turned on. I was never more thrilled. The next morning in Hauchowfu I met a man who gave me his card. He was 'Brig-General Su Shen Ting' and quite some boy. 'I order heat to attack this car' he said pleasantly, so the mystery of a comfortable night was explained."

"That was the last day of the Chinese year. 'Brig' was determined to get to Nanking that night. The engineer said the engine could not go any faster. 'Take off some cars,' Brig ordered. So after much pow-wow and swearing, the car he was in, and we too, thank heavens, was hitched onto the engine. The other cars were carelessly side tracked and left there until heaven knows when, but we went sailing on, passing all stations without stopping, tearing through the country so fast that we arrived at ten that night... and at two in the morning I awakened the family. They didn't expect me at all and I adored surprising them."

BEN

When Dorothy's poems were accepted for publication in _Poetry_ magazine, _Asia_ magazine, _Unity_ and other periodicals, they caught the attention of a young man in New York. A veteran of Army service in WWI and a graduate of the University of Chicago, Benjamin March was studying at Union Theological School, taking art history classes at the Metropolitan Museum and dreaming of travel abroad.

In 1923, he accepted a job teaching English and Latin to Chinese students at Hopei University in Paotingfu, China. He had never forgotten images such as this:

Red Candles and Incense
Between tall bamboo trees,
Stone step above stone step,
Up to the Temple of Secluded Light
And up beyond
To the Pavilion of Refined Elixir,
And all day the rain.
I passed no other pilgrims
And at the Pavilion there were none.
Yet in the Cave of Mystery,
Before the Red Cliff God,
There burned two crimson candles
And ten sticks of "fragrant smoke."
I wondered whence they came.

The following year, when Ben moved to Peking, he persuaded mutual friends to introduce him to the poet Dorothy Rowe.

Acquaintance expanded into a courtship that included picnics on the mystical grounds of the ancient Summer Palace and long, quiet conversations. They read poetry aloud, walked under willows near sacred temples and marveled at how many interests they shared.

She saved the notes he wrote to her – the first beginning "Dear Miss Rowe," then soon "Dear Dorothy" and then "My own."

As Dorothy shared her love of China with this intelligent, compassionate young man, Ben was captivated by the sensitive girl who had grown up amid enchanting natural beauty. It seemed to them that destiny had brought them together–as kindred souls–in this magical place.

In March, 1925, she wrote her sister Louise, "I have the most amazing and thrilling piece of news. It is more wonderful than the stories of all the adventures of all my life and more entrancing than all the dreams I had of future wanderings. I am going to be married. Gasp a bit. I too feel gaspy and unreal and whirled. Benjamin is head of the English Department at Yenching University. Since he looked me up we have played around a lot together, but I had plans to sail for New York in August and now I am giving that up for wedding veils and a home in Peking for another winter. And he, who thought only of settling into a life of work, is now ready to bum the world with me the minute his year's contract with the university is over.

"He is a poet, a dreamer and marvelously tender. He is a perfect pal and delightfully foolish. He has all the traits that I seem to want most in a husband. Just shy of six feet tall, he has a straight nose, high forehead, deep blue eyes and a mop of curly hair that sticks to my fingers whenever I am near. You might know I am no use describing the man I am going to marry. Ask someone else. I am so happy all the time that the days go by on swift wings and all the world seems beautiful.

"Write and tell me how you feel about this latest adventure of mine. We wish there were some way we could both have our nearest and dearest here for Our Day, but know that this love of Benjamin's and mine includes everyone we love.

"I have not given up my writing for Benjamin, nor my love of freedom and wandering. Simply, in him I have found the pal with whom to share them all."

Benjamin and Dorothy March on their wedding day - 1925

The two were married on June 30, 1925, in a simple evening ceremony in the rear yard of the family's home in Nanking–conducted by her father and officially witnessed by John K. Davis, United States Consul.

Dorothy wore a sleeveless, ankle-length dress of white-on-white patterned silk, with a deep collar of delicate lace hand-made by Chinese nuns. Her short silk veil cupped around the back of her head with a wide band of matching lace across her forehead, secured by hanging pearl ornaments at her ears. She carried a cluster of fragrant blossoms tied with lace streamers.

Ben's white summer suit looked equally handsome as the couple knelt face-to-face on a pale rug under festive paper lanterns strung high between the trees. They wrote their own vows, which included Shakespeare's sonnet beginning, "Let me not to the marriage of true minds admit impediment..."

For the next six weeks they honeymooned in Hangchow, on the coast south of Shanghai. Poems that the bride wrote there are among those printed at the end of this book.

...

It had been difficult for Dorothy to desert her housemate, Denny. The long-time friends had been happy living together. But Denny's decision to "go round home by way of India" made parting necessary anyway. So, when the newlyweds returned from their honeymoon they took over the place that the two girls had shared.

Later, from April, 1926, to October, 1927, the Marches lived in a spacious quadrangle home, called "Temple Court" at Number Two Tung Fu Jia Dao, which the bride adored. The living room boasted very high ceilings and a fireplace. Decorative latticed windows brought daylight into Ben's study. The addition of five "stoves" made winter weather quite tolerable.

Ben March in a winter Mandarin coat made of deep plum silk
"lined with the skin of unborn baby lambs" – Peking 1927

Ben's sister, Helen March, came over from Illinois to live with them for a year. It was a happy time, with many friends and shared escapades. And Dorothy acquired a lasting nickname.

All the young people were familiar with a major shopping street in Yokahama called "Bentendoré." The sound was irresistibly similar to the couples' combined names, and her new nickname, Doré (*spelled with an accent over the final E and pronounced Dorrie*), stuck forevermore. No one but her parents called her Dorothy from then on. Soon, it was Ben who nicknamed Doré's sister Louise, for reasons long obscured. She was "Lurry" to him and to Doré for the rest of their lives.

...

Ben encouraged Doré to write more stories about China for Western children. While she worked on her second book, he continued to teach English at Yenching University, the respected Harvard-sponsored institution later known as Peking University. In his free time he became fascinated with Chinese Art and embarked on intensive self-education. He became such an expert that he was often called on to speak to Westerners about Asiatic Art – including the arts of Japan and India as well as China.

"Migod!" Doré wrote Lurry, "Ben has given two more lantern-lectures for the Peking Institute and so we again have free tickets for a concert and a French play."

Some of her letters reached her sister while Lurry was traveling as a governess to the children of a family named Robertson. Highlights of that year, she once told me, were periods in Cannes, London and Devonshire.

...

When Doré became pregnant, she was less than thrilled. As she wrote Lurry, "I believed that Ben shared my zest for adventure and I expected a carefree life of travels. Now he spends so much time on his new passion for art that I often feel lonely. That's hard enough. The prospect of being tied down with a kid is not my idea of fun." In a poem she asked:

How can I bear to be bound
When Spring comes back,
Though the bond be the soft-grasping touch
Of my child's hand?
I shall miss willow trees dressed in green,
Though I play with small garments of white;
And how can I walk in the moonlight of spring
If my new born son cries in the night?

But she knew that Ben wanted a child. Because of his weak heart, which had been damaged by Scarlet Fever in boyhood, any infection was a threat and "even a touch of the flu," she said, could potentially be fatal. Because he would never slow down, and lived with such passion, Doré assumed that he could not expect a normal lifespan. Still, he hoped for an heir, and Doré had agreed to fulfill that dream, even if it meant rearing the child by herself.

As she anticipated the demands of motherhood, she rushed to finish her second book. Puffing on one cigarette after another, she typed furiously at her intricately carved desk in the corner of the bedroom.

"I've had an excellent spurt of writing," she told Lurry. "Stories just drop of me tongue, me Luv. I got all my teaching classes in the afternoons, so I have mornings absolutely mine. All but two of the 12 stories for the new book are done. An old obliging Lantern Street artist is doing pictures beautifully, and the name is chosen. It is to be <u>The Moon's Birthday</u>. Like it?"

By November, 1926, she could say, "I'm so hap. The darling book is done and mailed off to Macmillan, the company that published <u>The Rabbit Lantern</u> you remember. I'm free and bereft all at once. Ben is drawing the cover design and end papers. I will dedicate it to the wee thing that is now using my middle for his gymnasium! The infernal kicking drives me crazy, but I still feel like a million bucks and seem to have endless pep."

By early 1927, Lurry had had her fill of living with "the fam." She decided to spend a year in New York while she figured out what else to do with her life. Before long, Doré's letters alarmed her. The uneasy alliance between Mao Zedong's Communists and Chiang Kai-shek's nationalist party, the Kuomintang, had ruptured. "The fighting has made things a terrible mess in the Yangtze Valley," Doré wrote. "All foreigners are ordered out of Hankow, Kuling, and Kiukiang where the Cantonese are in control and mostly snooty. Dad writes that he is lying awake nights wondering what to do when they get to Nanking. Peking seems safe so far. No government at all, but no trouble from the population either. The Cantonese are decidedly anti-British, but the rest of us don't seem in the wrong yet…"

"Boy Blue"

Doré and Ben's baby boy was born on March 7, 1927. A week later, as she listened to the shrill of insects in the darkness outside her hospital room, she propped a pad of paper against her raised knees and wrote to Lurry.

"In the middle of the night, Wednesday, I yelled to Ben and we both sat on the edge of the big bed laughing, for every time I stood up I would leak buckets of clear juice. It was funny and seemed so near to the end of all the months of waiting, and life was such a gay gamble and we adored each other with a pash we couldn't possibly have talked about."

Nick Eastman, her doctor, said to meet him at the hospital in the morning. "Spring was everywhere," Doré wrote, "the sun just up made a warm goldy color. We went to what was coming with such giddy hearts."

"For three days I leaked away and the doctors did all they could to get me started on the job, but to no avail. I ate three fat meals a day, knitted and read and hadn't the vaguest idea why they were making such a fuss. Blissful ignorance. Ben came every five seconds and never could remember what the cook had given them for lunch. My luxurious private room was fragrant with flowers and everything just waited.

"Sunday they put me under gas and did enough scrambling around in my middle to make any cast iron tummy ache. It went on from six that night until midnight Monday – damnably slow and drawn out."

The problem, she explained to Lurry, was that, "The membrane surrounding the kid's private swimming tank was exceptionally thin, and after all the water leaked out, it was empty for 72 hours. The poor wee fish didn't like it a bit."

Sunday night the doctor told Ben and his sister Helen that it had come to a choice of risking Doré's life as well as the baby's by doing a Caesarian section, or taking a chance on normal labor which the child might not survive.

"Poor blessed Loverdee had to choose," she wrote, "and then to know all through that wild mad day how it would turn out. I can get maudlin in a minute thinking about it. I knew nothing and poor Ben was so sweet to me, sticking by thru it all. He looked so silly with a long white gown and a baker's cap over his curls, pushing his ears out.

"They kept the kid alive to the very last, and I did the whole thing myself. But each earthquaky birth pain made it harder and harder for him. When it was finally over, the fat little rascal simply couldn't make a go of it alone. He just sniffed at this funny world and decided he was too tired to stay…When I came out from the ether, I nearly wrecked Ben with questions:

It's a boy isn't it?
Of course, Doré.
Of course he has curly hair!

'Course, Dear.
And blue eyes, Lover?
Um hmm.

Then Nick came in, and seeing I was wide awake, he told me. I thought I was coming out of a dream and it couldn't be true. But then I saw Ben's face. Gee, how he wanted that boy child."

When Doré saw the baby later that night, she wished she could keep him. "Golly he was cute," she told her sister. "He weighed eight pounds and was so amazingly patterned after Ben, with dark curls pushing away in little points over his temples, Ben's nose and long fingers with straight competent little nails. His mouth looked like [*our brother*] Johnnie's as a baby, all cupid bowish and puckery. But he was awfully tired and white and dead, Lurry, and he nearly busted my heart because he was so cold."

Doré and Ben began referring to their baby as "Boy Blue" – remembering Eugene Fields' poignant poem about a dead child, called "Little Boy Blue." By the time she wrote to Lurry from the hospital, Doré said, "We are now quite rational and unemotional, except that we are crazier about each other than ever. Ben is so giddily glad that I am all right. Only when I know how sharply he is wanting our precious Boy Blue do I get low myself."

Doré had never been able to accept the notion that death was "God's will." She did not believe in a Supernatural Parent who controlled the forces of nature or the fortunes and fates of human beings. She thought that if there was a Creator who designed the world and its creatures, he left it to them to figure out how to live together on earth. And he certainly did not make decisions about whether or not to prolong life or to bring about a death.

…

Two weeks later, Doré wrote, "I'm home again and I feel gorgeous. My clothes thrill me to death, and I'm all set on exercises guaranteed by Nick Eastman to give my tummy muscles the boyish form look in six weeks. I can't believe today that anything has happened. The experience is vivid but sort of disconnected from me. I'm writing in the long chair in Ben's study, tea's over and Helen dressing. Ben's squatting on the floor playing with his scrolls.

"We had a pathetic, sad, religiousy letter from Daddy. His talk of Christ and God and The Father's Love seems so damn unintelligent and it's set me to thinking. Have you ever wondered if bumped up against what religious people call 'a sorrow,' you'd feel like looking for Divine Helps? Well, I have now lived through such a sorrow, and here I am feeling less than ever a 'need.' And it is such a struggle to be civil when someone tries to comfort me by saying 'Your son will be waiting for you in Heaven.' Rejoice Lurry that we live under no such delusions.

"Lord knows I wish we had something to show for all these months. I had counted on making the kid occupy some of the time that hangs on my hands here. Perhaps I'll get crazy about writing again. Just now I don't feel interested in anything but Ben. I love him so. He's all the world to me and that's a risky state. It makes me so subject to anything the gods feel like doing to us..."

To America

Doré did take pleasure in seeing <u>The Moon's Birthday</u> into publication, dedicated to her husband, but their tranquil home life in Peking was cut short when Ben said that he wanted to return to America.

He had been invited to lecture at Columbia University that summer, and he was excited by the prospect of going to work for an American museum in the fall. Eager to share his new expertise on Asiatic Art, he dreamed of becoming an "interpreter" between cultures. Advanced degrees were not required in those days. Broad, keen knowledge articulated with flair sufficed to persuade museum directors and boards of a person's qualifications.

Doré agreed to the move, her profound reluctance assuaged only by imagining that they might live in New York City, which had been exciting to her in that year after college, and where her beloved sister Lurry had settled.

The trip included a stopover in Japan, which Doré described to Lurry in a letter typed aboard the familiar ship, The Empress of Asia: "Living in Japanese inns—the take off your shoes and eat local food kind—was screaming fun. Kyoto was full of wonderful temples and theaters and book shops, but Nara was the place we loved best. Lord, what a beauty spot. Ben spent hours in the museums but I mostly sat in the old park under drippy cryptomeria trees and fed the tame deer. I got so inspired that I began writing a Japanese kid story book. Macmillan said a few months ago that they wished I could put them in touch with someone who could write a book of stories about Japan to match mine about China, so here we go!"

Passengers on the ship included returning missionaries that Doré described as "twenty fleeing mishes who are all so hurt, my dear, at having to travel third and keep telling us that they simply could not get first class passage, you see. We tell them that we did not try and that we find this third much better than third on other trips we have taken, on, well, say the Baltic Sea ships or even the Swedish American Atlantic boats. So all of us are snooty in our own way, and we like ourselves the best of course."

After docking in Victoria, Ben and Doré took a train to Chicago, where she finally met his parents and was welcomed into the March family.

"Lord it is pleasant here," she wrote Lurry, describing life in the spacious, light-filled stucco house centered on three fenced acres in the western suburb of Glen Ellyn, where she would spend August while Ben lectured at Columbia.

"Such peace and joy in this 'mansion,' with beautiful gardens and woods and a mother-in-law who is a marvel. She took me into the city yesterday and let me pick out a costume that took my breath away and gave it to me for my birthday. How they all fuss over me. We have done nothing but sleep long, eat much swell food and ride about in the car since we came. It's such a heavenly place and I feel like a new woman already. The only drawback is a feeble one but real to one of my kind. I don't feel married very much and night is the only time I see Ben alone. Considering my demanding nature, that is rather insufficient, but it has to be.

"It's good to feel sensuous again. Heaven only knows what we would have done with a kid in this hectic country. I see folks with newborns and I don't see how they stand it. If we ever weaken again it will have to be a year in the Orient for Dr. March to gather material for his book on Comparative Perspectives or some such spree. I get the most awful moments of blues when Ben shows the fam some pictures of Temple Court (*their Peking home*). I loved it so. But there will be other thrills in New York, when I can join Ben there, and I can't wait to see YOU...

"Because we must save cash, we won't stay long," she wrote, "but I yearn to see millions of people and race and chase and get sore feet… "

Meanwhile, she weeded her in-laws' garden and mowed the wide Glen Ellyn lawn for exercise and finished her Japanese children's book to be titled The Begging Deer. As she reported to Lurry, "It's off to Macmillan, and I have sent other stories to John Martin, Child Life, Junior Home and Everyland magazines and hope that a few sen may materialize… At least it gives me an alive feeling.

"Lurry, can we talk Chinese when I come to New York? It is already beginning to sound funny to me when I speak it. Only eight more days till I see you…. The important thing is to work all the pulls we can for a terrific job for our budding sinologist…"

A post at the Metropolitan Museum of Art was open, but Ben learned, as he wrote his wife, "A curator would be too busy with letter writing, seeing dealers and the care of collections, to have any time for study." He applied, but soon told the Met that he'd made another choice.

It was doubly disappointing to Doré – not only to hear that she wouldn't be joining Ben in New York that week, but that they would not be living in Manhattan, Philadelphia or Chicago. Her husband had accepted what to him was an enticing offer – to become the first Curator of Asiatic Art at the Detroit Institute of Arts.

Apparently she didn't show how let down she felt. He wrote her, "Your telegram brought me no end of happiness and stout courage. I go to Detroit (to sign on) with the knowledge that we will both be happy there and that we are wonderfully at one in our world."

While terribly proud of Ben and pleased for him, Doré did not feel "at one" about it, and faced her own future with active dread.

DETROIT

My mother was a woman accustomed to living surrounded by a landscape of semi-tropical effulgence and starry nights, with fragrant blossoms, delicate swaying bamboo forests and curved temple roofs mirrored in lotus pools. She'd had servants to cook her food and clean her rooms while she went off on lovely long hikes and wrote poetry. She found dirty industrial Detroit the ugliest possible place to live, the dark stuffy apartment confining, and the duties expected of an American housewife appalling.

Ben, who had been independent before marriage, taught her to cook and to iron the white shirts he wore fresh each day when he went jauntily off to succeed in his new career and left her to domestic isolation.

As she wrote to Lurry, "It's such a man's world. Ben is in raptures. The job seems to be all his heart desires. The museum is really gorgeous, each new room done absolutely in the manner of the country whose things are to be exhibited. Ben directs a crew of six men 'in the galleries,' placing the collection of jades, screens, bronzes, and paintings. He has a walnut office and an assistant who adores him. It does make him feel clever and authoritative to be adored.

"I need him to be happy, and I can't be alive and thrilly deep in me without him, so there you are. But I find it hard to think of my end of this job—housework and cooking and washing and dishes—as a real job. It's so piffly boring. Yet I want to do it well and I shall. Ben makes the money I spend but the difference is he loves what he does and I don't…"

I wonder if she ever reflected on how she had repeated her mother's life pattern. Doré hated Detroit as Margaret Rowe had hated China, and their fates were determined by a husband's calling. Nothing in her letters suggests that the parallel occurred to her.

…

Hoping to lighten his wife's gloom, Ben agreed to adopt a pure white wirehaired terrier puppy. Named "Yanger," he was a ringer for the dog they had to leave in Peking. As Doré wrote, "Ben knows I am restless still, so he has been stretching his blessed self to make me happy–getting tickets to concerts and shows and taking me to the biggest hotel for dinner and dancing to soft, cooey jazz and I loved it. It makes me wish I were a nicer girl, not so full of moods."

It did lift her spirits to listen, anonymously, to flattering audience comments after Ben's lectures. "He is really making a marvelous go of this job," she wrote. "One old dame said, 'What I admire most is his exceptional precision in use of the king's English'."

The formal opening of the museum's new Asian Art division was "a white-tie-beaded-evening-dress affair" full of celebrities and directors of other prestigious museums. "They are all crazy about Ben and nice to me," Doré wrote, "so the work of becoming 'March of Detroit' is progressing for Loverdee and I was hap. Ben's assistant went around telling people 'Mrs. March writes, you know,' which I lapped up, for just being someone's wife is not my idea of joy."

Writing saved her sanity. The Monitor invited her to send them an article about Chinese writing paper. _The Horn Book,_ a quarterly for a Boston children's bookshop, requested a personal profile to be published with a review of The Moon's Birthday. And Macmillan accepted The Begging Deer, about the children of Japan, with a one hundred dollar signing bonus in recognition of its being her third book.

Excitedly, Doré wrote Lurry, "Carl Bishop, the Smithsonian's expert on Japan, whom we last saw in Tokyo, has written a splendid introduction, and Macmillan agreed that Lynd Ward, the young artist I recommended, could do the pictures. Isn't it all too gorgeous? And it is to be dedicated to YOU."

Ben and Doré first met Carl Whiting Bishop when he was on assignment in Peking from 1923 to 1927. Ben's photographs of the distinguished archaeologist in his Chinese home were later very useful to Smithsonian scholars. Born in Japan in 1881, Bishop had this to say about Doré's book:

"This book has made the old days seem strangely real. Once more, out of the past, rise up pictures of the Japanese New Year with its feasting; of the Boys' Festival with its warrior dolls in ancient armor, and the great paper carp writhing and floating over houses; of the tame gentle deer of Nara, living testimonies to the all-embracing kindliness of Buddhism…All her characterizations are true to life….(The book) is delightful reading in itself, and it is a sincere and successful effort to help us realize the essential oneness of humankind."

...

Realizing that more physical exercise would help lift her moods, she started swimming at the City Club pool. But, as she continued to rail against the lack of natural beauty in her life, Doré said that she felt "condemned to penal servitude" in Detroit and wondered aloud to Lurry, "What in bloody hell am I doing here?"

When she sent her sister some poems about Detroit, Doré kidded that they would "someday be described as 'written during the period when our author was forced to let her sensitive nature be preyed upon by the crass ugliness of the then-new America etc. etc.' as quoted from my Complete Works compiled in 1998, the one hundred year centenary edition"

...

A year from the day that her infant son "went away" Doré wrote, "Part of me is shut inside, even from Ben, because to him Boy Blue never really *was* and to me, tho I am not morbid about it, his first birthday means so foolish much...Ben is happy in what he does, quite apart from me. I am not. I need people and he only needs books and me. It's funny. But, he is darling to me and understanding of my female ravings..."

During Easter week, spent with Ben's family in Glen Ellyn, Doré and Mother March went shopping in Chicago. "The most exciting thing happened," she wrote Lurry. "Coming out of the elevator on the third floor of Marshall Field's, I saw, above the heads of crowds, six lighted Chinese lanterns, the rabbit and the frog, the lotus and the goggle eyed fish. I gasped and we went to see. There was a huge table, covered with Chinese rugs and with the books of Dorothy Rowe featured all by themselves. The framed originals of all the illustrations hung about, and there was a huge poster with pictures of me and my life history! My books were spilled about in an artful manner and there were mobs of people. I introduced myself to the head of the department and she was thrilled. She said she looked forward to my begging deer book and raved about how easy it was to sell my stuff. O Boy did I ever feel as if 'the young authoress has arrived!"

To relieve her boredom Doré presented an idea to the educational director at the museum. After the Saturday morning movie, Doré invited the hundred kids to cluster around her in the Japanese art gallery while she told them ("and the rim of mamas") stories about cherry blossoms and little girls who compete in flower arrangement. "They seemed to love it and I was wildly happy. I'm going again...and may sell myself to the children's librarian and private schools..."

One day she and a new friend, Hope Vorys, took sandwiches and spent a whole afternoon riding the ferry back and forth between Detroit and Windsor, feeling "very silly and happy." Hope, a high school history teacher and mother of a two-year-old son, lived apart from her husband, who, according to Doré, "couldn't stand kids." Hope, Doré said, "loves her child but never prattles about him…"

A new children's magazine called _Boys and Girls_ came out featuring two of Doré's stories, "Red Threads for her Hair" and "Little Delight," and the publishers asked if she would break "Noodle Pagoda" into four serial parts for them. "Watch me!" she wrote Lurry. The same day she learned that Woman's Home Companion had accepted one of her stories and an ink drawing of Ben's for their children's page. "Isn't that marvelous? The nicest way to sell them, for we both get such a kick from it. And my savings account grows…"

The Rowe sisters were planning a trip to Paris in July. But when, in April, Doré discovered she was pregnant again, she begged Lurry to forgive her for backing out.

"Physically, I know I'd have plenty of pep, but I don't want to spend the money. I want us to have a house before the kid comes," she explained, "and some kind of car I can drive to escape the city now and then. I want not to be worried sick about paying bills. Ben wants me to be happy and says to use my royalties as I want, but if I want to live on a scale a little higher than it is sane to live on his salary I have to contribute to that. Yes, it has always seemed to me that adventure had it all over stability every time. But, you see, darling, I can't just take the adventure for me alone and thus deprive Ben of stability. If I use all my money for the trip it would mean coming back to a wobbly scrimpy year."

Lurry understood, invited a friend to go to with her, and apparently had herself quite an adventure. Responding to Lurry's detailed letter about Paris, Doré said, "I feel so much more near you, knowing that you have come to all those insane inexplicable sensations of physical love. For it is to have the up moments that we go thru the others. You say you don't love the guy. We can't know absolutely, but 'missing' isn't love, nor familiarness, tho they are some part, and you describe the emotions of all the women in the world. Sensations of anger and peace, of jealousy and maternal protectiveness, of beautiful sorrow and hilarious mirth. You have it intensified in two weeks versus years…

"I'm glad you were safe from feetees (*getting pregnant*). It does relieve me to know, for how anyone can love and fear at the same time I cannot imagine. Ben is worried about my having another baby, after what Boy Blue's borning meant. But I know he wants it, really, and I'm making it. I'm happier now than three years ago. Content is a word that is impossible to use, with the constant rebellion in my heart at almost everything in this city, but part of that word does tell of the companionship Ben and I have. Why such ravings? I feel as if I could talk to you more about such things now, since you know about how wildly much our pods (*bodies*) do to us. I wish you'd find a man you want to marry. Silly me!"

Lighting a late afternoon Spud, her chosen brand of cigarette, Doré concluded her letter with, "I wish you could come to have the baked ham and sweet potatoes and garlicky salad and blueberry pie that I'm about to put on the table for us. I don't mind cooking for weekends. It's sort of a feast day feeling."

...

Although not as exciting as Paris, Doré had "the most gorgeous time we have had in Detroit" one evening on a private yacht on Lake St. Clair. "The throbbing of the engine made my imagination come whole again and I sat on the front deck under the stars and was in raptures."

Soon she "jumped at the chance" to take a week-long boat ride on the Great Lakes as "chaperone-companion" for a young woman traveling alone with a reporter covering a sojourn of the Michigan Conservation Commission. Doré's role was a sham, but her way was paid and the pretense just made it more fun.

It surprised her to find that after the week away it was "heaven to be back to Ben, so much I love him," she told Lurry. "Comparisons help me. He seems so precious beside all the other men in the world. He had the apartment beautiful and full of flowers and a cool lunch waiting when I got in... I simply worship him...and it is some swell feeling to know that I am the most and only in the world for him"

Although my mother had never driven a car before, she learned easily and loved it. "Our Ford is a dream," she wrote. "It's a coupe, with a little shelf for Yanger [the terrier] to sit behind me. He licks my ear while Ben watches my every move from the passenger seat. The car is already bringing freedom. Yesterday Ben had to go out east so he dropped Yanger and me off at Belle Isle, a very decent park with water all around. We spent the whole sunny afternoon under willow trees, watching freighters go off to the Great Lakes."

An editor at The Detroit Free Press called to describe her ideas about newspaper promotion of <u>The Begging Deer</u>. She arranged to bring to Hudson's department store the display of Doré's books that had been used by Marshall Field's in Chicago, and she planned a rotogravure spread for a Sunday paper. When it was published, Doré told Lurry, "At least we have gone up in the eyes of the grocer and the dry cleaner… How easily is fame thrust upon one in this puny town."

Dorothy Rowe March – photo by Ben used in The Detroit Free Press

In October, their long search for an affordable new home finally ended well at 634 Ferry Avenue West. Doré wrote, "We love our house, Lurry. I had a screaming week before we moved, getting wall paper and paint and vamping decorators to make things turn out my way. The three front rooms (can you bear such swank?) were supposedly a dining room, living room and front hall. But by taking out the partitions and painting the walls all one color, we have produced a space that would hold a party of fifteen."

"Ben took snapshots you'll have soon. He thinks it's the nicest house on earth. He is so good not to mourn for gone places but to always love now things."

Having a home motivated Ben to take up his old interest in woodworking, which began when he was a Boy Scout. The small sturdy desk he crafted at age 12 is still used by his grandson.

For his new Detroit study Ben designed unconventional bookcases. "They are lovely red and black lacquered copies of the shelves that stand behind the throne of the Empress Dowager," Doré wrote Lurry. "Just off her bedroom in the Forbidden City, remember? But everyone says 'O how modern!' which amuses us. In addition, Ben created floor lamps resembling Japanese lanterns and small end tables that mimicked Chinese k'ang stools.

"Yanger is idiotic with joy over the deep wide yard," Doré wrote. "The kitchen is full of sunlight, with green Korean cloth curtains and pink geraniums. I don't really mind domesticating… but the best thing is that I now have a part time maid named Donnie who comes three mornings a week and does all the washing and ironing in the nice basement and races through the house and makes it shine. I just sit back and let her because I am so much happier writing…."

"I appear in the latest _Everyland_ and _Child Life_ and _Everygirl_. _The Monitor_ accepted two poems and _Boys and Girls_ magazine wants 'four or five stories of the life of American children in China.' _Woman's Home Companion_ has asked for another story too, so I have lots of work to do. It pleases me to sit here at the desk and hear the ironing board creaking under Donnie's hand. How I hated all the washy-washy last year."

MOTHERHOOD

After the train ride to Chicago for Thanksgiving, Doré wrote Lurry, using a nickname for her unborn child. "Pearlie and I, sitting on each other from 9 to 5 isn't so good. Pearlie punches very systematically: one, two, one, two, right foot, left foot, until sometimes I could wring her neck. But it is lovely to be here with Mother and Daddy March and the dogs and the roary fire and marvelous meals. I am resting and eating like a pig. Helen comes today and younger brother Don will come Wednesday and Ben on Thursday morning, so Mother will be utterly hap with all her angel lambs home...."

"Please don't send Pearlie any gift. I won't even take home the cute things Mother March is making. It's too risky. You know how we were gypped the last time. I'm probably being superstitious and cowardly, but I haven't bought a thing or even opened Boy Blue's trunk. I simply can't. We saw some perfectly beautiful nursery furniture, ivory enamel with just the places for Ben to paint small blue horses....but we aren't buying one thing until we're sure..."

Doré's doctor predicted that "Pearlie" might arrive as early as Dec.28, so he urged her to stay home for the holidays. Doré told Lurry, "It's bad enough that the poor kid will have to admit to being born in Detroit, now he will always have his birthday competing with Christmas."

"We made this one quietly festive; with a tree and holly wreath and tall red candles and a swell dinner we cooked ourselves. You know how I love celebrations and Ben is such a presh about it."

The doctors kept assuring her that she was doing fine, but she said, "Nobody knows how it will end. If anything goes wrong this time I'll never do it again and shall solemnly take up Art as a vocation and go to the museum and work right along with Ben and have a grand time. So, being philosophically minded for either situation, I feel very cheerful and rather hopeful too..."

When she went into labor on New Year's Day, she persuaded Ben to drive her around the park before taking her to the hospital, so, in case she died, she would have seen the snow-laden trees one last time.

"IT'S A GIRL!"

The Marches' healthy nine pound daughter was born about 12:15 a.m. on January 2nd, 1929. They named me Judith, after the first Judith March, wife of a pilgrim innkeeper, Hugh March, in Salem, Massachusetts.

Doré was relieved to see that I had "nice flat ears," and she loved the "sweet silliness" when Ben brought me a little corsage and a box of chocolate animals. He also treated his work colleagues to a quart of scotch at lunch, and rushed home to finish painting prancing blue horses on an ivory crib.

Doré felt just fine, physically, but motherhood was a huge adjustment for her. She would say how sweet and cute "Judy Pooh" was, and delighted in every new thing I did, but admitted to Lurry that "I like being babied myself and Judy rather forces me into a grown-upness I don't always feel. I'd give anything for an amah."

PART THREE

幸运

"Mothers may love their children, but they sometimes do not like them. The same woman who may be willing to put her body between her child and a runaway truck will often resent the day-by-day sacrifice the child unknowingly demands of her time, sexuality and self-development."
—Nancy Friday in <u>My Mother, Myself (Random House, Inc./Delacorte Press 1977)</u>

TRAPPED

Budget tightening didn't even allow funds for a maid like Donnie. A month in Glen Ellyn got Doré through the spring, with Mother March and other relatives doting on the first grandbaby.

But that summer, Ben was asked by the Carnegie Corporation in New York to survey all the Chinese and Japanese objects in American museums, for a book to be presented at the Institute of Pacific Relations in Kyoto in the fall. The Detroit museum gave him leave, because they knew it was "a feather in their cap," Doré said, that their curator was picked to do this work. The prestige and honorarium were wonderful to contemplate, but Ben had to visit eight cities. Doré resented being stuck at home "like the wife of a traveling salesman." She was still on the fringe of his life when he came home.

"I never spent two such mad weeks as the last before his book was done," Doré wrote to Lurry. "He came home at 6:30, wanted food at once, and went back to the office at eight. Imagine me with a husband like that. No loafing, no tea time, no conversation whatever. And as to affection, beyond 'well that's a good dinner and I'm off'' there wasn't any. Ben saw how funny it all was, and we begin to understand the life of big business boys. But I feel that if we had to live like that all the time it simply wouldn't be worth the struggle. I'd certainly never stick around any man for so little satisfaction and leisure. But of course Ben did a beautiful job. It's a creditable small book, beautifully written."

When the book was done, Ben celebrated by going on a relaxing fishing and camping trip with his father and brother Don.

In the flyleaf of the first published copy, he paid tribute to the months of Doré's loving support by writing:

"Ten words unsaid enrich the uttered one;
Ten strokes unpainted free the picture's soul;
The background's work, profoundly void, though done
in silence, formulates the final whole."

She acknowledged to Lurry, "It is almost worth being a background all summer for that isn't it?"

Yet, as her husband's career took off and his world widened into lecture tours and book contracts, Doré was increasingly left alone with "the kid."

"I find it fearfully hard to concentrate when Judy is jabbering away," she told Lurry. "She wants company, but she has to learn to be self-sufficient, for I can't have her with me every waking minute."

When I began to speak, Doré was determined to avoid "baby talk." She succeeded, but wrote Lurry "You wouldn't believe how easily I could say 'Wanna go bye bye?' instead of 'Shall we go for a ride in the car?'

Most young mothers have feelings of being trapped at times, but social conditioning prevents them from admitting it. Doré was honest with those who knew her best. "Sometimes I feel as if I don't belong to me at all." In a poem, she put it this way:

"I am a little child pressing her face
to the windowpane of life
wanting to go out.
The snow may be cold and bitter
but I would be in it and know!
The wind may be shrilly cruel.
I would feel it and be sure.
Perhaps the softness of snow
is its reality.
And the strength of the wind
its true meaning.
Open the door of life to me!
Let me go out!"

When Ben said that they could again afford some household help, Doré escaped from child care as often as she could to go shopping or to a movie or to just walk and eat lunch in a restaurant, jotting down ideas for stories or phrases for poems in anonymous privacy.

Gardening also helped her to "work off devils." She loved piling leaves and watching things grow. "There is a row of fat tulips and hyacinths along the fence, in front of the hollyhocks," she wrote. "The columbine has spread all over and the iris is thick with green shoots and the new peony bed looks swell. Next I'm going to buy pansies and stick them in everywhere."

Her self esteem received a much-needed boost with the publication of her fourth book of children's stories, Traveling Shops. The title tale told of the enticing street vendors she had known as a girl in China. She dedicated the book to me; and, with her first royalty check, she bought Ben the Buick he craved.

She loved telling "Dorothy Rowe stories" for children in bookstores, but loathed lecturing for women's clubs. She was always asked questions such as, "Is it true that the Chinese do not celebrate Thanksgiving or the 4th of July?" Yet when the women bought copies of her books to be autographed, it added to her "ten percent of sales" royalties. She would never speak before groups that raised money "to convert the heathen," because, as she told them, "There are no heathen in China."

Still, she saw the irony in her situation. "Ben, who loves hearth and home, is given adventurings. I, who want to wander more than any other thing, must stay put. But, from it, I think Ben will learn to love to adventure more easily, while I find a kind of peace in roots growing deep. Not easy, but then life isn't easy."

...

Ben and Doré had many friends and were popular guests at social occasions. She found a seamstress who could revamp clothes – such as taking old blue Peking gauze, adding matching crushed velvet for a long, fitted bodice, and creating a lovely, 'swoopy" gown with ripples touching the floor in back. It was so cheap that it felt to Doré like the old days in China, but, as she told Lurry, "This gal knows the new styles." And Doré had a flair for knowing what would enhance her lithe body.

One night Doré was included in a last-minute invitation to go out for drinks after a museum meeting of Ben's. She wrote to her friend Hope Vorys, "I called the girl who could stay with Judy and duded up. I like me for being able to leap off at fifteen minutes notice on some goose chase with the Boy Curator."

The Marches also loved entertaining at home in Chinese fashion. Ben drew raves for his home-made "chiaotzûs." The fat steamed dumplings are made by filling circles of thin dough with a mixture of minced pork, cabbage, scallions and ginger, held together with egg. Folded over with pinched edges, the circles become the crescent-shaped delicacies sometimes called dim sum – served with a sweet-salt dipping sauce.

When my parents moved to America, they shipped over a number of Chinese furnishings. A large red lacquer cabinet, called a zhougwi ("jo-gwer"), was the size of an armoire with carved and gilded scenes on its door and drawer fronts. A smaller zhougwi made of polished cherrywood, straight chairs with carved arms, k'ang stools used as end tables, low carved tables, a tall red lacquered stand, and glowing Oriental rugs all made their home seem exotic to Detroit museum patrons and artists.

If there is truth in the notion that "people are made of places," then Doré was indelibly shaped by China. All her life, she cherished her "treasures," not only furniture but pottery figures, carved Buddhas, and scroll paintings. She loved them not only for their timeless beauty and their power to evoke her early home, but for the awe and admiration expressed by friends and household help. She reveled in the way these possessions set her apart and made her seem unique in other's eyes–quite unlike other housewives–but she was never owned by them the way she believed that people she called "social climbers" would have been.

As a hostess, Doré relished appearing in embroidered silk costumes that enhanced her dark beauty and the air of mystery admired by all who met her.

SCANDAL

One of her admirers was a stock broker named Thomas Newton, who met the Marches because his father, a wealthy meat packer, lived around the corner from them. Bored with his own child-bride Esther, Tom began visiting

Doré whenever Ben was away. He learned that, despite the blessed security of Ben's love, Doré often felt neglected.

As she explained it to her sister, "When I married Ben, I thought he shared my zest for adventure, my wanderlust. His passion for Chinese art grew slowly, and, for me, that came at the expense of nearness between us. There is so much of me unburned. I am not ready yet to be old, quiet. Precious Ben is ready. He is so hap with the sweet settledness of having me once in a while. I can't accept that as the end. I know that there aren't many years of wildness left for me. I'm 32 almost. I feel sure that when I am burned out a little more, when the physical edginess is quieted, it will be the calm sure, utterly devoted love Ben gives that I shall want.

"Meanwhile, I'm restless. Tom adores me and I glow in the light of knowing I am still desirable and not too old for love. We go for long drives in the country and pretend such lovely foolishness. Tom has never played before and is crazy about it. He is so sweet and I love it."

She was also attracted to the kind of life Newton led – "a rich, lazy, selfish, well-dressed, pointless life." Tom persuaded her that "more years of Detroit the way you are living will kill the free, gay you."

In March 1930, when I was 14 months old, my mother ran off to Bermuda with Tom Newton. It was to be a month-long "experiment," known to Esther Newton and sanctioned by my father. Ben told a close friend that he had been "aware of the intimacy" and was willing to give them a chance to see if their love would last. He firmly believed that, "Forbidden fruit is perceived as the sweetest. If I ordered my wife never to see the man again she might always wonder whether she'd been denied greater happiness."

Ben's mother, now called "Granny" March, came to Detroit to take care of me while her son "lived through 17 million hells."

Three weeks later, after the lovers came to Miami, Doré wired Ben that she wanted to return home to him and their daughter. Tom wanted to make things permanent. He begged her to stay, but she was firm in her decision and left him there. The next morning, Tom shot himself and died in their hotel room.

Because of Newton's suicide, the adulterous affair made the front pages in Detroit. Headlines screamed, "Newton's Affair Revealed: Friend's Wife Tires of Experiment" and "Self-Aimed Bullet Solves Newton's Love Experiment" and "Love Tryst Wife Back." Exaggerated drawings of the exotic temptress Mrs. March appeared for days. Writers made our home sound like an opium den. Most sensational to the reporters was Ben March's acceptance of his wife's behavior and his quiet welcome when she came home.

He was quoted as saying "I did what I did because I love her and I wanted her to be happy. I told her that if she ultimately wanted to leave me she should have that privilege, but if she wanted to return to live with me, I would do everything in my power to make life agreeable.... It wouldn't be easy at first, but I saw no reason why we should not carry on with even greater confidence in each other and more mutual happiness."

He issued a statement asking the public and the newspapers to give them "privacy to reconcile behind their closed door." Although reporters left them alone, The Detroit Free Press kept the story going by asking readers, "What Would You have Done?" Society matrons were interviewed for their opinions of his forgiveness. Most considered Mrs. March a very lucky woman.

There is no way of knowing exactly what words the couple exchanged behind that closed door, but the whole affair must have been something of a wake up call for Ben. He must have realized that he needed to create a better balance between his career and his marriage.

Doré told Lurry that the getaway with Tom was "the kinds of fun young children have without a thought of consequence or cost. I willed myself to be happy and not think of my after-while-inevitable life and feelings. But I accept that to keep Ben's gentle, wise touch on the life of our child is worth whatever compromises I must make."

She understood that she couldn't rush restoration of trust. "I must be as much as possible self-sufficient and poised, quiet and calm. That will break certain defenses that Ben has put up against the old, over-passionate me... I know if I am sporting and unselfish I can keep Ben and I want to, because he isn't just any husband. He is a very unusual person with bigness enough to overlook my disloyalty and deceit and want me anyhow.

"It is being sure just what I want that is important. And it is determining to build toward that bit by bit. I've never built towards anything. I've grabbed at present happiness and been so hellish selfish. I've always snuck out of any disliked present by play-acting, glorifying my past, dramatizing myself. I'm not going to do that anymore.... I just feel a huge searching loyalty that I want so to bring to port. I need understanding of the real me with the ugly places unglossed and, too, not enlarged."

In May she went with Ben to a museum conference in Toronto. Though she struggled against feeling "subordinate," she pulled it off and ran slides for his lecture. "It was excellent and very well received." She wrote, "Ben is so sweet and flattered, so pleased and small boyish in his clever, scholarly way. He was so happy the whole time. He misses having people who know more than he does, to hash with."

Gardening was therapeutic for Dore, as before, and she started sewing – pleased about making two dresses and a little coat for me. "They really look quite decent," she said.

...

In New York that year, Lurry was hired as a receptionist/assistant at Huxley House Designers and Typographers. When she left China in 1927, she fully expected to go home again within a year. But conditions there had changed drastically. Doré had written her, "It looks as if anything might happen – peaceful turnover or the Cantonese roaring into Peking. God knows."

Dore and Ben left Peking just ahead of the brutal conflict between the Nationalists and Communists. But Father and Mother Rowe were still in Nanking where rampaging Nationalists soldiers killed six Westerners, including a university president, and terrorized the rest of the foreign community. In 1928, when Chiang Kai-shek made Nanking the seat of his Nationalist Kuomintang government, the Rowes were among those forced to leave. Lurry had to acknowledge that for her to return would be dangerously foolish.

She found the typography business creatively satisfying and Huxley House a congenial place to work. A fine writer like her sister, she was soon promoted within the firm, and she took advantage of New York's vibrant cultural opportunities. Unlike her sister, she loved classical music and always splurged on season tickets to Philharmonic concerts.

Lurry had the same pointed Rowe chin as her sister, and a long straight nose. Her steady dark hazel gaze was what people noticed. Her lively open expression let others know they were heard. Proud of her trim figure, she walked miles for exercise and pleasure. She dressed in what I think of as a sensibly stylish way. As far as I know, she never entertained in Chinese costumes or stressed her 'foreign" upbringing with acquaintances.

Doré and Lurry assert their Rowe chins

NURSERY SCHOOL PARENTS

In October 1930, when I was 22 months old, Ben and Doré enrolled me in the Merrill Palmer Nursery School. The "behaviorist" school was known for its scientific monitoring and guidance of every aspect of a child's social adjustment and character development. In order to be assured of admission, "Fetus March" had been registered while still unborn. Thirty children, ages

18 months to five years, were supervised from nine to four each weekday, with only three tots to a teacher, so placement was widely coveted.

With her child spending every weekday under the scrutiny of professionals, my mother had more time for reading and writing. She also found that she enjoyed me more in the evening. Bedtime stories and lullabies became special pleasures for both of us.

She gave up hiring a cleaning woman, in order to save money "for a sport roadster of my own next spring." She figured that the housework would be good exercise as well, but cleaning was never terribly important to her.

"Why is it," she asked her sister Lurry, "that to me a spot on the floor or a curl of dust isn't that vital? Probably it's a reflex against Mother's constant nagging of servants who didn't dust just so every dawn. Ah me, how much a mama is responsible for a young'un."

Apparently the school officials accepted my parents' "modern" decision to have me call them Ben and Doré, rather than Father and Mother or Daddy and Mommy.

But, maybe it's just as well that the school officials didn't hear when I asked my mother, "Who is Little Lord Jesus?" Doré dashed out and bought a nativity picture book, explained the Bible stories and taught me Christmas carols. Soon, she told Lurry, "Judy declared that 'Little Lord Jesus that didn't make any crying when the cattle is lowing, and Wee Willie Winkie, who ran right outdoors in his night gown, are my favorite stories'."

That winter, a number of Dore's short stories were accepted for publication in magazines such as _Child Life_ and _Story Hour_. She spent some of her royalties on a small upright piano, lacquered jade green with Chinoiserie-style painted figures and flowers. She felt genuinely happy playing and singing with her husband and child.

In the spring of 1931, the celebrated painter John Carroll asked Ben and Doré if they would allow their two-year-old daughter to sit for a portrait to be included in an upcoming exhibition of his work at the Rehn Gallery in New York City. As a thank-you gift, he painted a duplicate portrait of me which my mother displayed with pride all her life and hangs in my home today.

Some time that year, the Merrill Palmer headmistress called my parents in for a special conference.

"Judy is doing just fine academically and socially," she began. "But we are rather concerned about nap time."

"Nap time?!" Ben asked incredulously.

"Yes, well, you see, Judy sings herself to sleep with some very questionable songs. We are alarmed about the lyrics and we wouldn't want the other children to pick them up. Maybe you can help us to understand where she might have learned them."

Seeing Ben and Doré's blank stares, the woman explained. "She is singing things like 'Sixteen men on a dead man's chest,' she huffed. "and 'Yo ho ho and a bottle of rum'."

I can picture my parents struggling to suppress a chuckle or outright guffaw as they recognized the words to old sea chanteys that Ben sang to me at bedtime. Not exactly conventional lullabies but hardly subversive. Avoiding each other's eyes, they firmly assured the headmistress that they would suggest that I sing familiar nursery rhymes from then on.

PENTWATER

During the previous summer, Ben and Doré had been introduced to the resort village of Pentwater, on the Lake Michigan shore about 250 miles northwest of Detroit. They were invited guests of their friends, attorney Walter Nelson and his wife Rilla, who owned a vacation home in the community.

Among other "summer resorters," the Nelsons had been drawn to the wide beach of pale, fine "singing sands" backed by low dunes with graceful swaying grasses and warm hollows to huddle in on windy days. Behind rose taller dunes topped by a pine forest. From the beach, a long channel connected Lake Michigan to the inland Pentwater Lake, where Walter skippered his sail boat, "The Ripple."

Unlike a waterfront cottage, the Nelson's place was a solid two-story house in town. One evening after dinner, Walter and Ben were talking on a screened-in porch. As they gazed across a narrow side street at an old wreck of a house, Walter said he was tempted to buy it just to tear it down and improve the view. Ben then said, "Well, why don't I buy it and fix it up instead?" That he did.

The purchase was well-timed. In the spring of 1931, Ben was awarded a special grant from the American Council of Learned Societies that enabled him to spend six months in China studying the 13th century painter Ch'ien Hsuan and acquiring art and artifacts for the Detroit Institute of Arts.

During all the excitement and flurry of preparations for his trip, Doré found that she was able to stay fully supportive of what she saw as Ben's "glorious opportunity to sail to England and travel by train to Berlin and Leningrad and on to China."

Despite her longing to be "adventuring" with him, she felt surprisingly serene about the need to stay with me. She managed to tell herself that she would be glad to be free of wifely duties for a while and just be herself, and although she would miss Ben, she told Lurry, "It isn't as hard to let him go as it would have been two years ago." Moreover, the prospect of fixing up the Pentwater house gave her an exciting new focus for the time that Ben would be away.

The two-story frame house was probably at least 40 years old at the time and long neglected, so its rehabilitation would be a major challenge. But Doré adored the charming little village, and happily threw herself into creating a retreat from city life.

After spending Easter weekend up north with Rilla Nelson, Doré wrote, "It was heavenly. New leaves, red maples, pinky arbutus, crimson wintergreen berries in the woods, quiet and warmth. The beach was gold and the lake full of whitecaps. And my house is so absolutely right. I spent a glorious day in its emptiness with a notebook, writing down every single thing I'd like to do. I can eliminate later if I have to.

"I plan to tear off a crumbling front porch, put the door in the center with a colonial arch over a tidy red-brick entry, paint the ancient clapboard siding bright white with shutters of dark green, paint every inch inside, floors included, and paper it all gaily, put in plenty of electric plugs and <u>two</u> fireplaces. The one in the living room will be deep and wide, and upstairs in my room will be a tiny English-style grate like China days. I am mad with excitement."

She soon made arrangements to rent the Detroit house to a "sensible, middle-aged woman," and the rental income gave Doré needed funds for remodeling and decorating plus furniture, lamps, curtains, dishes and kitchen utensils. She loved scrounging at Detroit thrift shops, yard sales and department store clearances.

"Everyone I know says I'm utterly loony," she wrote to Lurry. "They can't see how I can 'shop around' and crow so over a dollar or two saved here and there. But I do. This first year, living room furniture will be six low-slung canvas deck chairs and two sawed-off card tables. Every cent saved on inside furnishings is that much more for filling in my garden and planting trees and flowers."

Off the kitchen, a cement terrace, bordered by low red brick walls, became the favored spot for morning coffee, sandwiches at noon and cocktails before supper. A long hedge of cedars screened the side and back yards from the road. Over the years that hedge grew nearly as tall as the house.

Inside, Doré used tongue-and-groove paneling saved from the porch ceiling to create an enclosure and drain boards for the wide kitchen sink. In the central dining room, the same paneling was used for wainscoting and a built-in china cabinet under the stairs. Since there were no wall cabinets in the kitchen, dry foods were stored in a separate pantry on shelves beside and above a small refrigerator with a round condenser on top. Serving suppers and putting dishes away were inefficient, time consuming tasks, but summer allowed plenty of time to be "wasted" on such chores. My mother also ignored the lumpiness of the kitchen floor, made of rolled roofing over boards of the old shed. She simply painted it bright red and saw it as part of the room's old fashioned charm.

For a corner of the dining room, Doré ordered construction of a wide built-in daybed. Although no charcoal fire burned beneath it for warmth, the wooden platform was modeled after a Chinese k'ang bed. A blue and white Russian spread was tucked in over a thin cotton mattress. A dozen small pillows, covered with Chinese cotton or colorful calico, were banked in the corner. This lounge, which Doré called "the jazz couch," became beloved by all who lived in or visited her house as long as it remained in our family.

Her color schemes were also unique. For the wooden floors she ordered a paint mixture that was somewhere between sailor blue and royal blue, and which became known to family and friends as "Doré Blue." She loved the color so much that she never cared how quickly it showed tracked-in sand and dust.

Woodwork was painted a soft rose, which harmonized with any shade of gladiolas she kept in tall vases throughout their season. The zinnias and marigolds she grew along the side of the house were arranged with ivy or cedar clippings in small pottery vases that marched up the edges of the staircase.

The first thing anyone noticed on entering through the front door was the enormous white brick fireplace. Doré loved to tell the tale of a remark made by a village character named Elmer McKinstry who came to check out the remodeling. According to her version of his visit, after gazing long and hard at the deep mantel extensions on each side of the prominent chimney, Elmer asked, "Whatcha gonna put up there? A gol-durn orchestry?"

Doré ordered only white birch logs for the fireplace, because they looked so pretty stacked by the hearth. Crickets that occasionally chirped from the pile were seen as good luck. Hands and hearts were warmed at that fireplace on cool summer evenings and in her later years, when Dore could stay on into September or October; those same fires were a daily delight.

Upstairs, each bedroom was known by the color of its décor. Unsurprisingly, the master bedroom was done in blue. The yellow room came to be called "Lurry's room," and the two sisters looked forward all year to her precious two or three week vacation in Pentwater.

My room was really two – a small passage with a single bed, opening to the large attic-like playroom at the back of the house. As Doré envisioned future built-in bunks, closet and dressing table, she told Lurry, "I can imagine my girl remembering its feeling all her life."

"Judy can't get over being able to wander about outdoors. She took her doll buggy ten blocks alone one day and came back feeling as if she had been to Africa. She brings me little stones and sticks and flowers, calling to me, 'O Honey, look!'"

...

Streams of house guests came north to enjoy long days on the beach with campfire suppers far north of the bathhouse concession area, while Doré basked in their approval of her retreat. The peace of mind and beauty in Pentwater filled her with contentment, and the quirky old house became Dore's sanctuary nearly every summer for the rest of her life.

At the end of her first August there, she wrote Lurry, "I really believe that my ridiculous need for romance has been baked out of me this summer. I'm not sure. The volcanic passion of my body is so real a part of me, and I haven't smelled that ravishing male perfume—a combination of shaving soap and the oft-mentioned tweeds and that peculiar masculine physical essence—all summer. I'm not expecting too much of me, but a wifely once-in-a-while may soothe my hunger. We shall see.

"The whole escape with Tom seems so far and unreal most of the time, that I can't make it close. I don't want to. I want to be elated because I have had all the body-joyings there are, but not to live backward. In my aloneness I keep the joys I've had as a part of me, for a sort of warming when I am cold. But most of my time I am dashing and keep warm without that.

"I am glad Tom is gone, for all the aching want of him that stuns me sometimes. I know that if he had gone on living I would have gone on being infatuated by his love and growing weaker myself. I might never have found me, and success, and determination to live as life is, no matter what it brings. I couldn't have been good for or with Judy, whom I really love.

"Subconsciously, I hated the way Tom looked at life. He was my child, too, and so needful of me that he asked for too much. It would have closed me to Judy's greater needs which I must sense now because she doesn't even know them herself.

"It all had to be."

PART FOUR

幸运

> *"If you want to understand any woman you must first ask about her mother and then listen carefully. Stories about food show a strong connection. Wistful silences demonstrate unfinished business. The more a daughter knows the details of her mother's life—without flinching or whining—the stronger the daughter."*
> —Anita Diamant in The Red Tent (Picador USA 1997)

THE GREAT DEPRESSION

Ben's China trip was perfect. He was thrilled over what he accomplished in Beijing, acquiring all the treasures he wanted for the museum and material for a book. Upon its publication, his complete glossary of technical terms to be used in the critical analysis of Chinese paintings set standards that earned him lasting respect in his field.

While pleased and proud, he was also delighted to be back. He had been very homesick for his wife and daughter and the museum and even Detroit. He brought Doré what she described as "the most beautiful pair of soft blue patterned silk lounging pajamas and matching coat I've ever seen!" She wore them for years, even after stains and holes from cigarette ashes rendered them fit only for private use.

Doré's re-entry into couple hood was difficult. After the blissful summer of eating whenever and whatever she wanted and going barefoot in "knickers and a yellow checked shirt," she had to "grit her teeth" to produce full dinners at an appointed hour and iron six white shirts again every week.

Her feelings would undoubtedly have been different if they'd had servants, but she wrote Lurry that she was happiest alone. "I'd adore Ben if I didn't have to live with him. That goes for every man I've ever seen so I guess I'm lucky to have even that feeling about the man I <u>am</u> married to. But isn't life funny? It's one huge eternal compromise. It's fun too, this silly business of being alive. No reason to it or purpose that I can see, and much weariness and loneliness streaking through it in some mad amusing pattern."

...

Meanwhile, the Great Depression was following on the heels of the Stock Market Crash of October 1929. The Detroit Institute of Arts reluctantly followed the example of other museums in making the difficult decision to lay off its curators or reduce their hours.

In January, 1932, Ben had to take a ten percent salary cut. Doré wrote Lurry that, "He has been hellish low over it all. He hates uncertainty in money matters. I say what the hell. I will not talk Depresh." Still, she economized by shopping at the downtown farmers' market instead of convenient neighborhood grocers, and gave up buying theater tickets or going to movies.

When I outgrew my crib, Ben built a "big girl" platform bed and dresser to match, painted soft jade green and yellow.

Doré was writing again, which always raised her spirits. "I get the spinach washed and the rugs swept and the flug out from under the beds while I am thinking up plots in a rapturous state all the while."

She took on the challenge of writing for 15-year-old boys in _American Boy_ magazine, which paid rather more generously than other publications. The plot she imagined was "about a Manchu boy in the 1911 revolution in Nanking, who escapes to the Yangtze in disguise. The idea being that this kid, who had been walled in by his house and the minds of his conventional tutors and the rules of his home, is suddenly thrown out into the midst of the rebellion of modern youth and how he handles the change."

Meanwhile, her earlier stories about Chinese children continued to be published in such magazines as _Child Life_. The $25 honorarium was a blissful fortune to her then.

The $100 lecture fees Ben received from the Chicago Art Institute, the Metropolitan Museum and the National Archeological Society in Washington, D.C. helped to tide them over a month of bank closings. And, despite continued financial pressures at the Detroit museum, he was kept on in a part-time capacity. Meanwhile, he was given a half-time appointment as curator in the Museum of Anthropology at the University of Michigan. As Doré put it, "Ben never has had a kick that wasn't up! But he thrilled me by saying that he couldn't have gotten through the last six months if I hadn't been such a good sport and kept telling him day after day what a swell guy he is"

Ben and Doré knew how lucky they were. Fourteen million Americans were out of work, nine million had lost their life savings and many thousands were forced to line up for soup and bread dispensed by charities. The economy had totally collapsed, but the country would always need teachers.

Around that time, Lurry and their cousin Pauline "Paula" Simmons decided to cut expenses by sharing a New York apartment. Related through their mothers, who were sisters, the two career women lived compatibly for many years, with Paula doing the cooking and Lurry the "washing up."

DEARBORN

In June, 1932, we moved to Dearborn, then a relatively small community between Detroit and Ann Arbor. The location was not only more convenient for Ben as he divided his time between two jobs; it pleased Doré to be out of the big city. My father had to spend most of July on a grant-funded research project, but first he was able to spend a couple of weeks in Pentwater.

Doré was delighted to find that all the trees and shrubs started the previous summer had survived and she threw herself into weeding and planting annuals. "I never had more fun," she wrote Lurry. "I shovel black dirt and wallow among the plants and get the biggest kick out of my flowers. To have six times more than you can do and be crazy about all of it _is_ living, I guess."

Granny and Granddaddy March came for a week while Ben was there, and Doré loved repaying the pampering she always enjoyed in Glen Ellyn. Moreover, as she wrote, "Father and son laid out all the plans for a 'forest' of new trees and bushes across the back of the lot, screening the neighbor's barn, plus rock ledges over which creeping juniper now cascades. There is a fairy tale of white birches, jack pines, hemlocks, white pines and cedars and the loveliest honeysuckle and cranberry bushes. My book royalties paid for them all!"

My father was able to return to Pentwater for three weeks in August. "We are so happy here," Doré wrote. "Ben is the dearest thing, bumming around in shorts and growing a mustache. He works at his desk all morning, then breaks for the day and we loll with Judy on the beach or on Nelsons' sailboat. In the evenings, after she's in bed, we have such silly fun by the fire, loving Pentwater and each other."

Although she hated the end of summer, Doré looked forward to living in Dearborn. Our pleasant rental house on North Monroe Blvd. was set on three acres of hilly land with a stream and willow trees. She told Lurry, "It means returning to a cool, green retreat instead of dirty old Detroit."

She was also happy to have her days to herself again, with me back in nursery school. "I love my child and she's loads of fun," she wrote Lurry, "but summer is a rather long stretch of unrelieved mothering." The serenity of Dearborn's rural setting made the chauffeuring back and forth to Merrill Palmer worthwhile.

The academic year brought invitations for Ben to lecture at museums in Boston, Milwaukee and Minneapolis as well as repeat appearances at the Metropolitan in New York. When a feature story about him was published in a Detroit newspaper, my parents found it hilarious that the reporter wrote so much about Doré as well. "Me, the erstwhile outcast and infamous as I was two years ago! We howled over every word."

In October, my parents were invited to view a University of Michigan football game from the president's box. The guests included two German princes, grandsons of the late Kaiser, so an elegant luncheon preceded the game, and police with sirens blaring escorted the procession to the stadium. Doré loved the pomp and circumstance, and did her best to show proper enthusiasm for football. "It was a jumble of figures," she told Lurry, "squatting or kneeling in worship of an elliptical leather ball – then suddenly all racing insanely down the field and lying down in a heap over their god. The worship was monitored by white lines across the field, and two huge electric scoreboards that flashed out the numbers to tell which color of worshippers had done best in their prayers."

...

That same month, Phillip Fu, a member of the Board of Recommendations of the Palace Museum in Peking, made a business trip to Detroit. His first request was a private meeting with Benjamin March. The following evening, Ben and Doré picked him up at the Statler Hotel and brought him out to Dearborn for a home-cooked dinner.

It turned out that one of Mr. Fu's two missions for his U.S. visit was to ask Ben to come to Peking for as long as five years, to take a position as Secretary

General of the Palace Museums. As Dore described it to Lurry, "They need a man trained in museum techniques to put the Palace Museum on the map as it belongs, as the center of all Oriental museums, to get out a Bulletin, to popularize their collections by publications, etc.... They will pay our way over and back and ship any household items we want, give us a house and a living stipend. I am breathless with excitement."

For Ben, the offer represented a major advance in his career. That the Chinese sought an American for this position was unimaginable, and was a clear affirmation of his professional expertise. As Dore wrote, "Isn't it staggering to think about – Ben in the midst of that precious collection and so gorgeously connected... He says there isn't a job like it in the world. He can have any post on earth after that."

"Isn't Ben really marvelous, for a kid of 33?" Dore asked. "How many times in seven years we've been married some great change has come that seemed stupendous and vital and he has leaped into it as if life held no greater chance. He feels able to do anything and he has no fear of work.... He is already subconsciously planning this gigantic organization job in Peking, step by step"

The timing, in the midst of the Depression was also ideal. The serious financial constraints on both the Detroit museum and the University of Michigan meant that Ben could surely arrange a leave of absence from both jobs. On reflection, however, he decided to resign. It would give The Palace committee more "face" to have his undivided attention, and if he were still buying for the Detroit collection, there would always be rumors of dealers getting commissions through Ben's position.

"Oh Lurry," she wrote, "Just imagine! To have a Chinese house, with a cook and servants and an amah for my child, and to have tea in my own courtyard with lotus plants and tons of chrysanthemums! And think what it will mean to Judy, from four and a half, to cross the ocean and learn to speak Chinese and to study at the Peking American School and learn that Detroit, Pentwater and Chicago are only bits of the big wide world."

As Doré and Ben considered what furniture to leave at Pentwater, what to sell and what to ship to China, such as "good beds," events in the Far East were determining another course for their lives.

Japan had invaded Manchuria on Sept. 18, 1931. Control of the area it renamed Manchukuo was just the initial step of Japan's aggression against China that would continue until 1945. However, in the early 30's, China's leader, Chiang Kai-shek, was so consumed with his fight against internal Communism, that he ignored the external threat and followed a policy of non-resistance against Japan. In Peking, the Palace Museum board, terrified of a Japanese incursion into China from the north, decided to move and hide all of the museum's priceless irreplaceable national treasures, for safe-keeping. Ben was informed that, regrettably, until the "messiness" was settled, and Peking was easy again, there would be no expansion of museum activities. And no new job.

Doré's letters to Lurry betray none of the anguish they must have felt. Perhaps she splurged on a phone call to hear her sister's supportive voice and talk over her disappointment. Whatever else happened that winter of 1932-33, no description remains. It may have been a difficult time in Lurry's life. When she left my mother's letters to me, she said that she had destroyed some which were too private for anyone else to read.

In the spring of 1933, Doré wrote of daffodils and tulips and hyacinths and narcissus poking up from under the leaves, and her plan to get out and rake so she can watch them grow. "Lilacs and forsythia have appeared from nowhere, and there is a soft green haze over the willow trees. The meadow is making the silly word *lush* seem real," she said. "Nature is the realist thing always."

As she looked forward to summer in Pentwater, she wrote, "Happiness we make for ourselves. Sometimes it is all runny and unsure, but we can see how mostly we make it steady and real. It has to come out from within us for it never comes to us from outside. I know that. And the thing that counts is personal courage. God, how I fight for that. To you it must seem as if I have everything, with love and book making. But everyone wants and wants...."

...

The major news in Detroit that spring was the controversy over enormous murals at the Institute of Arts painted by Mexican artist Diego Rivera. While the massive figures and depictions of machinery celebrating industry in the motor capital drew raves from art critics, segments of public opinion were in an uproar. Catholics said the panel portraying vaccination of a child was a desecration of the Holy Family. The mayor and city council lamented Rivera's Communist leanings.

Doré wrote, "Really, is there any place in Detroit for intelligent, unprejudiced people? Personally, I don't give a damn about the controversy. The murals are thrilling and they do convey the feeling of Detroit. If they wanted a picture of the spiritual essence of Detroit, I suppose a whitewashed wall would quite express it! Hey, nonny, nonny!"

The Depression ground on. The university paid Ben half time salary, but nothing came in from the museum. Doré wrote, "We let the bills slide and try not to care. It's no fun to have to watch every cent so furiously and to not buy anything but food and heating fuel and gasoline. This week we are eating nothing but beans and spinach so we can go to see 'Green Pastures' with the entire New York cast. Doing something so extravagant is such a boost."

Ben's ego was massaged by a request to consider a job as Director of the Walters Museum in Baltimore. Fear of losing him may have compelled the University of Michigan to finally get its finances straightened out so it could offer him a full time faculty position. He was hired as Curator of the Division of the Orient in the Museum of Anthropology, starting May 1, 1933.

ANN ARBOR: MORTON AVENUE

"Ben is a new man, so gay and free and at peace after months of uncertainty. He is closing up the Detroit affairs this week. I feel a certain sadness for him, horrible as it has been for months, because he <u>did </u>love that job, but he is swell about looking ahead and being content. The Baltimore job, on further inquiry, seemed very dreary in comparison, so I'm glad he took this and it's settled. And what a break that the salary starts at once, so we can afford Pentwater."

Doré's birthday presents that June included rouge, lipstick, a slim compact of face powder, and cleansing cream – costly luxuries that she had been doing without for months.

On June 15, they moved to Ann Arbor. Much as she hated to leave the "lovely outdoors" in Dearborn, Doré felt "lucky to have a much nicer house in a swell part of town, three blocks from Judy's school and within walking distance of Ben's office."

The grey-shingled rental at 1605 Morton Avenue had a large central entry hall. Off that was a long narrow living room with a fireplace and French doors opening onto a side terrace. The 12 by 20 ft space took all three Chinese rugs. Off the living room was a spacious dining room and an enormous kitchen with so many cupboards that Doré said, "I can't imagine a restaurant having dishes enough to fill them."

On the right side of the entry hall, wide stairs rose, turned onto a broad landing and rose again to the upstairs hallway. The front bedroom became Ben's bright spacious study. At the back was my cheerful room, where colorful East Indian Numdah rugs warmed the floor.

In the basement, Ben constructed a dark room where he could continue to develop the professional-quality pictures he'd been entering in photography shows. He also took many pictures of me.

Lurry once told me, "I believe that you were the most photographed young child that ever lived. Ben captured you on film with his true genius. He was very generous about sending me copies so I could watch you grow."

I remember my mother's description of sitting for a picture with me, both of us dressed in Japanese kimonos. I must have been about three years old. Ben told Doré to remain very still, holding her pose, while he clicked away, concentrating on the movements of their daughter. The most charming print he made reveals my frustrated attempts to get her attention.

Doré and Judy pose for Ben

After Ben decided which photos of me to enlarge for exhibitions and to mount in "The Book of Judith," an elegant Chinese-style album he kept, Doré saved the rest. She pounced on all the discards, fastening them with gummed corners onto black pages in smaller Kodak scrapbooks.

...

After settling into the new house and hiring a woman to do Ben's laundry, Doré tucked me into her car and headed to Pentwater for the summer. As always, the lake and cool northern air delighted us and this year Dore took greater pleasure in my companionship. "She's grown so much, in her head as well as her small pod, that she's really fun and no work at all," she told Lurry. "We eat at the red kitchen table and read poetry during meals. While I putter in the garden, she rides her trike or pushes her doll buggy about, visiting any house she thinks is 'insterting.'"

Ben came up for their wedding anniversary June 30th and his birthday – the always convenient holiday of the 4th of July. As a boy, he imagined the fireworks were for him. "Can you believe it's been eight years since we were married?" Doré asked Lurrry. "The last two have far surpassed the middle two, and I am so glad and proud." Ben was also able to spend August up north, playing host during visits by his parents and his sister Helen.

Before returning to Ann Arbor that fall, they stopped by Glen Ellyn and spent an exhausting but exciting day at the Chicago World's Fair. "The whole place is so glorious at night," she wrote to Lurry, "that we decided that Judy must see it, too. The next afternoon we did the whole Enchanted Island, rode the ponies, the train and speedboats, slid down the magic mountain, and saw them catch the beam from the star to light up the whole place. Judy could hardly bear to go home at midnight."

In September, I entered first grade in public school. After advertising for help and interviewing dozens of women, Doré found a girl who stayed with me if my parents had plans to go out. Our house also became a popular gathering place for artists and authors, including Carl Sandburg, plus faculty and graduate students. Ben was "on top of the world" over the new job, and Doré made compatible new friends.

My mother always adored having "new duds." When Ben allowed

her "$25 over budget," she bought "a hyacinth blue wool dress with bulgy sleeves and a smart cherry red velvet (very Thailand) scarf at the high neck. With blue kid shoes and blue hat as big as a peanut, it's a delectable outfit." For Christmas, Ben gave her "a juicy black pajama outfit." She told Lurry, "He's just the same darling of Peking days this winter."

...

For my major present that Christmas Ben painstakingly constructed a large wooden dollhouse which Doré hand furnished with calico curtains, grey velvet carpets and checked oilcloth for linoleum. "Honestly," Doré told Lurry, "We have had a second childhood making it. Ben put in electric lights, a hand-carved fireplace that looks like bricks and miniature paintings on the walls." The furniture included a piano, a tall radio cabinet, standing lamps and fern stand, and even "silverware" for the dining room table. Doré made cloth napkins the size of postage stamps, a bathmat and towels and put a tiny bit of real pink soap in the soap dish.

I played with that dollhouse nearly every day for the next seven years, until circumstances required that it be put into storage. It was saved and passed down to my daughters and granddaughters. I believe that Ben and Doré would be deeply touched.

The holiday in Glen Ellyn was particularly mellow, with a new baby in the family. Ben's sister Helen and her husband had just welcomed their first daughter, nicknamed Mimi. After the tree was trimmed and lighted, Ben sat with me on one side and his brother Don's three-year-old son Benny on the other, to read aloud from a beautifully illustrated copy of The Night Before Christmas.

"I may be sentimental and silly," Doré wrote Lurry, "but things like that really make the wheels go 'round in life, dontcha think?" How often, in later years, her thoughts returned to the bittersweet memory of that Christmas.

...

As my fifth birthday approached, Doré told Lurry that she had learned "It's vital to have more than plentiful food and games at a kid's party. You gotta have a program." So Ben put on two puppet shows with his Chinese marionettes, delighting both children and their parents.

My gift from my parents was a puppy–a purebred Scottish terrier whose kennel name was "Sandy of Peebles." Ben had long wanted a Scottie, and Doré said "Sandy is the swellest dog I've ever had. He is gentle and loving like old Duggan and wise and gay like Petey of Peking." I took charge of feeding my new playmate and keeping his water pan clean and full, and reportedly said he was "better'n any toy in all the whole world."

A cherished companion for many years, Sandy was a featured character in a slim handmade book that Ben wrote and illustrated, called "Pentwater Beach: Six Poems for Judy." Family members and friends still treasure copies of that wee volume.

During the winter and spring of 1934, Ben was more and more in demand as a lecturer. In April, when his travels took him to Philadelphia for meetings of the American Oriental Society, Doré invited her friend Brenzelle Hueseman and her son Bobby to come from Illinois for a visit in Ann Arbor. Bobby and I were the same age and best friends from shared summers in Pentwater.

The visit, however, stretched to three strenuous quarantined weeks when Bobby came down with a life-threatening case of the Measles! Brenzelle was an utter wreck, "helpless as a dishrag" with worry. Trained by being "school doctor" in Nanking, Doré took on all the nursing duties–ice bags for fever, sponge baths, bedpans, enemas, plus getting meals for everyone and trying to keep Bren sane. At night Doré sterilized everything Bobby had touched, but the pediatrician, Dr. Lichty, also recommended immunizing me with an injection of blood from someone who had had measles. Doré volunteered and that transfusion protected me enough that I was hardly sick when I developed the disease. I had already had the chicken pox in February, so Doré felt that an important phase of childhood had been survived.

"I'm glad to be growed-up, she wrote to Lurry. "It's a swell feeling. And when Ben got home he was his usual utterly dependable encouraging self. I thank god for our Oriental slant on life. Cause and effect, a bit of fatalism, a good shot of brutal cruelty, if that's needed, and a huge jigger of what-the-hell make the only potion on which to raise a kid."

Doré was invited to submit a description of her childhood for a thick volume called The Junior Book of Authors, to be published in 1934 by The H.

W, Wilson Company. With a photograph taken by Ben, her page appeared between Christina Rossetti and Carl Sandburg.

...

In mid-May, Doré took me out of school and "tooted off" to Pentwater for a week–to get the work started on built-in bunks and a closet under the eaves in the so-called attic bedroom and some raking done in the yard. "Ben is so busy I never see him," she told Lurry. "He is frantic getting his syllabus ready for California and exams and term papers approach. So he is all for us getting out from under."

The syllabus was for a summer post as director and lecturer on Fine Arts for a Seminar of Far Eastern Studies at the University of California, Berkeley. The session lasted six weeks, and, counting travel and visiting his parents, he was to be away for two months.

There was never any question of Doré going along. Ben would be so busy, and his wife and daughter would be much happier in Pentwater. I was given a two-wheeled bike and roller skates as a "California present." Lurry was able to vacation in Michigan that year, and with the visits of friends, Doré had what she called "a perfect summer." However, when Ben returned on August 15th, he was "in rotten health."

HIS LIFE TO LIVE...

Clearly, the heavy summer responsibilities had taxed Ben's heart and depleted his reserves of strength. Knowing that his heart had been weak since boyhood, Doré constantly worried about his health. But she kept her concerns to herself when he exhausted himself on lecture trips or took on something as demanding as the Berkeley seminar. Even at home, she swallowed her fears when projects, such as making a dollhouse or handcrafting furniture, and his consuming hobby of photography kept him in his basement workshop or darkroom far into the night. In a journal she used poetry to describe her private woe:

Sometimes at night,
Dreams come to me of losing you,
And I am tortured in my sleep.
And wake myself with crying.
There is no joy so wonderful
As finding you alive and warm beside me,
Hearing you ask sleepily,
"What is it Sweetheart?
What's the matter, Dear?"
I press against you till you sleep again
Then take the great white handkerchief
From your pajama pocket,
Wipe my eyes,
Laugh a little,
And go back to sleep.

When Ben arrived home from California, his doctor, Marianna Smalley, explained that, as one side of his heart took over all the work normally done by the damaged half, it had become grossly enlarged, which made his breathing increasingly labored. She told him not to walk even two blocks, to do as nearly nothing as possible. So Doré brought him up to Pentwater for a month of "staying in bed until two and then just sitting about."

On August 29, she wrote, "His heart is getting noticeably worse, and with feeling so tired, he's really badly off. It scares the hell out of me, for it can't go on indefinitely and I can't really face life without him, with Judy-Pooh to raise and all. Yet I do think of it constantly, waking up at night to listen for my darling's breathing. It's like a huge black shadow hanging over me always. No use grousing and there's nothing to do. But the waste of his life, for such a grand person, gets me all the time…"

When Ben went back to work in September, Doré drove him to Detroit or Jackson for lectures. She hated the city traffic, but was glad for something she could do to help. As she put it to Lurry, "For Ben, not getting tired is harder than it sounds. He is trying. He has classrooms where he can sit, and he sits. We have dinner on a card table up in his study, to keep him from doing any more stairs than he has to."

In late October she wrote, "It is so hideous for Ben to be moderate. Monday he went down to the darkroom after he came home, and worked on pictures. He was shakey white that night and it scares me terribly. He knew he was a fool, but we all hate admitting it and he's been mad at himself as well as draggy. This afternoon, he finally opened up and told me he hated his own limitations. I used psychology on him, as I do with Judy, and coaxed him to come home at two. He's in bed now, reading a mystery story and waiting for supper on a tray."

My mother knew what kind of man she'd married, and she loved him for all that made him Ben. Taking to a wheel chair might have prolonged his life, but she knew he was not willing to settle for that and would continue to push himself to do all that he loved. It would be unfair, she thought, to whine or demand that he think of her or of his child. She believed that, "It was his life to live," however he chose.

On November 20th she wrote, "A consultation of doctors decreed, gently but decisively, that Ben must stay flat in bed for at least five more weeks. His bosses and colleagues have been so swell about it that it almost made me sentimental. Blanket permission was given for any arrangement, 'just so Ben gets well.' For there is only one Ben March, they say, and he is essential to the university."

Ben's students were to come to his bedside weekly for assignments. A grad student who had taken his courses, carried on in the classroom. The museum sent a secretary over to take Ben's letters. "He needs mental repose too," Doré wrote, "and having his correspondence up to date seems to give him a chunk of peace."

Meanwhile, Doré handled "the up-and-downing of stairs and trays and liquids and what not," and kept her spirits up. "There is a funny challenge to being so goddamn necessary. Perhaps knowing that Ben, for all his grand power of seeing things through, does lean on me for humor and encouragement and hope gives me a real boost."

For my sake, Doré even stuffed a Thanksgiving turkey and roasted it as if she cared. "Judy was so excited about a celebration," she wrote, "that she made paper decorations and place cards for the card table and stayed out of Ben's room all day so he would be rested for dinner. He ate a sliver of white meat and drank 2 oz of cranberry juice. Judy stuffed herself and I haven't any idea what I ate. I thought before it was over I'd die of the goddamn lump in my throat behind the grin on my mug. Somehow, it all gave me a too vivid seeing of the three of us in relation to all kids who are not-yet-six and all grownups pretending whatever they must."

On December 4, the doctors enforced stricter orders. No callers. No secretary No bathroom privileges. Doré added bedpans, sponge baths and alcohol rubs to her routine. Ben lost interest in life, wouldn't read his office mail or look at the Christmas presents Doré had been buying for his family. Soon he was so discouraged and fed up with being an invalid that he had to be mildly sedated during the day. At night he yelled and cursed repeatedly and talked of suicide.

"Yep," he said, "that was a smart fellow who said when you're done, quit."

When the noise woke me, I knew I must not call my mother. "Judy is really amazing," Doré told Lurry. "She just turns on her bed light and sings herself back to sleep. I turn her light off when I get around to it."

The following week, the most celebrated cardiologist in the state told Doré, cold and straight, "I do not feel that Mr. March will come through this."

Ben's mother, Granny March, came in time to see her son before he died – at 11 p.m. on Thursday, the 13th of December, 1934.

Doré was sustained by knowing that he had heard her say good-bye. She wrote Lurry, "I said good night, my darling boy, sweet dreams. He looked right at me and nodded his head and was gone to dreamings that no one ever shares. But he knew that I was strong and there to see him off. He was not like a grown up lover, but like such a little, little boy, and it's good to know that he is not in pain any more or afraid of anything at all."

Then Doré woke me to say that Ben's poor sick heart had stopped and he was dead. She let me climb up on his bed and kiss him goodbye. I had been prepared to accept his death as a blessed relief.

"No more suffers," I said. Without tears, as was expected of me.

It gave Doré peace of mind to insist that Ben's body not be "stuffed into clothes" or laid out in a casket, but taken immediately for cremation in an old white shirt he loved.

A very simple memorial service was conducted by a good friend of

Ben's who was a Unitarian minister. "There were gobs of flowers," Dore told Lurry, "and candles, but no prayers – just the idea that life is rich and grand and real for however long it lasts. I chose three poems, translated from the Chinese, from Ben's favorites, and Harold Marley read them well." Friends and colleagues shared their memories of the remarkable man who died too young.

I wasn't allowed to go to the "remembering meeting," as I called it. I accepted my mother's wishes and did not complain, but I never quite understood my exclusion, particularly when I heard that the music included "Home on the Range," a favorite song of my Daddy Ben's that he sang to me so often as a bedtime lullaby. I don't know whether my mother or Ben's mother wept during the memorial service, but I later understood that neither of them wanted me to see that.

I was sent right back to school and told that Ben wanted me to carry on normally. That was the beginning of my striving to live up to what Doré said were his expectations.

...

When droves of mourners came to call on her after Ben's death, Doré found herself "having to lift so many pitifully desolated ones out of their abject grief." She had that way of pointing up her Rowe chin and asserting her belief that death is a natural part of life, and of urging others to celebrate the days or years that they had had with Ben, rather than wallow in their loss.

Although Doré was raised by devout Methodists, she chafed against the way that religion dominated her early life. "We had to read one chapter of the Bible every day and five on Sunday," she told me. She came to view organized religion as "a crutch for the weak."

The notion of a personal God who paid attention to individual humans, answered their prayers or decided who lived or died seemed bizarre to her. She and Lurry poked fun at such traditional beliefs by concocting an imaginary faux deity that they called "*Kind-Dirty*."

"Sometimes he's kind. Sometimes he's dirty," she would say. So, if she hit a rough patch in her life, she might mutter, "*Kind-Dirty* is playing one of his nasty tricks again." And when some unexpected blessing befell her, she would say, "Thank you, *Kind-Dirty.*" A committed Christian could argue that the dirty things in life are the work of Satan, and that God is only kind. But Doré didn't make that distinction. To her, *Kind-Dirty* was a capricious personification of Fate that tested her again and again.

Christmas in Glen Ellyn was both supportive and nearly unbearable, with Ben's absence painfully palpable to his whole family. But for Doré, her sister Lurry's arrival was "the sweetest gift."

PART FIVE

幸运

"Endurance can be a bitter root in one's life, bearing poisonous fruit, destroying other lives. Endurance is only the beginning. There must be acceptance and the knowledge that sorrow fully accepted brings its own gifts. For there is an alchemy in sorrow. It can be transmuted into wisdom..."

—Pearl S. Buck

LIFE GOES ON...

Once all tributes to Ben were read and all the medical bills paid, Doré faced her widowhood. She realized that she couldn't keep renting the large Morton Avenue house and would have to go to work to support herself and her child. The university paid her Ben's full salary through February, which eased immediate concerns, and Granddaddy March, who was a Chicago attorney, took over the business of investing Ben's life insurance proceeds. Dore's landlord agreed to a reduced rent from January to June, so she had the spring to make decisions before her summer in Pentwater.

As Ben's condition had deteriorated, he and Doré talked about what might lie ahead for her alone. He knew her well enough to imagine that she would want to return to China. He asked her to promise that she would see to it that their daughter was reared and educated in the United States. By educated, he meant until I graduated from college. Keeping that promise became one of the most difficult tasks of Dore's life. To her friend Hope she confided that if she hadn't given Ben her word, "I would have tucked Judy under my arm and tooted off home to Peking."

It is useless to speculate how her life, and mine, would have unfolded if she had done so. China was soon to be invaded by Japan, enmeshed in World War II and overtaken by the Communists. But in 1935, as a young widow, she accepted the consequences of her life choices and set out to raise Ben March's daughter alone.

...

That first winter, she went over to the university museum every afternoon and made herself as useful as possible. Her knowledge of Ben's work and her own organizational skills were greatly appreciated. "It is swell to be busy and using the bean," she wrote to Lurry, "and to *have* to go someplace every day,"

"Lonely as the devil at night," she managed to live through each empty hour, and face another day. "I am learning to be alone, but I miss being loved and silly and protected," she wrote. "Nothing makes much sense and the struggle to feel that living is worth the effort wears me out. I feel old sometimes and horribly responsible. I would love to run away, but I know you can't run from yourself, so it's better to stay and face the music."

Her work at the museum became increasingly rewarding and valued. She finished a manuscript on two magnificent Chinese bronzes, for which Ben had compiled copious notes and recorded technical details. She prepared it for publication and wrote Lurry that, "Everyone seems pleased with it and it does sound like Ben. I loved doing it and I feel as if he would be pleased, too, at the way it turned out."

She sold both cars and bought a blue Ford V8 coupe, which she drove as fast as 85 mph on the highways. For spring vacation, she drove with me to Glen Ellyn, where it was restorative for her to "sleep late, read silly magazines, eat Granny's rich food, and be doted upon by others." The weight she dropped during Ben's illness was slowly being replaced.

She was anxious then to be done with living in the Morton Avenue house, where bittersweet memories dragged her down. "I want to get away to rooms that Ben has not known. I will not live backward, but it's harder looking ahead while still in this house."

During May, she endured the weary, endless process of chucking, sorting, packing, cursing and drinking alone. "The worst was Ben's desk drawers, his closet, his dear old darkroom, tools and trunks of childhood treasures," she told Lurry. "It makes him so very dead. I found myself holding things in my hands waiting for him to yell, 'For god's sakes, kid, I want that. I might need to use it some day'."

There were moments when she felt "as if I could not decide one more thing all by myself, but I'd recover and decide and then be quite inordinately pleased with me!"

Ben's enormous mahogany desk was sent to Pentwater. The top surface measured six by four feet–too big for any apartment. Ben had designed the desk in Peking and had it made to order by Chinese craftsmen. The deep drawers and brass drawer pulls bearing the Chinese character for his name made it a stunning conversation piece. As a child I loved to examine his Chinese pens and brushes, sticky red ink in porcelain dishes and other items used by Oriental scholars. Along with the contents of the desk, his old books, portfolios and photo albums gave the Pentwater study a sweet musty odor. Anytime I am around venerable volumes and artifacts today, that characteristic smell evokes poignant memories.

Other furnishings that weren't moved to Pentwater were put in storage for the summer. The price Doré got for Ben's cameras and darkroom equipment paid for a new red roof on the Pentwater house and a coat of paint on the siding.

In some ways, Doré was prepared to be single parent. She had often cared for me alone during Ben's many professional absences and then his prolonged illness. But, now, with the stress of packing and moving, it was a great help that she found me increasingly "companionable." She told Lurry, "I need her as a friend and a nice, casual, swell pal. It's so much more satisfying than the mama-baby relationship."

She had never played with me. Although she always took an interest in my school work, writing or drawing, she saw "play" as something children did by themselves, with their toys, or with other children – their "playmates." Almost certainly, as she was growing up in China, Doré never saw adults play with children. Neither did I.

Throughout her life, Doré prided herself on keeping true feelings to herself and showing only a serene, untroubled face to the world, and most of all to her child, whom she wanted to protect from pain. That's one reason that writing letters to Lurry was such a valuable outlet for her. As Lurry explained it to me years later, "I was the one person to whom she could tell anything, though not always everything." With others, she would "never let the Rowe chin quiver where anyone can see it."

That chin was long remembered by Pat Nelson, Walter and Rilla's daughter, who observed my mother on their sailboat that summer. Clad in loose-fitting white ducks and a sweatshirt, Doré sat quietly, her pale, thin face framed by a royal blue cotton bandana. Pat described her as "a Modigliani sort of figure….the profile of her determined chin seemed to forbid conversation." But her impassive blue eyes had crinkled at the outer corners in what Pat saw as "a mute message of reassurance" before they became "inscrutable under slightly fluttering eyelids."

Doré had asked the Nelsons to help her fulfill a promise to Ben by taking her out on "The Ripple" so that she could bury his ashes in the depths of Lake Michigan. After a while, when Pat and her brother were preoccupied, she leaned over the stern, her head bowed. "Only little puffs of gray dust, rising in our wake," Pat remembered, "gave evidence of the silent requiem…."

Slowly then, Doré turned to the others, saying," There's no need for sadness. Ben would have loved the sail today. In the long days when he was dying—it seemed an eternity to us—he was so ready to go—we sometimes talked about this sail. It comforted him and made him happy—and it has been just as he wanted it." On her face, Pat remembered, was a look of fulfillment—of peace.

Dore's financial future was secured when the university hired her as a full time assistant to the museum director, Dr. John Winter, to start in September, 1935. In addition to some research, cataloging and organizing, she would help with student conferences and other tasks as need arose.

SWELL APARTMENT

After a peaceful, restorative summer in Pentwater, we moved into a comfortable two-bedroom Ann Arbor apartment. The landlords, Mr. and Mrs. Kempf, lived on the first floor of the large, traditional house, while the second and third floors were divided in half, creating mirror-image apartments. A few years later, I would keep my big two-wheeled bicycle in the detached garage.

I can picture my mother walking through our apartment for the first time. She would be thinking how well the big, red lacquer Chinese zhougwi ("jo-gwer") would look in the dining room where it could also be seen from the living room. Her jade green upright piano would fit on the long wall of the living room. Opposite, she would back the davenport up to the bank of windows for good reading light when she sat in her favorite spot at one end. A landing at the top of the interior stairs would hold her desk, which she would use primarily for storage of stationery and household records. Letters she would type on her lap downstairs.

The other apartment was occupied by a divorced woman, her mother, and her six-year-old daughter. Other than being parents of "only" children, Doré and Marjorie Johnstone had almost nothing in common. But Patsy and I were classmates in school and played together until suppertime almost every evening of our shared childhoods.

Best of all, the house At 612 Church Street was located within reasonable walking distance of Eberbach Elementary School and just a few blocks from the university campus. That first year, a young woman named Virginia came in afternoons to do dishes, light housekeeping and stay with me until my mother got home about 5:30.

For Doré, the psychological adjustment to "punching a clock" wasn't easy, but she soon slid into the routine and felt "really keen" about her work. She particularly enjoyed the young graduate students she got to know in the Fine Arts study hall, and before long she invited some of them over to the apartment. She not only wanted to fill a few lonely hours, she needed to create gladness. It seems quite possible that memories of her mother compelled her to be as different as possible. "Mother was always so wretched and weepy," she recalled in a letter to Lurry.

"I don't want to be hard or sour or crabby," she wrote. "At 37, I've had experiences that could do all of those to me, but then I wouldn't be me, would I? I've always been so romantic and sentimental. I try to control that, to let it come out in some small, gentle ways. I have learned so much about tolerance. I see so many people needing me to be tolerant and kind. That makes me glad.

"With the kids who come to study, I will not be a grey-faced, unlipsticked flat person behind a desk. I insist on being real to them, and, in return, I make them real, with names and a thought or two, and always a smile. It is the most exciting part of my days. It leavens the business of research. I've never leaned to scholarly pursuits, really. I enjoy the effort of digging into books and pictures, but I vastly prefer organizing and interacting with human beings."

By devoting herself to learning and to meeting the needs of others, she slowly healed. "Sometimes it doesn't seem possible that I've been without Ben for ten months," she wrote, "but lord how I've grown up!"

The two-week break in Glen Ellyn over Christmas was welcome – with its chance to sleep late and eat good food that she had neither purchased nor prepared. Beloved relatives were gathered, and over the New Year's weekend her dear friend Bren Hueseman met her in Chicago, where they attended plays, ate in unique restaurants and sat up drinking and talking for hours. But she was also content to go back to work.

"Except for Pentwater summers," she told Lurry, "I don't think I could go back to the life of leisure. It seems strange to me, but I went back to my desk feeling so gay and happy. Judy is in school, the house is clean and in order, with everything running smoothly. I like it. I like belonging to me."

In the spring of 1936, she organized and catalogued all of Ben's books, photographs and papers, preparing "The March Library" to be moved to the university. There was also a certain sadness to it, when memories would take her "off to the day we bought the Chien Lung writing paper or the time Ben simply had to have those pictures from the Palace Collections."

So it was cheering for her to look forward to a vacation with Lurry in New York City. The sisters, who were as close as intimate friends, relished time together, and Doré thrilled to the additional prospect of seeing friends and watching Helen Hayes on the Broadway stage. Rilla Nelson, who planned to go east to see her daughter Pat, invited Doré to share the driving and costs, which made the trip affordable. According to Dore's letter, "Judy is tickled pink" about spending the week with Alice (a family friend).

Preparation for Dore's trip to New York included painting her fingernails bright red. It was the kind of "vacationy" gesture she loved. Even when her nails went unpolished, Doré usually wore large rings – silver or enameled, as opposed to small gemstones. My own hands resemble hers, with long slim fingers and deep nail beds – and I now wear those rings.

...

Toward the end of the school year, Doré helped the leading professor of Asian Art, James Plummer, mount an exhibit of ink rubbings from China. Preparing wall labels, writing and typing the catalog and handling publicity were a pleasant change from routine research. Jim said she saved his life, which was nice to hear.

The Pentwater summer held its usual joys of no schedules, spontaneous beach suppers and yacht club dances. On the 4th of July, we celebrated what would have been Ben's 36th birthday by singing his favorite old songs around the fire after a beach supper. "Judy was thrilled to sing at the top of her voice to a small new moon over the warm lake." Dore wrote. "She held tight to my hand. We both knew why."

Throughout the 1930's, my mother attracted an eclectic assortment of friends of varied backgrounds, hues and sexual orientation. All can be presumed to have been liberal in outlook. Some were drawn by Doré's connection with the fabled Orient, but to all she was appreciated as frank in her opinions and uninhibited in her lifestyle. Our apartment once again became the center of quiet weekend gatherings. Among those who sought her company were a number of eligible men.

During the summer of 1936, the darkly attractive widow was seriously courted by a businessman named Syd Chapman, who made frequent visits to Pentwater. His regular features were cheated of being handsome by a scarred complexion and thinning hair. Appearance probably wouldn't have counted against him if it had not been for other detractions.

"I like him," Doré told Lurry, "but I pity him more each time he comes. He is too old, too dependent, too gentle and far too impressed by money. He has showered and embarrassed me with gifts unsubtly given. I am surfeited and a little bored on this pedestal of his making. No one can buy me or even appear to. I am too easily pleased by my small, personally-achieved security."

By late August Doré decided to reject Syd's proposal of marriage. Crushed as he was, Syd stayed a devoted friend for several years, always willing to squire her to an upscale restaurant or to drive her somewhere in his Cadillac with no strings attached. Granny March convinced her that it was not unfair to help him spend some of his dough, since it gave Syd so much pleasure.

The other significant man in Dore's life was David Stewart, a sandy-haired University of Michigan law student with boyish good looks. Raised in China by missionary parents, he not only spoke Chinese, he had a solid appreciation of art and literature and responded emotionally as she did. "With him," she told Lurry, "I have color, humor, brilliantly alive conversation, respect without maudlin gushing and a give-and-take that gives me joy. I feel quite young and enchanting."

Doré on Pentwater Beach 1936

As always, summer seemed to end too soon. Early September had been unusually warm, but, as if the weather gods knew Dore's needs, the day she left was cold and grey. "I always have a hard time leaving," she wrote Lurry. "I wander about the rooms and pat things, go and say goodbye to the trees and the blessed flowers, and generally let myself have a field day of sentimentality. I picked marigolds and zinnias to bring along."

That year, a mature Pentwater woman named Ora Freeman came back to Ann Arbor with us. She lived in a nearby furnished room and came as close to duplicating a Chinese amah as possible in America. "Ora is the answer to my oft-muttered prayers for a servant," she told Lurry. "She gets a big kick out of everything and has no thought but to help me."

Whether or not Doré had domestic help or plans to go out with a suitor, she always tucked me into bed at night, with stories that evolved from nursery rhymes and Winnie the Pooh to classics such as Alice in Wonderland, Uncle Remus, Pinocchio, Wind in the Willows, and pages of poetry. After lights out, lullabies included her sentimental favorites "Little Pink Rose" or "Little Boy Blue." I knew that both syrupy songs referred to dead children. Much later I figured out that if her own "Boy Blue" had lived, I wouldn't have been conceived, but as a child I tried to share her sadness over the loss of my "brother." I requested the songs so often that the lyrics are still embedded in my memory. Nearing Christmas, she sang traditional carols. She also taught me a few Chinese folk songs.

Years later, Lurry told me that my father intended to raise me bilingual. After he died, Doré probably couldn't envision my ever having reason to use Chinese and she didn't try to teach me. The sisters enjoyed speaking their childhood tongue whenever they were together. They also used it to say anything they didn't want me to understand. I knew that xiao haiza ("shaow highza") meant child, so I caught on when they were talking about me, but beyond a few other expressions such as hello, goodbye and thank you, that's all I learned.

Ben's father continued to handle investment of life insurance proceeds. In June Doré told Lurry, "Dad sold 2000 shares of something or other that leaped in price with the Republican hot airing, and sent me $218 as profit." A tidy sum to her then. Her financial stability was also improved by sub-letting the Ann Arbor apartment for the summer to two responsible grad students. She knew that Ben would have hated the idea, but she was willing to pack away most of the Chinese treasures and she felt confident that all would be okay. "Still, it is strange to make a decision like this alone and realize that it's no one else's affair but mine!"

In the fall of 1936, my mother was offered a position in the Department of the History of Art, as assistant to Helen Hall, the supervisor of photographs and slides. Doré not only received a raise in pay, she negotiated an unusual contract for a staff member. She was allowed to work the nine month academic year so she could have summers off in Pentwater.

The job consisted of cataloging and filing all the "lantern slides" used to illustrate the professors' lectures and the mounted photographs used by students in the study halls that she monitored. The "librarian" aspects of the job became a pleasant routine, and colleagues in the department became her friends.

In November Dore's mother died of cancer. I regret that I never even met my Grandmother Rowe. Since their return from China in 1933, she and Grandfather Rowe were living in California, near their youngest daughter, Caroline (or "Barbie" to Doré).

Doré begged Lurry to write to their father, who was so depressed after his wife's death. "I know it isn't easy," she said, "I ask myself why I should do it and swear that I won't get involved in the emotions that bend me to the fam. Then it seems as if I must, because it is kind.

"I have known hideous loneliness in these last two years. It comes as sharply in crowds....Once or twice a small gesture of tenderness from a person who understands the ache of loneliness has comforted me for weeks. There is a meaning to tenderness between people that ranks it high in human qualities I would achieve. It's such a two-way working quality between people. It so seldom hurts either one, unless you fight the softening of the crusty edges of our hearts...

"Life is complicated, and sometimes seems so futile. What point is the going on of it at all, and to what end when we do? Yet it has flashing moments so good that all the rest are forgotten. I suppose it is with eternal painful hoping toward those few that we live out the many."

...

In early 1937, Lurry arranged for the printing of book plates for me, a black-and-white woodcut following a design that Ben drew the last evening before his fatal illness confined him to bed. The depiction of a pilgrim girl with a long scarf flowing out behind her was based on the story about the first Judith March, who supposedly shocked Salem by wearing a red scarf to church on Sunday. "The book plates are lovely," Dore wrote, "and it means so much to have this last idea of Ben's carried out for his girl. She is very prideful about pasting them in her books."

Dore's friend David Stewart graduated from law school and began his practice in Mt. Pleasant in mid-February. His absence left "a hideous void" in her life. By this time, the two had acknowledged that love was what they felt for each other, and she was "so alive and happy" with him. "He is so wise and gentle, infinitely considerate, and always sincere," she wrote Lurry. "Judy adores him and, in fact, she suggested that I might marry him!

"But so damn much stands in the way of a for keeps future," she admitted. David was just starting his career, studying for his bar exams and dreaming of going into the foreign diplomatic service. "What of Judy then?"

Dore wondered.

By early April, David decided to end the relationship. "The decision had to be his," Dore wrote. "He knows that I would wait to marry him if he wanted me. But he is young and I think afraid of permanence, and he does not love me in that way. He had pretended to himself, as well as to me, that he did.

"I never guessed, so his letter, brief and cruel and final, was a shock.... Death is easy compared to this. Death puts the one you love beyond any reach we humans know. But David still lives, smiles, speaks and moves through days apart...

"I am so empty and dull and the feeling of being old is frightening. I think I am cured of loving. I have so much to give and I like giving. I think the intensity of my love frightened him... I have no feeling of unworthiness or fault. It's good to be sure of that. But I want now to be hard boiled. If I ever marry, I'll make decisions with my head."

During the university's spring vacation, Doré left me with friends and drove the blue Ford to Springfield for a week of pampering by her old friend Brenzelle ("Bren") Hueseman. By the time she returned to the job, she had found herself again, and although life was not gay or exciting, it was bearable. She helped a friend face a divorce, and felt proud of the mature wisdom she could share.

In mid May, David telephoned and asked to see her. Wild as she felt inside, she maintained her characteristic exterior calm when he came. It turned out that, because he knew he was not going to marry her, he believed that he should, as she put it to Lurry, "hit me hard enough to free me of him entirely." After many sleepless nights, he had realized it didn't have to be all or nothing. Reunited on an open, realistic basis, they resumed a companionship that fulfilled them both. Lurry worried that her sister was headed for further heartbreak, but Doré convinced her that she could not be broadsided the same way again, and that her here-and-now happiness was worth the risk.

Come June, Doré had her blue Ford coupe packed for the road the night before the university semester ended. The very minute she could, each year, she headed north for Pentwater. Our dog Sandy rode on the shelf behind my head, and seemed as eager as we were to get back to a real house with a big back yard. As we drove through Whitehall, Montague, Shelby and Hart, Doré swore that she could begin to smell the pines and the "Big Lake" and she thrilled to catch glimpses of sand dunes.

I remain grateful that my mother's choice to work a nine-month academic schedule and her wise year-round money management made possible our long summers in Pentwater. I didn't envy classmates who spent two weeks crammed in a car to see Mount Rushmore or Old Faithful. If anything, they envied me – spending three months at a "summer cottage."

Weather permitting; we spent every afternoon at the beach, usually with Bren Hueseman and her son Bobby. The heavy fringed blankets that Doré spread on the sand had once been, she told us, "steamer rugs" that kept passengers' knees warm as they reclined in deck chairs on ocean liners. One was navy blue, the other a green and yellow plaid. As our mothers stretched out to work on their tans, Bobby and I would create a vast metropolis of packed-sand buildings and roads for our toy cars. Tips of dune vegetation, snapped off by the city planners, served as wee trees among the houses. Windy days found us squealing with glee as Doré and Bren lifted us over the rolling Lake Michigan waves. Venturing further out, as we grew older, we could belly surf the bigger waves as they crashed ashore. Sometimes, in the late afternoon, Doré would give in to our plaintive pleas to stay longer. She would drive back to the house and bring food to the beach for a sunset supper. Her justifiably famous chili con carne was our favorite picnic fare.

My mother's former beau Syd Chapman visited often the summer of '37. Doré told Lurry that she felt so cherished and peaceful in his care that, although she did not love him, she considered agreeing to marry him. Reading this, Lurry was alarmed enough to telephone.

"Oh Doré, I just can't see you being married to Syd. Please be very sure that it would fill all your needs," she urged.

"I will Dearest," Doré promised. "I know he's a bore and certainly not much fun to talk to. But it really is nice to be loved so boundlessly. Can't you understand? I have loved so hard myself. I have not often been the one best loved."

"Yes, of course I do," Lurry replied. "I've never been adored myself, but I can imagine how it would feel. And I'm sure it must be nice to have someone so rich paying court to you. But, Darling, you don't need to settle for someone as dull as Syd. Please take some time about this. You deserve someone that you love."

"Yes.... well...since you say that, it brings up the other thing I'm wrestling with...and that's the deep feelings I still have for David Stewart. He is still the man I <u>like</u> best in my living world."

"Oh, Doré!" Lurry cried, "He's made it very clear that he can't make a long-term commitment. I've always been afraid that you were going to cause yourself real heartbreak if you keep hoping for more from him."

"I know. I know," Doré sighed. "But that's my personal burden and my skinny shoulders are strong. I promise to go slow about Syd. I've told him I need time to decide."

As it happened, Syd was patient, not pushing her to make up her mind, and Dore's relationship with David remained on the level of loving friends.

Although Lurry told her sister that she had "never been adored," I know that she was admired and loved by a man she worked with at Huxley House. A mature bachelor, Gebhard Stoeckler was called "Uncle Geb" by his sister's family and "Steck" by co-workers. Frequently enjoying plays, concerts and dinners together, Lurry and Steck were regarded as a couple for years to come.

...

During the summer of 1937, Japan carried out merciless attacks on Chinese cities. Hundreds of thousands of people died and a humiliated China collapsed. For Doré and Lurry and their family, the infamous "Rape of Nanking," their home, was almost unbearable.

Japanese brutality was also pointedly directed at intellectuals. It grieved Doré to learn that the campus of Yenching University, where Ben had taught in Peking, was gutted and converted to soldiers' barracks, bars and brothels. Americans expressed public sympathy over the plight of China, but our government remained neutral for four more years.

...

At the end of the Pentwater summer, Ora Freeman came back to Ann Arbor with us again, much to my mother's relief. Having household help was an added blessing that September, because Doré suffered excruciating headaches, which were finally traced to severely abscessed teeth. Ora played nurse, kept the house in order, and saw me off to school, while Doré recovered from several bone-deep tooth extractions.

In October, because I had been faithfully practicing the piano, Doré took me to see Sergei Rachmaninoff perform at Hill Auditorium. It was my first professional recital, and excellent third row seats gave us a clear view of the virtuoso's unusually long fingers as they caressed or pounded the keys. I had looked up the composer/pianist in the encyclopedia, felt proud of my knowledge and was thrilled to see him in person. As Doré hoped, I never forgot that rare experience.

November brought Doré "more agony of pain" than any she had ever known. The well respected dentist explained that the extent of decay required him to pull two more teeth. He wondered whether her childhood "in the Orient" had impaired her dental health at an early age. At the time, she didn't say anything to me about her pain, but when I had to go to the dentist, she taught me to take slow deep calming breaths and let my hands lie open, palms up, never clenched.

...

Christmas in Glen Ellyn that year was emotionally draining for Doré. Ben's mother was, as always, sweetly caring, and his brother Don's visit was a pleasure because, as she told Lurry, "He is such a dear person, full of understanding." And Doré gained much-needed rest. But she missed Ben more than ever there in his family home, and she simply went through the motions of holiday festivities for my sake.

"I lift it as high as I can for Judy," she wrote. "I smile and act gay and cover my private loneliness and pain for the sake of the whole family, but O my dearest, it is not fun for me. I am so alone in the crowd. I wish so much for just one person to whom I am of first importance."

The stationery reproduced on the following pages used a favorite design that Ben adopted as "the March horse." His surname in Chinese was the same as the word for horse. The brief letter shows Doré's unusual handwriting and distinctive signature.

hurry, my very dear, we are close so much closer than it is usually possible for far apart humans to keep. Never fear about that, please.

And don't worry about me, for I am able to keep going & my spirits are good most of the time. It is some moments, hard to like my particular treadmill & being almost forty, & feeling always tired, but I get on top after such drear times. The beauty of snow on this lovely campus is sometimes enough, a dark

pine against an oak whose leaves were
gold is still remembered from a day
last month, and Judy prospering
very well in every way is satisfaction.
My doldrums, when they come, are from
wishing with a deep passion for some
one to love me, to hold my hand &
say no words for cheer. How awfully
many others are without that, too. & all
who are are missing one of the dearest
forms of happiness I think.

No more now, dear. I shall be
hearing your voice on Monday.
O, I love you so, dear heart.

Jon.

Nevertheless, creating my ninth birthday party brought her profound satisfaction. "It is good to make a small girl happy," she wrote. "There's nothing quite like that, I guess."

To my sentimental mother, all anniversaries mattered – of births, of deaths, of marriages, of all life-changing events. Birthdays, especially mine, were festive occasions. As I grew older, she usually asked me what sort of present I wanted, and did her best to buy it, or asked Lurry to find it in New York. I learned the importance of making her June birthdays special too.

...

Doré rarely told Lurry about the times that I let her down in some way – maybe by making a mess, forgetting a chore or being sassy. Her annoyance was never expressed through a raised voice or scolding. Tight-lipped, reproachful, she became silent as stone, freezing me out with emotional withdrawal that perfectly conveyed her disappointment.

Stories about mothers who routinely cursed or beat their children remind me that I was lucky. But Doré's icy discipline did have consequences. To this day, the "silent treatment" in a relationship is anguish for me.

In my mother's effects when she died was a scrap of paper with my penciled scrawl: "Dearest Doré, Please forgive me for being rude to you. I am truly sorry because I reilise (sic) that you are wery (much erasing and change of spelling) and I agree one hamberger (sic) will be fine and because I was nasty you don't have to let me have ice cream. Love, Judy." On the reverse, Doré had later penned, "O Lambie, I sorrow you have to know so soon that mothers get weary. But there must be ice cream for you always, please *Kind-Dirty*."

Frequent reminders of the perfect behavior expected of Ben March's daughter also served to control me. Doré transformed him into a god-like figure that could witness my every act and pass judgment from on high. Her need to deify a dead father is not unique. Soldiers' widows often do the same. But, I grew up believing that my life had to make up for my father's death.

He was a brilliant scholar, a gifted teacher and an unusually vital man. In The Michigan Daily, a student editor had written, "...Nor was his scholarship the dry pedantic sort...He was alive to life. The university has lost a foremost expert on Oriental art—this is a minor consideration. The loss of Benjamin March the man leaves a niche that will never be filled."

According to Lurry, everyone who knew my father well adored him. His friends couldn't bear losing him, so they consoled themselves by telling Doré that he would "live on in Judy." Moreover, Doré needed to believe in the rightness of giving up her dreams of far flung adventures. In order to justify her sacrifices, I had to be the perfect daughter that she imagined Ben would have wanted. We were both stuck with fulfilling what she believed were his expectations.

Later in January 1938, Doré lost one more tooth. The dentist hoped to save it, but it had to come out under anesthetic due to its deteriorated condition. The rest of her winter passed in a blur of illness and added parental responsibility.

My right hand was severely burned when the protruding handle of a pot of boiling soup caught in the belt of my snowsuit and tipped as I reached behind. I was kept out of school for four weeks, and Doré was "driven crazy by the whole mess" of changing lumpy bandages soaked in gentian violet and summoning appropriate sympathy at the end of her own tiring work day. Then Doré had a strep throat and Ora had the flu, so she couldn't help for three weeks.

In March, one of Ora's sons died. After attending the funeral in Pentwater, Ora wrote to tell my mother that she had decided not to return to Ann Arbor. Despite being "sunk" about this loss, Doré adapted with customary acceptance. She shopped for groceries on her way home from work, and she and I divided basic household chores. To Lurry she wrote, "Judy is delightfully particular about how to wash the dishes."

Doré had neither the money nor the energy to go to New York for spring vacation, but she did leave me with a caring family for two days so she could visit old friends in Detroit. It seemed strange, she said, as she kept expecting Ben to arrive at the familiar haunts, but she had her hair done by a prestigious stylist and relaxed into the support of dear companions.

In May, she had to have several more teeth extracted. "I really think it's gonna be store-bought dentures for old Grandma before long," she told Lurry. Indeed, two days before leaving for Pentwater in June, she had a "fancy bridge" put in.

Summer began with the familiar schedule: Bren Hueseman feeding her son Bobby and me breakfast while Doré slept 'til noon, then Doré getting lunch for everyone before an afternoon at the beach and another of her delicious suppers. After we kids were tucked in at night, she and Bren would sit by the fire and read or talk as they sipped applejack brandy. "It is all so wonderful and peaceful," she wrote Lurry. "I love every minute."

However, still feeling as if she were "full of poison," she needed more rest than usual and felt very low on energy. "My body reacts badly if I overdo at all, and I'm not just slim but painfully lean. I hate it."

In late July, a family reunion raised her spirits. Lurry arranged for their father to come from California to share her vacation and stay on to spend the following month with Doré. A tall, stately man with white hair and goatee to match, my Granddaddy Rowe was slowed down by a stroke that left one arm paralyzed and his leg draggy. Still, he loved going into Lake Michigan, where he felt no fear of the water. It took every ounce of Doré's pep to walk him in and out, but she did it gladly, for his sake. His other wants were few and his company a delight. "He will not go to bed as long as I sit and listen," she reported.

One Saturday, Doré made an effort to go to a Yacht Club dance; doing up her finger nails and toes with Lurry's "Lady Lillian" polish and struggling not to mind being alone. "Detachment is excellent, I know," she said, "yet I like the high road of intense highs and lows so much better. It takes definite control for me to go a middle path."

As others got tight and boisterous, Doré felt removed from the scene. "Others' moods are very vivid to me, because I refuse to have any sensations that are personal and poignant myself," she wrote Lurry. "When I left early the moon was so lovely that I made a drink and took it and a cigarette to the back terrace. You seemed to be sitting in your chair across from me, loving the beauty of a cool night breeze and moonlight on the trees."

In August, Doré's brother Davey and his bride, Kit Ingram, made an unexpected stopover in Pentwater, en route from a year in China to a faculty position at Princeton University. Doré was quite smitten by her pretty new sister-in-law, who had big brown eyes, red-gold hair and a gentle nature that seemed absolutely perfect for Davey. Doré truly enjoyed giving a buffet dinner for the 16 guests she invited to meet the newlyweds.

In September, Doré wrote Lurry that, "Summer is quite over here. Rain and cold wind keep us from the beach. Some of the maple leaves are already red. The dear village is deserted since Labor Day, and by ten at night the main drag is dark. I hate the nearness of my own going, but I love these quiet days. My house is mine after weeks of company and I do just as I please with no one on my mind. Sandy lies practically in the fireplace, and Judy and Bobby are playing with toy cars on the dining room linoleum."

Upon her return to Ann Arbor, she scheduled a medical checkup, to see if anything could be done about her feeling so damned tired and wobbly. On Sept. 26, she wrote Lurry, "Sit down and hold your breath, for instead of this being the end of my first day back on the job, it is my first night in the hospital. I have the most unromantic ailment, _diabetes_. At least it's better than other possibilities."

FIRST SEPARATION

By a lucky coincidence, Granny and Grandaddy March were scheduled to stop by Ann Arbor after a trip. The timing allowed them to be in on a conference with the doctor. The decision was for Doré to spend six weeks in the hospital, for me to go with my grandparents to Glen Ellyn for the first semester of school, and for little black worried Sandy to enter a kennel.

The diagnosis meant that her pancreas wasn't producing enough of the hormone insulin which the body needs to convert the glucose in foods to energy. Sugar was building up in her blood instead.

Although Doré was critically ill when admitted to St. Joseph's, injections of artificial insulin, high carbohydrate foods laden with butter and heavy cream, plus much-needed rest, soon had her gaining weight and feeling more alive than she had for months.

"The whole pattern of my days has been rewoven about my weary shoulders with startling suddenness, and I am neither warmed nor chilled, but just numb and utterly tired," she told Lurry. "The university was swell, saying that my job waits for me and pay goes on. Judy was a perfect sport about accepting this jolt in her life and made me very proud of her, and Daddy is selling one of my bonds to pay for the hideous expense. My Rowe chin is firmly up and I am doing everything I can, mentally, to adjust to weeks in bed and obeying orders absolutely. Send me old _New Yorkers_ and a silly nightgown for my fall wardrobe and please, please, write."

Doré loved being "spoiled" by the hospital caregivers, and she was less lonely there than in her usual life. "You can't be bored in a hospital, unless you're a complete fool," she said. "There are so many human dramas to watch and hear. People are so interesting to me, and you never know what will happen next. I have my radio and piles of books and magazines, and it's swell to have chosen chrysanthemum season for my rest cure. I have two huge pots of yellow and bronze ones. I get lots of mail and have gotten two cartons of Spuds.

"When I left Pentwater," she told Lurry, "I felt so sick and scared that I had an indefinable feeling I might never be back. I even left a sealed envelope on my desk for you–telling you silly things to do when the place was yours. Now I'm sure once more that I will live to a ripe old age and have ravishing white hair so I can wear Marie Laurencin pastel blues and carry a glint in my eyes and an insulin hypo in my reticule, with tiny white saccharine tablets clinking against it, to slip into my coffee.

"You and Judy and I are going home to Peking someday. It's the dream that I hold to despite everything, and I am so certain we will go that I sometimes amuse myself by planning details."

When Doré's insulin dosage was regulated to the doctors' satisfaction, she was allowed to go home – but not back to work. The university gave her an extended leave of absence for the rest of the semester. Her challenge was to learn the percentage of carbohydrates in every fruit and vegetable, and how to weigh every portion of her food on a gram scale. The 3173 calories she was required to eat seemed to dominate her days. She also learned to inject insulin in her own thigh, a ritual she performed every day for the rest of her life.

At first, a painful "diabetic neuritis" developed in one leg. She was restricted to the downstairs davenport, only climbing stairs once a day, but she was glad to be home, among her own belongings. Friends dropped by often, and a simple, reliable woman named Bertha came in for an hour each afternoon to clean, wash dishes and prepare vegetables and fruits.

Dore found the urge to write poems again, and character sketches of nuns and nurses she had observed in the hospital. She brought out her old sheet music and played the piano and sang by the hour. Although she had resisted staying home from her job, she acknowledged that it was best, as her leg was improving.

By mid-November, she began taking short walks outdoors. One day, she enjoyed a three block stroll to June Grey's tiny hat shop and ordered a small chapeau of blue-grey suede trimmed with a bit of grey baby lambskin which she had saved since China. Designing the hat with the Russian milliner reminded her of the days she and a Chinese tailor worked together on the enclosed back porch of her home in Nanking.

Highlight of the month was bringing Sandy home from the kennel. He nearly knocked her over with joy, so she sat down in the vet's big chair and let the delighted dog lick off all her makeup. At the apartment, he tore up and down the stairs, woofing into closets, and then settled down by the front door to wait in vain for me to come home for lunch.

By Christmastime, Doré had gained 20 pounds. To Lurry, she described one of her office dresses that had a zipper up the front. "On me now, said zipper comes just to my belly button, and, above it, my satin slip pushes out as if it covered two muskmelons. You should see it! I nearly fell down laughing." But the doctors were happy that she had reached the goal of weighing 129, and she certainly felt healthier. The new diet was less complicated and easier to maintain, so she was actually hungry before meals. Weighing her food had become automatic by then.

When she arrived in Glen Ellyn for the holidays, Doré discovered that I had not believed any of the adults and thought, absolutely, that my mother was going to die. "She even had nightmares about it, poor lamb," Doré told Lurry. "Even now she'll touch me or kiss my hand and say, 'Oh Doré, I'm so glad you're alive'."

My mother decided to take me back to Ann Arbor after Christmas, even though my school semester didn't end until late January. She wrote Lurry that, "The sooner I get my girl back in the peace and sweetness of our own life the better. Judy knows she will have to help and protect me as never before. And my shoulders are strong enough now for the old load. It's a wonderful feeling."

Home Again

For my tenth birthday, I was allowed to invite "three quiet girls" over for games, birthday cake and hot chocolate. Doré had a surprise for us. As she told Lurry, "These ten-year-olds are getting very grown up, so I ordered tiny colonial corsages for each of them. If you could have seen the pleasure! 'Pearl pins, too,' said Judy."

Doré felt elated at how well she picked up the threads of her pattern without their becoming snarled or snagged. Work went smoothly, and by sleeping ten hours every night and lying flat for an hour every noon, she got happily through her days. Her leg pain finally subsided and she could walk at a normal gait.

"Nothing seems to get to me and I am amazed and pleased," she wrote Lurry. "If occasionally I feel a bit dull because I have no activity beyond my job and the home and Judy, I think how near I came to ditching all three forever, and I don't want that. It must sound queer to you, having known me always as restless and reaching, but this contentment is very real and lovely. Soon there will be time and energy to spread across some of the non-essentials I have always loved. But for now there isn't and it's quite all right."

...

That winter I joined the Girl Scouts, which amused Doré no end. "She has a horrible green uniform she adores and a pin I'm sure she would wear on her pajamas if I didn't giggle. Her investiture beat anything sorority sisters ever imagined for glory and drama. All promises, even not to walk in the snow drifts at noon, are sealed with Scout's Honor and fingers over her heart. She loves it all, and I play too... She is a baby one second and adult the next. It keeps me blinking. The other night she told me, 'You are such a softly person. It makes me feel good and I want to be like you.' I glowed, for her blue eyes were large and comprehending. The softly Doré refuses to be perturbed by anything."

...

115

In February, my mother's old admirer Syd Chapman stopped by the office one day, full of admiration for how well she looked. "He was all for a date," she wrote, "but when I said I was busy for days ahead, he got the point. I could use dressing up and being taken places, but not by anyone who wants to get serious."

In late winter, an acquaintance that popped back into her life developed into a new beau. Don Lake had been a young admirer of both Ben and Doré in Detroit. She described him to Lurry as having been "tall, dark and bitter" at that time. Now sleekly handsome and cultured after worldwide travels, "He has become a charming man," she wrote, "but not yet old enough to understand why my wandering feet must be set a while longer in my chosen path. I was touched to have him wish I could pick up and go with him as he took off last week for Hawaii, Japan, Korea and China."

Spring vacation meant lazy days of sleeping 'til noon and taking me out for Chinese food. "For Easter, we dyed hard boiled eggs all over ourselves and the kitchen," she told Lurry.

In June, after I sang a solo in a school program. Doré wrote, "Her teacher wants her to start private lessons. That is way beyond our means, but migod! Such unexpected moments make it perpetually amazing to be a mama."

The Pentwater summer started with gloriously warm weather and, with her restored health and energy, Doré relished swimming again. "I feel so wonderful I can't quite believe it sometimes. I positively gloat, and everyone raves about how well and young I look."

Grandaddy Rowe came again for a month, overlapping for a week with Lurry's vacation and a visit by their brother Davey and his wife Kit.

The Ann Arbor tenants left the apartment in excellent condition, so the September reentry went smoothly. Doré's letters to Lurry were filled with reports of new back-to-school wardrobes for me and for herself. "I feel so set and at peace and rested and well that nothing can daunt me. I'm so damned lucky to have a swell, not too urgent, job, a lovely home, and Judy so easy."

Both Doré and Lurry worried about their father, who still lived unhappily with their sister Caroline and her family in California. They sent him a little spending money every month, for newspapers and magazines he enjoyed. It annoyed them that Davey would not contribute a cent, because he believed that Caroline's husband poached any money Father Rowe had.

The younger Rowe sons, Harry and John, who never married, also lived in that household, where their sister was surrogate mother for many years.

One Saturday night in October, Doré wrote that she had spent the afternoon doing some mending and polishing her nails while hearing a University of Michigan football game on her small table radio in its pale blue plastic case. It would be no surprise to read that she listened to popular songs or dance music by her favorite Guy Lombardo and his Royal Canadians. But she felt that she had to explain to Lurry about the football.

"I learned to find it fun a year ago in the hospital. Imagine 80,000 people watching, the band playing 'The Victors,' and the roar of the crowd. And me, who yearns to wander to far places where I will be a foreigner again, getting a sharp, deep thrill of American pride. Very funny! But there is something childlike and lovely about this collegiate crowd, so young and careless, so free and foolish. And U. of M. won the game!

"Afterwards, Judy and I went to eat Chinese food at Lantern Gardens, where the owners have made a fuss over her ever since she was a tiny blue-eyed girl eating with chopsticks. We walked across campus in the mobs returning from the game and felt gay and silly with weekend relief."

On the way home, my mother bought me a half pound of chocolate fudge at Mary Lee's candy shop on State Street, near the Arcade. This would be my breakfast the next day. The weekly bribe kept me quiet on Sunday mornings while she slept until noon.

When I was invited to five Halloween parties, Doré grew "fed up with the costuming rituals," but told Lurry that she was glad that her daughter felt popular. Soon, she enrolled me in a small ballroom dancing class.

"I sent her off the first night in a deep blue frock and a drop of lotus-lavender perfume on her ears and sat back smiling," she wrote to Lurry. "How early the young of now learn tricks, and how easily I loose my fingers and let her go. She meets her problems with good grace and wisdom, and I love sitting back and watching."

It's probably just as well that Doré never knew how much I hated those classes. Unaware of my discomfort in that chubette "frock," Doré seemed oblivious to the awkwardness of my pre-adolescent years. She mused to Lurry: "A child is probably the most satisfying creation in the world, and mine has been almost completely my responsibility, so I delight in my achievement as I both mother and father her these fateful years. My alone ways with Judy could never be as Ben's and mine together would have been, but I am proud of her and feel the pattern is being woven with reasonable beauty."

...

In the fall of 1939, Dore's young admirer Don Lake finished a job in San Francisco and came back into her life. "It's fun having a social whirl again," she told Lurry. "We heard Jussi Bjorling, the great blonde Swede, sing a beautiful recital, and this week the Boston Symphony. Don is grand fun to be with. We like the same nonsense and the same poetry and drink the same drinks and he is very keen about me, which, of course, is flattering. I don't know what the hell it's going to mean, but it's exciting. Don't laugh at me. Just hope when you're 41 you can get the same kick out of life that I do. And don't worry. I am so happy and secure that it will have to be the very tops to budge me out of my treasured independence."

In early December, Doré wrote that she was teaching herself to read Italian. When asked to find information on third century Etruscan sarcophagi, she discovered that the best books on that "amazingly hideous" sculpture were in Italian. So she just decided to fall to and read them. "It has been fun and strenuous and successful and the weeks have spun past me so quickly I can't believe it's nearly Christmas."

My mother and I took the streamlined "Mercury" train to Chicago that year, a luxurious extravagance we both savored. I loved sleeping in the Pullman bunk and Doré enjoyed the privacy. Grandaddy March met us at the station with traditional sweet treats from Stop and Shop.

"Christmas seems more precious to me this year," Doré wrote, "because only in America will there be any peace at all." Nazi Germany had taken over Austria, Czechoslovakia and Poland. Hitler had further clear designs on the Netherlands and France, and Japan was terrorizing China. World War II was imminent.

"I am trying to make Judy appreciate her security and good fortune more deeply in contrast with the awful horror in the rest of the world. It's one small good that I can squeeze from the mess..." she told her sister. "I suppose, not to go mad with thought, each of us must embroider some tiny designs of stability on the crazy quilt of our minds. Without awareness of how lucky I am to be an American, I could not bear to read the papers or listen to the radio."

Her decision to spend only a week with the Marches proved wise. It was just the right length for loving reunion without boredom or heartache. "Everything went smoothly," she wrote, "and the family couldn't get over my vim and vigor. Last year I was still leaning on things; this year I washed dishes for twelve and dashed about.

"I spent one lovely adventure day by myself in Chicago, at the Art Institute and Marshall Fields, and window shopping up and down the Loop in the tearing wind, loving the crowds and holiday excitement."

Back in Ann Arbor, New Year's Eve was "nice and giddy." Don Lake arrived in a tuxedo, whistled at Doré's silver lamé evening dress, and escorted her to a festive party. Later, it was his idea that they come home to see the New Year in with me.

It's surprising that she agreed to that. Doré was always gentle and soft spoken, but she could never be called meek or self-effacing. And she certainly wouldn't have chosen to stay home with a child on New Year's Eve!

Don was making a great effort to court the daughter as a way of winning the mother. For my eleventh birthday, he gave me a lustrous small pearl in a six-prong gold setting. I still love that ring, but the gift was symbolic of the fault-line developing in the adult relationship. Doré wanted Don to understand her responsibility for me and to like her child, of course, but, when it came to a man's attention, she needed to be the "one and only."

...

At work, she had fun "digging into" Greek and Roman sculpture. "It's a whole new world for me," she wrote. "I've never known much but the few famous statues, such as the Victory of Samothrace or the Venus de Milo."

That winter of 1940, the death of a professor of Fine Arts left budgeted salary money that Doré realized would just go back into the general fund if not used. So, as she wrote Lurry, "I went to (*the chairman*) Dr. Winter, with Oriental humility and American blueprints, and 'suggested' that Bruce's cluttered old store room be turned into a Far Eastern Seminar space. I said I hoped he didn't think me presumptuous, whereupon the darling old guy gave me the go ahead for the whole project."

Not only did Asian Art Professor Jim Plummer receive all the equipment he had so needed for years, the university provided special locked bookcases and folio cabinets for the Benjamin March Library, and put Doré in charge of cataloging and lending out books. "It's a dream I have had for years," she wrote. "The books are still mine, but will be available now to scholars who need them, and I will be surrounded with the volumes that Ben and I slaved to buy."

Meanwhile, she enrolled in a course in Contemporary Art, taught by her good friend Adelaide Adams. "Not for credit, but for joy. I simply love learning all I can about the new field I'm working in."

Feeling so fit, Doré decided to spend her April vacation with Lurry in New York. My uncle and aunt, Don and Helen March, offered to have me come to South Bend to spend a week with my cousin Benny.

My mother's dreams were nearly scuttled when I came down with the mumps. After consultation with the pediatrician, Doré decided to go ahead with her plans. As she told Lurry, "Judy is past the swelling/ice packs/liquid diet phase and feeling chipper, but still has to be quarantined for two weeks. So I've hired Virginia, the young woman who worked for me before and is willing to spend her own spring break with the young patient."

It was undoubtedly a wise decision. I accepted the arrangement, understanding that my mother would have gone "quietly nuts" staying home. She treated herself to a berth for the train trip, and had a wonderful vacation, riding the Riverside bus, going to the theater, eating authentic Chinese food, shopping for bargains on summer clothes, seeing old friends, and talking endlessly with Lurry.

"It was heaven," she wrote her sister on the returning journey. "Change always rests me and I go back to the known pattern on feathered wings that shine in eastern sunlight and do not mind the rain or April snow. I loved it all and never could tell you what it meant. I will be glad to see my daughter tomorrow, and when I left I was so sick of being a mother. See what you and New York did in nine short days!"

In late April, her suitor Don Lake took a job in New York City. He was thrilled over the prospect of working for the Ford Motor Company with Doré's old Detroit friend Fred Black. My mother said nothing in her letters about being sorry to see him go, but I remember missing him. Years later, she told me that he was the sort of man best described as "a charming rotter."

...

After a successful piano recital in May, I decided to stop taking lessons. Daily practicing had become more punishment than pleasure. Characteristically, Doré left the choice up to me. "I'm not one to say 'Now eat your <u>lovely</u> spinach, Dearie," she told Lurry.

That year, 1940, Doré invited my old friend Marilyn Lexen to spend the summer with us in Pentwater. Our mothers met when she and I were in Merrill Palmer Nursery School together. Marilyn's father had died and her mother worked, so she had learned to be responsible, as had I. My early Pentwater pal, Bobby Hueseman, had become more interested in playing with other boys, so Marilyn proved a welcome companion. She and I turned the two adjoining "green rooms" into a dormitory, assumed all the upstairs housework and dish washing duties around the edges of blissful days on the beach. Doré, who slept around the clock, grew rested and tanned.

The only time my mother ever let on that my Daddy Ben was less than a saint sticks clearly in my mind. While making beds, she laughingly remembered how he would insist on the crisply folded sheet corners that he had learned to make while a soldier in World War I. He also let her know that it was utterly unacceptable to place an old khaki blanket on the bed wrong-way to. That is, the large insignia "U.S." must properly be read from the foot.

Lurry's vacation coincided with perfect July weather, and, as usual, she came generously laden with presents. My "Pentwater present" was almost always a new dress, purchased at some alluring place such as Lord and Taylor's or Saks Fifth Avenue. Because the one time I knew I would wear it was when she took us to the village's only upscale restaurant, I called it my "Jenny Wren dress."

In August, Marianna Smalley, Ben's doctor, paid her first visit to Pentwater. After his death, the capable caring woman with dark eyes under bushy brows and hair styled in what was called a "mannish" cut, had become one of Doré's best friends. Sharing the drive from Ann Arbor for this visit was Adelaide Adams, the professor of Fine Arts who befriended Doré at work. A sweet-natured, tightly-permed spinster who lived with a dominating mother, she couldn't have been more different from Marianna, but they both loved Doré. And to her delight, they enjoyed every aspect of her house and summer lifestyle.

"ROGER"

Meanwhile, a dashing new man had entered my mother's life. In late June, Roger Cluett, whom she met through Don Lake, came north to take her to the first Yacht Club dance. Doré didn't write to Lurry at all in August, which suggests that frequent late summer visits were leading to a serious romance. And, back in Ann Arbor one fall morning before school, I walked in on him in our bathroom.

Six years Doré's junior, this handsome suitor was a Clark Gable look-alike who had, in fact, been a bit player in Hollywood. Roger Cluett was his stage name, which he was using when first introduced to Doré. His name was actually Don Goss, but to avoid confusion with the other Don in their lives, Doré continued to call him Roger. In November, she surprised Lurry with the news that she was going to marry him.

Why had she never let her sister know that this relationship had become so serious? Close as they had always been, the two sisters differed markedly in character. Doré was the kind of woman often called "an incurable romantic." In contrast, Lurry was the practical type who worried that Doré's impulsive leaping after love would lead to heartbreak. Doré must have remembered how Lurry warned her against settling for Syd Chapman or wasting her tears on David Stewart, so she probably feared further disapproval. Yet, she certainly longed for Lurry's support.

"I have been aching to tell you but would not until every detail was settled and sure. I am marrying my Roger, whose real name is Donald J. Goss, on December 21, at high noon. He is the son of a well-to-do family that owns an estate outside Ann Arbor. He drives every day to Detroit, where he works for Advertising Services, Inc. and has a definite future. Personally, he is one of the best, a lovely sense of humor, a tenderness and understanding of me that constantly surprises me. Best of all, we like each other so truly and enjoy the same things. He and Judy get along, and I think he is equal to the first time when, I fear, her small nose will be out of joint."

Indeed, I resented him mightily and begged my mother not to marry him. I much preferred Don Lake, who had been so attentive to me! Fortunately, Doré did not listen to her eleven-year-old. She wisely believed that her own happiness would make her a better mother and lead to my well-being in the long run.

To keep my life as much the same as possible, the couple planned to live in the Church Street apartment for the rest of the school year, and let the future take care of itself.

"I am so utterly content," she wrote Lurry. "I know from the quiet and peace this man brings to me that I have found someone to go along with through the years ahead that we all get to dreading in our forties. He makes me happy, but a sane and softly happy. He has never been married. It is grand beyond these words of mine to say, and I do so want you to be happy about it with me."

Lurry fulfilled Dore's dearest wish by agreeing to stand up with her at the simple ceremony in a side chapel of Roger's mother's Methodist Church. His 27-year-old brother Kelly Goss was best man. The only guests, besides me, were his widowed mother, his sister, and Doré's best friends Adelaide Adams and Marianna Smalley.

Doré wore a soft blue crepe dress, with a side draped skirt and elbow-length sleeves, and a matching feathered hat over her deeply waved hair. She didn't smile in their wedding pictures. She might not have wanted her teeth to show. But there is contentment in her eyes, and Roger is grinning widely, showing off the dimple in his cheek.

I had finally accepted the whole idea of the marriage was happy for my mother and felt important in my holiday dress of wine velvet with a white eyelet-edged collar.

After a toast of scotch all around, the newlyweds and their daughter caught a train for Chicago. We ate on board and they dropped me off at Niles, where my uncle and aunt, Don and Helen March, with cousin Benny, picked me up and got a brief look at the bridegroom. With other revelers, Doré and Roger sang Christmas carols all the way to the windy city.

Don and Doré Goss – wedding photo 1940.

At the Congress Hotel, their spacious room was full of flowers and their honeymoon week was all the "utter joy and silly fun" they wanted. Doré later wrote Lurry, "I can never tell you how glad I am that you came and were with me for our wedding. It was wonderful that you got to see our apartment and my office, and to see the three of us together. I'm so glad that you liked my Roger. He has all the things I want and need, and we are so happy."

They were invited to spend an evening in Glen Ellyn, where the whole March family surprised them by turning up in force. Doré said, "It was a considerable test for my Roger and he did me proud." When the newlyweds returned to the big city, I was content to stay on with my grandparents, aunts, uncles and cousins for the traditional Christmas festivities.

On Christmas Eve, Doré and Roger dined with friends at "The Beachcomber." Doré wore a new deep blue velvet dinner dress with a gardenia, both gifts from the bridegroom. "I had my first zombie," she told Lurry, "and the highball is not overrated. We came home very late and when we walked into the hotel room, it was filled with fresh flowers and lit softly by a tiny Christmas tree Roger had ordered.

Sleeping late on Christmas morning was at treat, and they loved having dinner alone, in full dress, in an unreal escape from pressures and schedules. "A hotel is like a boat in port, isn't it?" she asked in a letter to Lurry. "I love the feeling, the rest from everyday living, the pampering of a hotel. To have it with this man I love, who plays my way, was beyond all words to tell."

Although Roger had to go back to work, they had a week alone at the Church Street apartment before I came home for New Year's. When our three schedules resumed again, all went smoothly.

"I have never known such peace and loveliness, Lurry. It is nice to be 42, to know what makes the wheels go round, and to be so adored and protected and cared for. It still continues to surprise me that there is someone to take over the big and little chores, who is always trying to save me and do for me. Judy is turning to Roger for help in many small ways, from asking him to suggest which clothes she should wear to helping with math. I love watching it, and I feel that having a man in her life will iron out any problems that a mother alone could not settle too easily or well.

My work goes beautifully. I shine, and, of a morning I often think of Edna St. Vincent Millay's lines:

'Be not discountenanced, O my love,
if the knowing know
you rose from rapture
but an hour ago.'"

125

RAPTURE CUT SHORT

Three months after the newlyweds and their daughter settled into harmonious daily living, Lurry was surprised and alarmed to receive a phone call from Roger. He wanted to tell her, not just wire, that Doré had collapsed and had been taken to the hospital in a coma.

Lurry was on the next plane. For three nights, she stayed beside her beloved sister and a frantic new husband – both of them willing Doré back to life. Although running a high fever and coughing as if to turn her lungs inside out, she came out of the coma. The diagnosis: advanced tuberculosis.

Tuberculosis (abbreviated as TB) is an infectious disease that usually attacks the lungs. Doctors had first noticed "a shadow" on Doré's right lung in 1938, during the examinations leading to the diagnosis of her diabetes. They guessed it was scar tissue from the illness she'd had as a child in China. At age 12, her activities had been restricted and for months she'd slept alone on a cold screened porch. When she recovered, no one understood that the illness, which was almost certainly TB, had merely been arrested and remained dormant in her body.

While adjusting to living with diabetes, Doré had also received pneumothorax treatments to rest her lung. In that procedure, air is pumped into the chest cavity through a long needle between the ribs. The air pushing against the lung collapses it, with the hope that disuse will arrest the TB. But diabetes is one of the medical conditions that make the body less able to protect itself from TB.

Because Doré had annual chest x-rays, it was a shock to hear that a huge tubercular "cavity" had developed and that she would be sentenced to complete bed rest for at least six months. Worse yet, her confinement had to be at the Michigan State Tuberculosis Sanatorium in Howell, forty miles from Ann Arbor. Not only would the newlyweds be torn apart and separated by such distance but they were faced with what to do about me.

For a month, while they waited for a long-term prognosis, Roger rose to the challenge, maintained the apartment and kept my life as normal as possible. Then his widowed mother, Gertrude Goss, eased his burden by inviting him to bring me with him to live in the family home.

The Goss homestead was an enormous white mansion known as Skylodge, about three miles out of town, on vast acreage with expansive lawns and a tennis court. It was home not only to Mrs. Goss, but to Roger's unmarried sister Dorothy, called "Do" (*pronounced Doe*), who taught piano, and his younger brother Kelly, who ran the family business, a dairy farm called The Oaklands.

Their father, who had been a Kelvinator Co. executive, had taken his own life a year or so earlier, after a series of personal financial reverses left him deeply depressed. Fortunately, whatever investments he had were sufficient to allow his widow to keep their extensive property.

Perhaps it was healing for Mrs. Goss to subsume her own grief in caring for me. Certainly she couldn't have been kinder, and I became something of a buffer between her and her daughter. Do, who believed that she was forever denied true happiness when her father prevented her from marrying some Italian "count," took out her bitterness by aiming shrill complaints at her mother.

Kelly's two large Dalmatians, "Herman" and "Hero," caused enough uproar in the Goss household without adding an aging Scottie dog. So Roger took on the sad task of having our Sandy, "put to sleep." Heartbroken, I deeply resented being informed after the fact, and, although he and Doré undoubtedly made the decision together, I held it against my new stepfather. Not for long. Eventually I accepted another loss and forgave him.

For Doré, giving up the apartment was a painful symbol of all that had changed. "It's the damnedest feeling not having a home," she told Lurry. "I hated it terribly, but am getting used to it now. While waiting for my darling to come last weekend, I lay still as a mouse in this hospital bed and packed the apartment 'in my head,' so I was able to tell him just where and how and what to do before the movers arrived"

Roger then bore the entire burden of having all of our belongings, including Chinese furnishings and artifacts, put into commercial storage or his mother's basement.

"He was simply amazing," Doré wrote. "He is so calm and sure and cheerful, and none of the messy details stopped him at all."

Roger's devotion to Doré extended to me. He took on the role of "Papa San" with flair, teaching me to ride horseback and ice skate, and soon won my affection. Now that we were living with his family, who naturally called him Don, I stopped calling him Roger, and, soon, so too did Doré. My nickname for him became "Poppy."

127

Howell

As an impersonal state institution, the Howell Sanatorium was staffed by underpaid, poorly trained employees who usually treated the patients as faceless objects in bed 1B or 2A. Doré loathed being there, but with her habitual acceptance of her fate, she knew she must not rebel. "Dutiful adherence to doctors' orders will be the fastest route to recovery and dismissal," she wrote Lurry.

Even as she endured the frightening life-threatening illness that left her weak with coughing, Doré's interest in people served her well. She asked about the nurses' lives, showed them that she cared, and soon earned their interest in her. She could see that patients who were crabby and demanding were usually ignored. "They don't seem to understand," she wrote, "that patience, grace and a little charm win sympathy, and then indulgence, and, finally, perhaps, help.

"But, I don't believe I would like to be sick at home with a private nurse," she told Lurry. "Here, the sounds other patients make, of pain, or exasperation or of gratitude keep my hours in proper perspective. It's always good to remember that I am quite unoriginal."

She lived for the weekends, when her husband could drive out to spend the brief visiting hours with his chair pulled up close to her bed and her hand in his. Don's love and tenderness fortified the courage she needed to face their uncertain future. Together in hope, they strived to be optimistic.

Doré's sense of humor helped to keep her spirits up and also to keep the doctors interested in her as a person, not just a case. Once, when the head physician saw Don in the hospital lobby, Dr. Finch told him, "It's a perfect marvel to us all where your wife finds something to be cheerful about every day. We do appreciate it."

In a letter to Lurry she wrote: "Living in a hospital room is a placid form of shipwreck. The bed is my island, flat and compact in a sea of pale green walls and grey floor. On either side are smaller islands on which are conveniently arranged all the things a lackadaisical refugee needs. My pen and paper, books and radio are on the left. Kleenex, perfume, tooth paste, comb and mirror are on the right. My man Friday wears a white uniform and can walk on water to bring me food, wash basin, bedpan and sundry necessities. Together we hope that someday I'll get to the mainland again."

One Saturday, the whole place was aflutter with the importance of an official Open House. Patients were on exhibit for three hours, "like animals in a zoo," Doré said, while legislators and other bigwig visitors came by on tour. "This is a four-bed ward" intoned the guide. "Notice that the bed tables are of an unusual design and all the windows are open wide."

Doré found those hospital tables that extend across the bed an ingenious convenience. "Don kids me about not being able to get along without one," she wrote. "He says he is designing a huge one to fit over our double bed, with a wind-up arrangement to raise it up in case we are doing more than sleeping. He is such a lovely nut."

As June 20th neared, Lurry asked what Doré wanted for her 43rd birthday.

"How funny to imagine spending it here instead of Pentwater," Doré answered. "But, since I will likely spend the rest of this year in pajamas, I can't have too many. Cotton, please, and square necks look nicest because collars rumple. And if all this is a burden to you, send me a bottle of 'Whisper' cologne and your love!"

After starting to read a new book, she wrote, "We have practically no conversation in this room, and nothing really interesting. So I read from 7 a.m. to 9 p.m.—as I eat, and while the others nap from 1 to 3. I don't want to sleep in the daytime, because I would go crazy if I lay awake at night. I go to sleep at 9, wake for the bed pan and washing at 5, curl down again and sleep until 6:30 when my insulin arrives and I do my hair and face. I can't eat breakfast unfixed and messy as the others do. Della sleeps six hours a day and envies my sleep at night. The others sew or knit all day, so you see why I read so much. Lucky me."

That June, Dore shared the wonderful news that Don had been offered a terrific job with Chrysler Motors Company. "It's just the sort of promotional work that Don loves and can do best. He has to go to Montreal for six weeks of training, but the bosses said he can come back every other weekend to see me, and ultimately his office will be in Detroit. I am wrecked to have him away, as I've leaned so hard and will miss him much, but the future is rosy as to promotions and raises, and the starting salary, with car provided, is so swell I may never have to punch a clock again."

Don enjoyed the job, and took advantage of the training locale by studying French conversation.

Meanwhile, I spent the summer in Glen Ellyn, with Granny and Grandaddy March. I had good times at a swimming pool, riding my bike and playing with my younger cousins. But Doré had promised that I could return to Ann Arbor for school. This was just fine with Mrs. Goss, who said she missed having me at Skylodge and looked forward to my return. I also looked forward to being with my "Poppy" again. I wrote Doré, "To tell the truth, I miss him almost as much as I do you."

Just before school started, I was allowed to see my mother for the first time in five months. Don, who had come home from Canada, drove me to Howell and Doré was wheeled on a stretcher to an office where we could be alone. There could be no embrace, of course, because TB is highly contagious, but even seeing each other across a room meant so much to both of us.

A concept that helped Doré endure her confinement was that of "pushing past time."

"It's not too hard," she wrote Lurry. "When you let go and let time wash across you, either you get sunk beyond recall, or you swim with a determination of desperate quiet power. I won't let myself go under, and my body can't be more important than my spirit.

"I really am cheerful, an almost nutty gaiety that burbles to the amazement of my room mates. Mostly I like my own thoughts pretty well. If I don't like 'em, I change 'em as fast as I can."

She was always able to push outside her windows with her mind and stretch her horizons to far off places. "I pity my young room mates because they have not lived enough to do that. But when I lie here after supper and see the evening star beyond the west wing of this building, I can remember endless other places I have watched its particular haunting beauty – over Kuling, over the Yangtze in June, in Nara with a cryptomeria branch to veil it, on the edge of the Gulf of Finland in a tiny fjord town, over the walls of Peking, and in Pentwater countless nights.

"When activity is practically stopped for you and about you, you find out if you have enough saved up inside you to live on day after day."

...

130

During that summer, Dore's empathy for Lurry seemed to increase. In earlier years, she usually just wrote something such as, "I was glad for your news," and hurried on to describe her own activities or feelings or current crisis. Now she wrote at greater length, expressing concern.

"I hate knowing that you are so beastly tired, and wish again that you could take your experience into a company that didn't try to kill you off and work you such foul hours."

Lurry had risen to third in rank at Huxley House, behind the owner Walter Huxley and vice president Franz Hess. Franz not only became her mentor, he and his wife Flora became her close friends. It wasn't that the business forced Lurry to work overtime. Her own high standards motivated her to stay late or come in on weekends to complete a project to her satisfaction. Years later, when I was behaving that way in my own job, she told me she wished she had been able to accept when something was "good enough" to just leave it and go home.

In early October of '41, Lurry came from New York to see her sister. Every minute they were allowed together was precious to them both. Lurry was glad to be able to envision the four-bed ward and meet the room mates and have a sense of hospital routine. For Doré it was "almost too wonderful."

Lurry accepted Mrs. Goss's invitation to stay at Skylodge, which gave her a chance to spend time with me and with Don. Her admiration and appreciation for him grew immensely, and he felt the same way about her.

"You're damned right in saying they don't come like him too often," Doré later wrote. "He has been such a one to lean on all these strange and unexpected days. He had such a little time of us so close and gay and happy together before I was stuck off here, and yet he misses it as if he'd felt that always. As you know, he went through hell when the chances of me living were slim and he felt so alone. Now he looks at me sometimes with a tinge of fear and I have to quick get it out of his brown eyes.

"As you could see, having Judy leaning on him and loving him helps Don so much. I am so glad they have each other now until I can come back again. I am lucky beyond all saying to mean the world and all its shining stars to such two as those."

Thoracoplasty

In late October, Doré was taken to University Hospital in Ann Arbor. She delighted in the ambulance ride through the autumn landscape, but what she faced at the end was the first two of a series of major operations called thoracoplasty. Before the advent of antibiotics such as streptomycin, such drastic surgery was commonly used in advanced cases of TB.

By removing ribs to permanently collapse her right lung, the doctors hoped to arrest her existing disease and prevent a relapse in the future. "Poor Don is sick about all the pain ahead for me," she wrote Lurry. "But I'm not afraid."

Through large incisions in her back, the surgeon, Dr. Cameron Haight, removed two ribs at a time in two separate operations, 20 days apart. Don was able to be there when she came out of the anesthetic, and watch her smile as he kissed each fingertip of the hands he loved so well. Doré feigned annoyance at having to remove her red polish so the doctors could watch the color of her nails during surgery.

She did not complain about becoming a member of The Short Rib Society. "I don't guess I'll miss a few," She wrote. "And I know I'll keep my husband even if my body has a hole or two not designed by nature."

She was so glad to be in Ann Arbor instead of Howell. "Here in University Hospital," she reported, "good hot food, real coffee, expert care, two daily backrubs, fresh beds, and fluffed pillows make me purr."

Not only could Don and his mom and siblings come up to the hospital often, but so could friends. Visits from Adelaide Adams, Marianna Smalley and others were so cheering in those winter weeks following her surgeries.

Officially, I was not allowed to visit. But dear Dr. Smalley snuck me in just before Christmas, by garbing me in a coat and hat of her own and pretending that I was a friend of hers. It meant so much to me to see that "Mommy" was as cheerful as always and optimistic about coming home again. I had stopped calling my mother by her first name because the conservative Goss family referred to her as "your mommy" and I went along.

...

The holidays that year were overshadowed by the Japanese attack on Pearl Harbor and America's entrance into World War II. "I will make no petty groans over my sore back," Doré wrote. "That we should be experiencing our second world war is unbelievable."

On their first wedding anniversary, December 21st, Don brought Doré a unique, modernistic table-top holiday tree. Made of curving wire, it held eight small red candles, which they lighted together on Christmas Eve. He also gave her a deep blue pajama outfit with matching quilted robe, expressing his unspoken hope that she would soon be able to be up and around. "I hope I can make it up to him for all his devotion and sweetness," Dore wrote. "He pours his love and strength into me."

I was sent by train to Glen Ellyn for the traditional holiday gathering of the March clan. "Poppy" was happily surprised when I phoned him Christmas morning. Later, Granny March told Doré that she felt that family life with the Gosses had been good for me, as an only child, and that Don was "making a wonderful father." Both comments pleased Doré immensely.

For my 13th birthday, Mrs. Goss allowed me to invite six girls for dinner at Skylodge. It made me feel quite special to show off the mansion that was now my home and treat my friends to a party around a vast oval table in the elegant spacious dining room.

On New Year's Day, 1942, Don had given Doré "a great lovely gardenia" that made her feel desirable and adored even though she wore it on pajamas. Thankfully, she didn't know then what lay over that fresh horizon.

PART SIX

幸运

"Can you stand your mother's sadness? We believe that if we had been better children, or even right now could do or say the right thing, we could make it go away."
—Nancy Friday in <u>My Mother, Myself</u> (Random House, Inc./Delacorte Press 1977)

WHAT MORE...?

On the morning of February 6th, Dr. Haight came into Dore's room and, uncharacteristically, pulled a vinyl chair up close to her bed and reached for her hand.

"Doré, we've just been notified of terrible news."

Feeling a nameless fear, she sucked in her breath.

Keeping his voice low as he struggled to continue, the doctor choked out, "I don't know how to make this any easier, but I have to tell you...your husband...was killed early this morning in a car accident."

Releasing the breath she was unaware of holding, Doré groaned, "Oh........NO!" and then, grabbing a Kleenex, she whispered, "How?"

"We've been told that he was driving to work about six a.m." Dr. Haight said, more comfortable with facts. "It's really frigid and slick out there. His car apparently struck a patch of black ice and skidded off the road into a tree."

As Doré tried to take this in, the doctor hurriedly added, "They say that he died instantly–of a skull fracture and cerebral hemorrhage. He wouldn't have suffered at all."

Still cocooned by shock, Doré accepted the doctor's condolences and managed to thank him. He told her that Don's sister, Do, was on her way to the hospital. Young Kelly was seeing to all the arrangements to have his brother's body taken to a funeral home, the car hauled off by a wrecker, and was standing by their mother.

Absorbing what she could of these realities, Doré asked the sorrowful physician for a special favor. Dr. Haight agreed to let her be the one to tell me. He ordered that at three o'clock Dore's bed be wheeled to a sun porch at the end of the eighth floor corridor. Do Goss offered to pick me up at school.

As the hour approached, Doré searched numbly for a way to break the news. As always, she was determined to give me no hint of her own inner despair. This is how she later described it to Lurry:

"Judy was so surprised and thrilled, at first, to have been allowed to see me. I felt so cruel to fill those blue eyes with tears. We had to keep our distance across the room from each other, so it was hard to comfort her, but then I told her that I had work for her to do. I said that if she and I felt as awful as we did about Poppy going on to far adventures without his girls, to imagine how much more difficult it must be for his mother, who gave him life and had loved him so much longer.

"So I asked her to take care of Mom Goss and cheer her up and help her in every way she could. Do says I was inspired, for Judy did just that and helped herself as she was considering Mom.

"Judy has met more trials than most 13-year-olds, and gracefully. She told me, 'Don't you dare cry. Gosh, that would kill Poppy!' and then let out a little gasp of embarrassment, smiling ruefully at what she'd said. A bit later, sighing, she said, 'I guess we're just fated not to have a husband or a father.'

"So it seems, Lurry, and yet you know I'm not railing. I know there must be a pattern and a reason in it all, even if I can't see it or understand. I just feel a kind of hopeless loneliness. Don's complete devotion and adoration helped me so during these nine months of hell and this marring surgery, which I've hated. He only minded the ugly scar because it hurt me and my vanity. His kind of love is very rare. I truly came before all others and all things. I never quite believed in that kind of love between men and women until Don came. And it was such pure gravy to have a lover like that at this stage of my life."

Don had always laughed at her for worrying every day about the winter driving and slippery roads. She would feel eternally grateful that he never knew what happened and did not suffer at all. It also helped her, she said, to know that he "went away happy, knowing he was deeply loved and confident of our future together."

On Sunday, his mother told her, "You know Donald was never really happy until he found you, Doré." It was a poignant surprise to learn that Mom Goss knew this.

"She seemed comforted by seeing me," Doré wrote. "Her son's death coming only two years after her husband's suicide is so shockingly near in time. And her religion, so steadfast and conscious on usual days is not much help in a crisis. She admitted it that night, wishing she had my wise ways and lack of bitterness. I was so touched."

Lurry observed that she and Doré had been blessed by their Chinese upbringing. They absorbed, at an early age, that ancient culture's acceptance of suffering, heartbreak and even death as commonplace, daily occurrences – to be expected as a part of life.

"You are so right," Doré replied. "Our background gives us something that those raised over here have never been able to learn – about being fatalistic in the face of life's slaps. I'm grateful for that."

A traditional Methodist funeral, held at home with Don's gray casket covered by a spring-like blanket of freesia, iris and mimosa, seemed to console Mom Goss. And she assured Doré that she wanted to keep me on at Skylodge. She and I had grown to love each other, and having me there may have filled her need to be useful. Doré gratefully agreed, as long as Mom would accept payment for all my board and expenses, which would be repaid out of money Grandaddy March withdrew from invested savings. Although the Gosses were relatively wealthy, Doré did not want to be beholden to them financially. Their willingness to take care of me was largesse enough.

"THAT'S MY BRAVER"

Although Doré would only allow her tears to flow silently in late night darkness, her sense of future promise had collapsed along with her sick lung. And the fragrant flower-filled vases and blooming plants that crowded her hospital room had yet to fade before Dr. Haight hit her with more bad news. On Friday the 13th he told her she was being sent back to the Howell Sanatorium.

Determined not to whine, she put a bright red ribbon in her hair for Valentine's Day, just to show him. But, as she watched the nurses pack up her belongings, she could hardly bear the disappointment of having to return to that wretched prison.

At Howell, the head nurse and dietician warmly welcomed her back, and, with the dreaded move behind her, Doré settled back into the institutional routines and set about to know her new room mates. Unfortunately, Flossie, Gertie and Delia were "deadly dull."

"It's no fault of their own that they are happily ignorant. I am, of course, friendly and gentle, but their aimless chatter and pointless gossip is hard to take, and, at first, the choked jailed feelings of returning here were awful."

Other aspects of her situation were equally distressing. At the state "san," as staff and inmates called it, seriously ill patients with virulently positive sputum were put right in with negative ones like Doré. Delia, in the next bed, coughed constantly, without covering her mouth, even into the faces of young ward helpers.

Moreover, nurses were routinely careless, picking up a dropped blanket from the floor and putting it back on a bed, failing to wash their hands from patient to patient, even between changing surgical dressings, unless called on it. The shortage of nurses, due to military recruitment for the war, meant even less attention to patients than usual. Beds were changed only once a week and Doré had to sweet talk for fresh towels. "We are reduced to one bath a week, too," she wrote, "so we certainly overwork the little pans of water that appear at the strange hours of 5 a.m. and 3 p.m.

"When Dr. Haight came out to check on my incisions," she told Lurry, "he asked after my happiness. He knew I hated being moved, but he had the nerve to remark that anyone who had taken what I had so gallantly when my husband 'passed' could certainly stand Howell. It made me furious! There are times when being stoic gets you no place. But I simply won't weep or plead."

On Friday the 20th, Mom Goss and Do came out with flowers, home made foods, piles of magazines and word of what I had been saying and doing. "I needed them that two-week day," Doré wrote, "and I'm so grateful. It's a hell of a trip out here and Mom is still shaky about driving on winter roads since Don died."

"Long visiting hours are usually an advantage here," she wrote Lurry on the first endless empty Sunday without Don. "Swarms of visitors make the day festive for so many who lie day after day shut in with the small, dull details of a bedfast life. Company makes one important, gives such a feeling of protection, and spins a tenuous thread between us and the outside world.

"Delia will cry when her farmer husband and two fat children leave, so I am thinking of stories to make her laugh. It's a source of pride to me to keep existence alive and gay in here. I get a thrill from coming into a dismal room like this and lifting it up by the heels. Flossie said last night that it seemed so different and happy here since I came. You'll do a great deal for a soft, heartfelt remark like that. And in lifting these three I lift myself."

One morning, the sanatorium doctor in charge of her case came to her bedside.

"Mrs. Goss, I have good news," he declared enthusiastically. "Your x-ray shows a remarkably good collapse from your thoracoplasty"

"That IS good news," Doré said.

"I thought you'd be glad to know that there were no unfortunate results from the strain of your recent bereavement. Your control in the face of great tragedy is most gratifying to us all."

"Thank you, Dr. Finch," Doré answered, as she smiled inwardly, imagining Don chuckling at the stiffly formal words. In her mind she could hear him saying, "That's my braver." She remembered what pride he took in the way her Rowe chin refused to quiver where anyone could see it.

...

Being exiled to Howell so soon after Don's death, meant that, when she needed them most, Dore's friends could no longer just pop in for a visit. Writing letters to Lurry became an almost daily way of feeding Doré's hunger for someone close to talk to.

In late March, the sisters used their letters to explore an issue that neither had spoken about before. It went back to after Don and Doré were married, when they didn't hear from Lurry for two months. Don had finally wired her a telegram of concern. Lurry responded with tales of office parties and a weekend in Princeton with Davey and Kit and their little son, Andy, but wrote not a word of happy reminiscence about Dore's wedding.

It wasn't until the exchange of letters in the spring of '42 that Doré told her sister how much that had hurt, and Lurry finally acknowledged that she had felt "shut out" after Dore's marriage. It wasn't that she felt jealous, Lurry said. It was just that she didn't feel needed any more. She felt as if she had lost her sister. This sense of things was confirmed in her mind when she didn't hear back from Doré.

Doré begged Lurry's forgiveness for never telling her the reason for her own long silence. Don had lost his old job.

"His discouragement and anguish were so terrifying," she said, "but I couldn't write about it and I couldn't think of much else. His mother was cruelly critical of him, giving him the feeling that she viewed him as a failure, and refusing to lend him any money. This attitude was such a shock and hurt him so. He seemed to be waiting for me to jump him and complain. He started misinterpreting what I said, not believing my words of support. It was horrible. I was working long hours, running the house, trying to keep Judy unaware and out of his way. Finally I just closed up and couldn't talk and never really slept. I didn't know how to prove that my kind of love went steadily through anything. Then I got sick and nothing else mattered for weeks and weeks.

"In all the confusion and worry about money, I did nothing about comforting you. I guess I believed that our love would hold until I had strength and time to give it thought. But my old pod gave out very badly on me while I was trying to see my way through. Forgive me if you can.

"When Don and I finally talked it out, here at Howell, he understood what his moods had done to me, and I realized that he had been in terror of failing me. He needed to be responsible for me and Judy. It didn't work for me to take on that load. His capable shoulders straightened at once with the new job. He had to feel good about himself in order to make a steady foundation on which to rest all the lyric loveliness... All I could do was to say that I trusted enough in him and in our love to do everything I could to get well and come home to him. He came through so gloriously, being a rock of strength for me, doing so beautifully with Judy and learning to walk softly with his family."

My mother told Lurry that she would never understand the Goss way. "Dollar signs over the eyeballs pattern life so oddly. The hardest tragedy for them now is knowing, too late, how they failed Don and hurt him. Even his mother never saw that praise was what he needed so deeply. She had high hopes for him, but her criticism undermined him. He didn't even tell her of the raises he was getting in the new job, or the nice office that he was given just two weeks before he died. 'Hell,' he told me, 'to them that would be just peanuts. You're the only one who knows what it means, Dorritt.'

"Poor Mom said to me, 'You are so peaceful because you never brought him anything but happiness.' Now, they would give me their shirts which I do not want or need, and a little gesture to Don a year ago would have helped him so. I'm not bitter, but he was hurt and bewildered…"

Both Mom Goss and Do were faithful hospital visitors, often bringing small bouquets of flowers for Dore's little blue glass vase that I had given her long ago for a "Saturday present." Now it was a treasured touch of home. Sometimes Mom brought fried chicken and stacks of new magazines, or fragrant soap and stationery. Doré was glad of the gifts, but sad, too. "I know she is giving it all to Don, wishing so that she had been gentler with him. If he somehow knows, he will be glad that I am lacking none of the little things he used to bring."

One day, Kelly broke down and wept with Doré, saying that he hated himself for always berating Don about money. "It had been petty and ugly," Doré told Lurry, "but I got him calmed down by telling him that I was sure Don knew he was sorry and forgave him.

"I did say, 'Kelly, try to learn from this to see more clearly what things really matter. If Don's death can teach you that, it's some good from the tragedy.' He seemed to appreciate that."

"I am determined that they shall not try to pay off by doing for Judy what they would not do for Don. And I am aware of the danger of them thinking I'm out for the Goss gold. I want them to understand that I want only their affection and respect. They seem to be learning. They are so touched by Judy's careful records of every dime they lend her. Mom says she never dreamed a child could understand money so easily and never ask for it unnecessarily. I'm glad we never had riches. It takes rare character to have them and still see clearly."

…

When Do Goss brought me out to Howell to visit, Doré was so glad, for she knew I was feeling less secure since Don died. I had written her, "I try hard not to miss you too much and to do my share, but now with Poppy gone, I guess I worry more about how you are and when you will get well."

Doré was taken by wheel chair to a quiet doctor's office, where we could talk alone. "I tried to give her the hope ahead of a little home for the two of us again, of our own things about us and the love and peace we would share," Doré wrote. "We talked of Pentwater, which has been such a solace before. It helped us both."

I was invited to spend spring vacation with my uncle and aunt, Don and Helen March in South Bend. When Mom Goss brought me to the san the next month, Doré could see that I was happier.

"I can rest my heart about her now," she told Lurry. "but I long to be closer to help her as she faces the consuming job of growing up. It is my last job to do and my greatest reason for going on."

In April she wrote, "It is good to have sunshine today. My special bit of sky has been so blue, with white clouds scudding. It made me remember Pentwater skies and I could almost feel the warm sand. I don't often lie remembering. When I do, I make it happy. It's good that grief and pain are what we forget first. That's why the past seems mostly happy and good in our memories.

"Some days I feel restless because I don't know anything about when I will be free. got so used to having Don to help pull me out of the doldrums. He did it with such eagerness to help. He loved the days here with me, even as others watched and either envied or rejoiced in our love. Sometimes I can hardly bear the yearning to see him walk through the door and cross to my bed saying 'How's my darling?'

I can picture her removing her glasses to blot a few tears. I imagine her huffing open-mouthed over one lens to fog it and then lifting a corner of the bed sheet to wipe it clean. After repeating the ritual with the other lens, she would have breathed deeply and continued writing.

"Losing Don now has been so much harder because I can't be busy and tired after productive days. But this thinking out loud to you eases my heart and I feel you pulling me up. Just one little day at a time is all I have to face. The Fates keep trying to beat me. I've never given in so they go right on

141

pounding, and the more they pound, the more I fight back. I'm made that way, I guess."

Lurry's letters meant so much to Doré, who loved hearing about Broadway plays and Carnegie Hall concerts and even office intrigue. "I mull over every word you write, filling out pictures."

Although no letters from Lurry to Doré survived, I know from the way she wrote to me when I was grown that she could vividly express her support. One letter from her that I saved was eight single-spaced pages in conversational style. "I never had any doubt that you would succeed," she wrote, "with your talents and ways of working with people." I valued such compliments all the more because she never spared me honest disagreement with some action I'd taken.

...

On Mothers Day 1942, Kelly brought me for a visit. Doré was glad to see that he and I had become pals. Kelly loved to tease me–especially about how much I liked his mom's chocolate chip cookies and chunk pickles, saying that I would soon have to buy my clothes at Fox Tent and Awning Company. But he never made me feel as if I were a burden when he drove me to and from town each school day.

Fed up with all the stalling about her fate, Doré asked Dr. Finch for a private interview in his office. Cool and determined, she put on full makeup and wore her luscious quilted silk robe to shore up her ego. The doctor agreed that after six months since her surgeries, it was time for more x-rays and a clinic session on her case.

As she waited the week to face a panel of eight physicians impersonally viewing her films on an illumined panel before them, she held onto the hope that she would be able to start getting up and counting down to dismissal. She also dreaded the thought that the clinic would bring her "the bitter business of facing more painful operations and long months more in bed. If so, I can take it. And at least the uncertainty will be over, which in itself will be no small gift."

The verdict was more surgery. She would need to have more ribs removed, to ensure a total collapse of her lung and prevent further disease.

Initially crushed at having to give up the dream of getting to Pentwater that summer, Doré met the news with her usual grit, even rejoicing in the prospect of returning to University Hospital.

BACK TO ANN ARBOR

A few weeks later, she described the pre-surgical prep. "They shave me all over my torso, slosh on ether and alcohol, and then wrap me in sterile cloths and a garment like an old-fashioned corset. I sleep in that straight jacket until 6 a.m. when they go through the ether and alcohol washing again. No dull moments, certainly. But I feel loaded with courage. There are no unknowns, and it's easier to face the familiar even if it's awful, isn't it?"

Afterward, she explained what had been done. "My fifth rib was removed and my shoulder blade tucked in under my 6th and 7th ribs to help out the collapse. It will stay there until the final operation.

It feels a bit odd, but doesn't hurt. Haight wants to take the sixth and seventh ribs next time, and then I'll be done."

Within a month, he said that Dore's sixth and seventh ribs should come out right away, and her shoulder blade released. He said that the diabetes was such an added hazard to her health when she got out, that they didn't want to leave any chance of further trouble. "I don't want that either," Doré wrote. "I really think I would kill myself if I ever came down with active TB again.

"It's quite possible they might not finish up this time. Haight is so cautious. I feel strangely casual about it. I guess when there has been so much punishment you don't feel very deeply any more. I don't really give a damn. And the silver lining is escaping the heat and flies of Howell a little longer."

The night before her July 2nd surgery Doré wrote, "I asked for Hogan, a swell nurse who has prepped me twice before. Now if only I have good nurses and lots of hypos for four days afterwards, I will be over the worst and able to take a deep breath and realize I am 44! Bless you for all your love and tenderness. Until after the ball...."

The post-op pain was intense. Doré never complained to others, but in her letters to Lurry she told the truth. She was deeply grateful that Do Goss was there when she came out of the anesthetic and stayed all day two days, wiping her brow, putting ice chips on her tongue, and doing countless other little things to make her comfortable.

"She was a marvel," Dore wrote. "She said I kept begging her to get Don. That couldn't have been easy to hear. She really cares for me deeply. She said she had always wanted a sister but never dreamed of one as dear and brave as Doré. That means a lot to me."

Meanwhile, I was spending the summer with Don and Helen March in South Bend. As my mother recovered, my letters amused her. "Judy has a crush on a 16-year-old that she herself calls puppy love," she told Lurry. "What heaven and hell is still ahead for her I wonder? I want her to have it all, for contrasts are important. Sometimes I get desperate to get back to her. There must be many things she needs to talk about casually that can't get into letters.

"Even after she comes home, it's a concern. Mom Goss is rather old-fashioned, and Do is decidedly abnormal in her notions about men. I want Judy to be genuine, with no prudishness and no gimme. Don was very sane with her. I know he used to tell her to be like me, to give generously and be really interested in other people. She said once, 'Poppy thinks you are just perfect. I guess he's a one woman man, isn't he?' We were so amused"

In August, Dr. Haight told her that he wanted to go ahead with the final stage of thoracoplasty – removal of her eighth rib through a frontal incision under her right breast. Of the 21 days since the previous operation, Dore had only felt completely pain-free four of them. She so wished that he would give her more time to rest and get stronger. But he had scheduled a ten-day vacation, and he wanted to do the surgery before he left.

"I'm definitely not ready in the mind," she wrote, "but I guess the quicker the better. I can't go on spending the rest of my life in bed."

The post-op pain was less than after the huge back surgeries, but when she came out of the anesthetic, Doré was unable to move her right arm or hand.

"Lucy, the Idiot Child"

During the operation, her arm had been positioned above her head on the table, with her elbow bent. The wires that secured her body in that pose had pressed into her armpit for so long that they crushed nerves and paralyzed her arm.

I can just imagine the shock and chagrin experienced by the whole medical team. Lucky for them that their patient was Doré Goss. She not only didn't sue them, she summoned the courage to take on yet another challenge–to get back the use of her arm.

 She named the useless limb "Lucy," and told Lurry, "She is a hell cat as well as an idiot child. For two days I had no feeling from the shoulder down, but then the torture began. The regeneration of damaged nerves creates pain like you wouldn't believe. With my arm paralyzed and my ribs missing, I could not even sit up by myself for 17 days. I lay as I was put, day and night, watching for my next hypo. But nothing stopped the pain entirely."

She wrote that letter slowly, painstakingly, with her <u>left</u> hand. The penciled lines angle up and down on the page, their words writ large but legibly. Doré said that she had to visualize every word before she started it, but she was determined to give Lurry the details she knew she yearned for.

"Everybody is being swell to me," she wrote. "They feed and wash and brush me. In return I laugh and kid and smile. The one good thing about all this is that I won't be sent back to Howell right away. Lucy has to have her baking and massage and manipulation. After a week of physical therapy I can wiggle my fingers a wee bit. So Lucy won't be sent to Reform School, and we can both stay here.

"The operations are over, and each day is one off my rest cure. The pain defies description, but my tail wags and I can snicker. Everybody who enters my room asks about Lucy by name, except Dr. Haight, who is subdued and apologetic. Judy says his name should be spelled H-a-t-e."

Signing off that first letter, Doré wrote, "I must stop. This took me two hours. Try it sometime. The mental contortions are something," she said, "but at least it is a letter, and you know I love you."

As the weeks went by, Lucy learned to pick up a small Kleenex box. "Of course she had a temper tantrum and threw it on the floor at once," Doré wrote. "I wish she would learn something useful like cutting meat or rubbing hand lotion on my overworked left paw. I can lift my arm, but I don't know where it will fall. The use of my hand will come back last, they say."

Dr. Marianna Smalley gave Doré the good news that her x-rays showed significant shrinkage in her TB cavity. Resting her lung was working. Marianna also commandeered an overhead reading rack—the sort that fastened to the bed frame and swung out over a patient on steel rods. A book could be positioned on a slanted wooden surface and held in place with heavy metal clips. Light springs held the book's pages, which could easily be turned with one hand. This was such a blessing, as Doré had not been able to hold anything heavier than a New Yorker. Additionally, Marianna prescribed "a pill for Lucy that was pure magic." Doré slept through the night for the first time since July 2nd.

Near summer's end, Lurry came to Ann Arbor for a long weekend visit, to reassure herself about her sister's condition. She had felt sure that Doré was sparing her the truth. As she watched Lucy get her lessons, Lurry was relieved to see that, although paralysis was indeed a handicap, there was every reason to believe that therapy would eventually restore the use of Doré's hand. During their long talks, Doré was also able to listen to the details of Lurry's life, and offer her the kind of loving support that only a big sister could provide.

Lurry's primary burden for years was her whining, fault-finding apartment-mate, their cousin Paula Simmons. That summer, Lurry also faced moving their father into a Methodist retirement home in Pennsylvania. Doré knew that it made Lurry feel guilty when Daddy Rowe resisted the arrangement, saying that he hated the thought of "a dull, abnormal life with a lot of old men." Lurry took such laments personally, always being more like their "sensitive" mother in that respect. So it was a relief to them both when he finally made the decision, as he put it, "in favor of security and peace." And after Lurry spent her vacation getting him settled in, he was content and made friends.

...

Doré's ability to use her left hand improved markedly. She was able to use a pen to sign checks. Being able to pay her bills gave her a lovely sense of achievement.

Lucy's pain was soon restricted to the last joint of each finger, bearable much longer between codeine capsules. "I made her butter bread last night," Doré wrote. "Then she threw the knife on the tray and broke a cup. I guess she wants to be a kept woman all her life."

The next week, Doré wrote, "Lucy can hold a matchbox while I strike a match or an envelope while I open it. She let me cut and file her nails and Do [Goss] put on Burma Red polish, so we think she is entering adolescence. She gloats over the bloody color, the slut."

The matches were for cigarettes. Smoking was common in hospitals then. Even for patients who had tuberculosis, unless their illness was so advanced that constant coughing made it intolerable. Scientific research had not yet made any correlation between tobacco and disease.

...

In September, Mom Goss was pleased to welcome me home. She told my mother that she had felt lost without me all summer and didn't know what she would do when Doré was out of the hospital and took me away.

"Judy enters ninth grade this fall," Doré wrote Lurry. "I can't bear not seeing her and sharing it all, so I asked Hate for permission to have her come up on Saturday, and he said that since my sputum is negative, there is no reason she can't come. He even offered the use of his private office so we can be alone." The day after this visit, Doré wrote, "She asked a million things about Lucy and devoured me with her eyes. She is so eager to have me back, but understanding about the time it will take."

It was a big day when Lucy learned to use a spoon, cut a fried egg, and even hold a mug of coffee. Doré weaned her off codeine at night and put on fresh nail polish – Dorothy Gray's "Ripe Cherries." Do gave her a new lipstick to match. "I feel a yen for a date," Doré wrote. "So you know I am coming out of the long fog, don't you?"

Mom Goss gave her a stunning new bed jacket, white crepe with blue and fuchsia flowers and shell pink lining. New hair ribbons too. Doré loved hearing about all the new clothes Mom got for me. Don's Social Security benefits provided a small check each month for his "surviving child." Doré had saved it for my fall wardrobe and school books. His mother was so dismayed by what she considered the poor quality of ready-made clothes that she also bought wool cloth to make me a skirt and dress so that I "need not look shoddy," she told Doré.

"Judy's a young amazon, Lurry. 5 ft. 8 inches tall, size nine shoes! Can't you see me dwarfed by my girl when I get out? I hope *Kind-Dirty* lets me shop with her next fall. I think often about the future for her. It isn't a pretty world we have to hand over. She and her children will be paying forever for this war, and our mistakes of omission and commission… I know it is good for the soul to endure pain and understand suffering, but, like all who bear young, I sometimes weakly pray, 'but not for mine, please *Kind-Dirty*!' I know better, but right now I have too much thinking time and am rather close yet to large prices paid in pain of heart and body to get my arithmetic straight.

"Having Judy makes it easier to grow old. It gives life a sequence that makes it possible to look ahead, even to the terrible loneliness of no Don in her life or mine. While yet I am necessary to her, I plan on not looking back or too much ahead. After that, well, no deluge!"

…

My uncle Don March, who had been in the ROTC at the University of Illinois, enlisted for ground work in the Air Corps, expecting, at age 37, to be kept in this country. But when his training ended, he was made a 2nd Lt. in the Judge Advocates Division and sent to England. Billeted with a family near Birmingham, he enjoyed the experience and his work. Doré wrote Lurry, "I do hope he keeps safe. Ben used to worry about him, saying 'He will be in the next war and it won't be a pretty one.' How right he was. Friends of Ben's, who were too old for service, are doing U.S.O. jobs or recruiting or selling bonds."

Kelly Goss was called up by the draft, but to his mother's vast relief, he failed the physical due to the spinal fusion he had at age 17 after his back was broken in a car accident. Mom Goss couldn't imagine how she would have managed the farm without him, and she dreaded the thought of any harm befalling her only remaining son.

…

One day, "Lucy" was tested by a neurologist, who not only wiggled and pricked her but made her identify objects put into her palm while Doré was blindfolded. She passed with high grades. But Miss Faye, the physical therapist, refused to give "Dr. Hate" a date certain for Lucy's "graduation" because nerve injuries were always unpredictable, she said. Doré rejoiced that a return to the Howell sanatorium was further postponed.

Meanwhile, Doré's paralysis had, at least, inspired a transformation in the way patients were positioned for frontal stage thoracoplasties. From then on, thick sponges were placed under those armpit wires, so no more patients would have to go through what she was experiencing. In the future, doctors would learn how to remove a badly infected lobe of a lung, leaving a TB patient's ribs intact.

By early October Lucy was writing well enough to write a letter to Lurry. "She still tires easily, but I told her she had to show off for you. Dr. Waring, the floor superintendent, whom I call Lucy's godfather, told me that at first he thought it might be three months before she moved. How kind he and Marianna were to not answer my pitiful 'How long?' We don't need to know too much, do we?"

The following week, Doré crowed, "Today I combed my own hair! It is so long that I am wearing it in a coronet of braids that looks neat and is comfortable in bed. One more hurdle is past. Lucy's fingers are still swollen, but, as you see, she remembers how to write."

"I recently read a sentence that seems true to me," She told Lurry. "'Hope wears silence like a protective covering to hide it away from reason.' I've reached the point where <u>my</u> hope is very articulate!"

...

To her surprise, Doré was moved to the west sun porch. Not only was it a large, bright area, but her new roommate was a private patient who was "well read and congenial company." Anne had fought TB for ten years and returned this time for more major surgery. "After three years of draining, her thoracoplasty just never healed," Dore explained. "She faces a re-opening of the whole incision, cutting two inches off her shoulder blade, grafting muscle into the drainage hole, and sewing her up with prayers and sulfa drugs.

"I have Lucy's fingers crossed for her, as I remember that others' fate can be worse than mine. Good old Hate simply beamed when he told me that my latest x-rays show the good lung still perfect and the collapse of the other just as they want it."

On November 1st, Doré marked the anniversary of her first operation. "What a helluva year it has been," she wrote. "But I am at peace. As I watch a gorgeous wintry sun setting beyond the eight tall windows of our sun porch, I only have nine weeks and three days left of my sentence. And as I maintain detachment, I like this saying: 'I am not what I think I am, rather, what I think, I am.' Don't you agree?

"I amuse myself with thoughts. Some thinking ahead is fun, some escape by reading, some news of the world which is a deep concern for all my helplessness, and a fragrant whiff of my really vivid rich past, which I use sparingly, as a good drinker uses Napoleon brandy in a snifter which is beautiful to hold. Balancing all these thoughts is tricky, but I've become quite a juggler."

...

When I was asked, with two classmates, to talk in school about our "foreign" dolls, Doré asked Lurry, "Can't you see her holding forth on Chinese clothes and customs as portrayed by Ben's family of cloth dolls he had made in Paotingfu so long before she was born? He must be pleased that she carries on not just his blood, but also his favorite enthusiasm of making China and her people vividly alive for Americans. It is strangely satisfying to see the early flowering of seeds we planted in the dark but nourishing soil of her young mind and heart."

In mid-November, Do Goss played a critically-acclaimed piano recital in the Lydia Mendelssohn Auditorium. I was thrilled to see her picture in the newspaper and to be trusted to hand out programs at the door. The following day, Do brought Doré five dozen red roses from the flowers she received. "Their vivid color and fragrance brightened up the sun porch no end," she told Lurry.

At the end of the month, Dr. Haight came in, with his usual serious demeanor, and said, "I know you are enjoying this set up, but I wondered how much you would mind having to leave it?"

Doré sucked in her breath. She felt sure he was finally sending her back to Howell. As she struggled to swallow her fear, she realized that he was saying, "I would like to move you down to Seventh Floor, the medical TB unit, so I can move a surgical patient up here on Eighth."

Of course she agreed. Describing the scene to Lurry, Doré wrote, "Marianna says this proves that Hate can't send me to Howell as long as Lucy needs therapy. He realizes the hospital is responsible for her and must make good. It is such a relief to know I don't have to spend another Christmas in that dark, impersonal hell hole, far from family and friends."

When Do Goss and a hospital orderly moved Dore's things downstairs, she got another surprise. She was ushered into a private room with a window looking out across campus, and her own bathroom.

"I still can't believe it. After a sweet young nurse tucked me in at night, I wept like a fool. After 18½ months of far-too-intimate living with strangers, this is too lovely for description. To be expecting Howell and land on this peaceful floor all alone was such bliss. I laughed even as I bawled, and then I slept through the night."

She continued to relish the privacy, even as she lay listening to all the familiar hospital sounds: the clanging of bedpans, the rattle of food tray carts, the clank of mop buckets, the slight squeak of rubber soled shoes, nurses' low voices exchanging information, call bells, elevator doors thudding and clicking open or shut. The smell of a hospital that often bothers visitors–the sharp odor of ether, rubbing alcohol and disinfectant–had become unnoticeable to her.

...

I asked to stay at Skylodge for Christmas of '42. Doré explained it to Granny and Grandaddy March on the basis of wartime travel conditions being so difficult. Lurry shopped in New York for the presents that Doré wanted to give others, including a red leather shoulder bag for me.

For herself, she asked if Lurry could find a bottle of Lentheric's "Shanghai" cologne. "This fragrance is bound with happy memories." She wrote. "I sniffed it first with you in New York, remember? I planned to buy it later. Then, when Don met my return train, the fragrance filled Mom's big black car. I asked, 'Does your mother use Shanghai cologne, Roger?' He laughed his merry roar and said, 'No, it's my new shaving lotion, for you, China Girl,' and leaned his clean-shaved cheek toward my nose. We had a lovely secrety feeling, as lovers-to-be, because we'd both discovered the same fragrance the same week.

"I wore it for our wedding and ever since. Sometimes my heart wavers, smelling it, because Don's cheeks are no longer here, nor any crisp white breast pocket handkerchief scented with Shanghai, waiting 'if you ever have to cry, Sweet.' But I still love it and can take it alone better than doing without. If it isn't available, it will be my small wartime sacrifice, and if I get it, I know we can't take baths in it anymore."

Dore's private room was not a lonely one. Friends were anxious to see her new set up and crowded the visiting hours. Anne came down from the sun porch with 8th floor news, including her own hopes to be home by Christmas. Seventh Floor nurses pampered Doré with fresh sheets every day, two daily back rubs and every effort to increase her comfort.

In those days of crisp white uniforms and white rayon stockings, nurses surely couldn't have imagined the bright patterned tunics that women wear over pants today. In the forties, nurses also wore starched white hats which distinguished one nursing school from another. Some tidy caps were bobby-pinned on top of curls. Others were great winged creations that threatened to take flight. Hatless ward helpers wore grey and white striped uniforms with beige cotton hose. Almost all were kind and helpful.

Lurry had always said that the nurses were Dore's devoted slaves. "You're right," Doré agreed. "It's because I won't beef and I've made a laughing stock of Lucy, my idiot child. It's well worth it. I need to be liked or I wilt."

...

In December, Miss Faye brought Doré a small live table-top Christmas tree and trimmed it with red and silver balls. It set Doré to reminiscing: "Peking trees at Temple Court the year I had Boy Blue, Judy's first dolls under the ceiling-high trees at Glen Ellyn, the tiny tree in our Chicago hotel room two years ago, and the modern metal model last year with real candles Don lit for Christmas Eve. With all the happiness I have inside, saved and cherished, I know I can get through hearing sentimental old carols once again.

"Mom Goss brought Judy to the hospital Christmas Eve afternoon and again after dinner Christmas Day," Dore told Lurry. "She and I were alone here in my small room and happy together knowing that in just a few months I will be free and living with her again."

One of my gifts to my mother was four new "stair step vases" for Pentwater, each a different pastel shade. "I love them," Doré wrote, "for the hope they bring that I shall see them filled with flowers as I rest on the Jazz Couch next summer.

Do Goss came up on New Year's Eve, bearing two little glasses and whiskey they drank together, deciding that the coming year could not scare them after the one they had just lived through.

I was allowed to give a "luncheon party" for my 14th birthday, and afterwards took my six guests to the movies. "Judy came to see me Sunday in a new blue sweater and lipstick," Dore wrote. "She looked very grown up."

…

In early January, 1943, Doré was allowed to dangle her feet over the side of the bed for five minutes twice a day. Her feet were purple and stinging and her toes swollen when the five minutes ended, but soon after that preparation she was able to get out of bed and sit in a chair. The next week the time was increased to ten minute periods. As she eased her feet, unaccustomed to slippers, down to the hard linoleum floor, she was astonished by the wet noodle feeling in her legs.

"Lurry," she wrote, "You wouldn't believe how wobbly the old pins are after so long flat in bed. My calves are positively flabby, with no palpable muscles at all. I can see why the docs say it will take time to regain strength and you have to take it slowly." Using a toilet for the first time was a milestone, and being able to shuffle a bit in the corridor was like an Olympic event.

One Sunday, when her hands were black from reading newspapers, she took soap and towel into her bathroom and washed under running water for the first time since May 1941. "I was most ridiculously pleased with myself!" Soon she wrote that "my first tub bath was a thrill beyond words to describe."

Doctors were pleased that a little exercise meant they could reduce her insulin intake, and Dore was so grateful that her blood sugar level was being so carefully monitored, something she felt sure would not have happened at Howell.

Doré admitted to Lurry that, as the end of her two-year ordeal approached, she was missing Don terribly. She believed that others would not be aware of her physical limitations and her need to be protected from overdoing. "Don would have hovered over me, cradling my strength and guarding me from those who, not having shared the paying, can't know the price. But I've thought it out carefully, and I know I can manage among normal people with their natural obliviousness."

When I saw my mother get up for the first time, I was relieved by her appearance. As Doré reported it to Lurry, "Judy told me 'Your back is perfect, and your shoulders are level too.' It made me realize that she had been wondering about that.

"When I am well again, I know I can make life beautiful and rich for my girl. It's so contrary of me, with so precious and wonderful a child, never to have been satisfied with her. I shall be now. My mind knows that seeing her through will suffice for the emptiness and loneliness ahead of me. Sometimes I get a frantic longing to be loved and to have someone to grow old with me. But this is how it is now, and I have the courage it takes to go on living and make it meaningful for Judy."

Bath privileges and "up time" were gradually increased during late February and early March, with each excursion taking less and less effort. She was happy to be more and more independent before going home to Skylodge.

The swelling of Lucy's fingers was down enough for Doré to get her favorite Mexican silver ring on the correct finger, a fitting symbol as she went to her last lesson with Miss Faye. "With her diploma in hand, I bury the name and all its hellish and amusing memories," she told Lurry. "Almost nine months of the idiot-child is enough!"

The next week she wrote, "Spring is coming in my window on soft warm air. I've really fought for the privilege of having this one, and I don't intend to let anything destroy it, no little confusions at Skylodge, no backward glances, no personal loneliness or tiny fears. I am all set to love all my tomorrows and find them good."

Skylodge

In his moving novel <u>Angle of Repose</u>, Wallace Stegner wrote, "At once, like a milldam opening, her ponded life began to flow again." That perfectly describes what Doré experienced when, on March 19th, she discovered that coming to stay with the Gosses was easier than she had expected. After Do picked her up in Mom's big Cadillac, they drove around campus by her old office building, past the stores on State Street, as she gloried in her freedom.

"The climb upstairs left me breathless but not tired," she told Lurry, "and it was bliss to pile into a real bed. The things that thrill me most are rugs and curtains, Mom's Wedgwood china and sterling forks and spoons. Food tastes so wonderful with seasonings. I love Mom's garlic salads and fresh vegetables. I make out my menus from what the rest are to eat, and Judy weighs things on the gram scales and brings my meals up on a tray.

"I have a toaster by my bed so I can have really hot toast in the morning. The family is so good to me, and my room is a gathering place for everyone. Do has her first cup of coffee with me in the morning, Kelly brings his coffee and a cig up after dinner, and Judy does her homework in here after she helps Mom with the dishes.

"Mom is lonely and tied to her domestic pattern. Do is selfish and moody and violently emotional with her mother. Judy warned me that Do and Kelly fight a lot, too, and I might have to be a peacemaker. We shall see."

On May 21, Doré wrote: "My checkup x-ray was perfect and tonight I can dress and go downstairs for dinner. In an hour I will don bra and girdle, hose and slip, and a white gabardine sport dress and eat at a proper table again. After two months upstairs, I'm in such a state of excitement I can't think…" The next day she reported, "It all went perfectly and Judy was so thrilled. We ate on the sun porch with lilacs and tulips in bloom beyond the bank of windows. It was a moment of real achievement for me. I look fine in clothes, with no sign of my caved-in chest. It was worth slaving over my posture…"

"There isn't the slightest question now about our going to Pentwater. Four weeks and we'll be there. Judy had a great idea of getting a big red express wagon she can use to lug the laundry and groceries. Bless her, she's going to be busy and I think happy doing such necessary chores this year."

In late May, she wrote Lurry that "Judy is off for the weekend at a girlfriend's house and I miss her sharply. I must watch my step not to hang on too tightly."

PENTWATER AT LAST

On June 15, Mom Goss used some of Kelly's gas rationing stamps to drive us to Pentwater. As Doré reclined in comfort on the wide back seat, she felt such a song in her heart to be returning at last to her very own home which had always been such a haven of peace.

The old house had happily lapped up two coats of fresh white paint, and the terraces had been cleared of grass and weeds. Inside, the rooms had been thoroughly cleaned, and the first thing Doré did was arrange iris in her favorite tall blue vase.

Marianna said she could start walking outdoors, make her bed, do dishes and cook simple meals. July 1st she was able to go up and down the stairs twice a day, but she assured Lurry that she would not overdo.

"You must know how careful I will be of what's left of me for my remaining years. I've learned at an awful price to go slowly. No matter how much I may want to move furniture or lug garbage pails to the dump, I can't, ever again, and I hope I can be happy in less strenuous ways."

She was, and she enjoyed a blissful summer, with all the usual gang of friends throwing cocktail parties and fish dinners on the upper deck of Nelson's boat house.

The red wagon proved as useful as I had expected. Grocery shopping was complicated by the wartime ration books everyone had to use–with different colored stamps for different products and the number of stamps assigned by individual needs. Doré's status as a diabetic meant that we had plenty of red stamps for meat, milk, butter and cheese. Green stamps for vegetables were also adequate. Blue stamps for clothing were sufficient as long as one's wants were reasonable. I quickly learned to tear out the correct stamps and present them to clerks along with dollars and cents.

I rode my bike to pick up the mail at the post office and run any light errands before meeting friends at the beach in the afternoon. It was a big change for Doré to have to stay out of the sun, but of course she accepted the restriction, feeling nothing but gratitude for just being in Pentwater. At that time, doctors erroneously believed that ultraviolet rays would re-activate TB.

Our old friend Rilla Nelson, who with her husband Walter introduced my parents to Pentwater, sometimes drove Doré to the beach at twilight, so she could at least walk into the water and take comfort from seeing and hearing Lake Michigan again.

While my mother was hospitalized, Lurry had spent her two-week vacations on the Connecticut shore with their brother Davey and his family. When she returned to Pentwater in August of '43, it was a heavenly interlude for the two sisters, and special for me to have my aunt's companionship again.

Lurry was a crisp up, no-nonsense person, very precise in her habits. She was an early-riser who loved the luminous first hours of day, the greetings of mourning doves and the sweet fragrance of honeysuckle on the crisp air. I basked in that time with her while Doré was still sleeping.

After making coffee in the old chrome percolator and sipping the first cup on the back terrace, Lurry fixed me the same breakfast that she had every day: a small orange juice and one soft-boiled egg with toast. For herself she added lemon juice in hot water "for regularity." By 1943, a streamlined, automatic pop-up toaster had replaced the small triangular-shaped model with manual "doors" that held slices of bread near open wires. But if the electricity went off in a summer storm, the broiler of the bottled gas stove did the trick.

On the wall over the kitchen table was a small framed print of a benevolent Chinese kitchen god. He was supposed to bring blessings upon the household. In China, children place bowls of rice in front of their kitchen god scroll paintings, to bribe him to bring good luck. Our family god still watches over my own kitchen today.

In the afternoon Lurry and I took long walks along the singing sands watching the rhythmic waves caress sandpiper tracks, climbed together to the dugout in the tallest dune, or swam across the broad boating channel that connected the "Big" and "Little" lakes. Lurry was proud of her trim figure and "worked on" her summer tan. In the back yard she stretched out her long bare legs in madras plaid shorts, relishing the relief from city clothes. In Pentwater, dressing up meant adding a wraparound cotton skirt and canvas slip-on shoes.

My Aunt was like a second mother to me—or put another way, the sisters seemed to be two halves of an ideal maternal whole. Because she was athletic,

Lurry balanced the more sedentary, contemplative gifts that Doré gave me. It never occurred to me that my mother might wish she could be out on the dunes. How poignant it was to learn from her letters that she loved to hike and swim in her youth - from China days on.

When I had children of my own, their excitement equaled my own as we looked forward to the summer highlight: when Lurry comes! She not only repeated with them all the dune climbing adventures she'd had with me, she took them on "expotitions" (*as Winnie-the-Pooh called long walks*) around the village, sneaking into empty "haunted" houses and making up fanciful tales about the families that had abandoned them. The year she turned seventy she swam across the channel.

...

Despite the pleasure of the final weeks in Pentwater, Doré worried about finding an attractive apartment when we returned to Ann Arbor in September 1943. She knew it wouldn't be easy. The college town, just as every other community in the area, was overflowing with southerners who had moved north to work at Ford's nearby Willow Run Defense plant. Automotive factories had been converted to produce bombers for the Allied war effort. Doré knew that the choicest apartments would already have been taken, but friends were searching for her, and she did hope for a pretty place where I would feel proud to bring my friends.

It didn't work out quite that way.

Doré didn't write to Lurry until late October, when she explained that she had been "far too low in the mind" to describe what was going on. In order for me to start high school on time, we took a dingy furnished place while continuing to search for something nicer. Our choices were limited by the need to be within walking distance of school and office. Doré didn't know when she would be allowed to go back to work, but she wanted to be in a convenient location when that day came.

The unspeakable railcar-style dump was two narrow rooms off a dark hallway, with a kitchenette at one end, sofa bed at the other, a smelly shared bathroom across the hall, and a mildewed old-fashioned ice box on an adjoining porch. A dripping block of ice delivered daily offered very iffy keepage of milk or meat.

Over the dry cleaner

Dore's relief was palpable when, after six weeks in what she called "the hovel," she located a small apartment at 516 East Williams Street, only three blocks off campus and four blocks from the high school. What she didn't tell Lurry, when she finally broke her long silence with this good news, was that it was up a long, steep flight of stairs, over a dry cleaning shop.

Never mind. It was adequate, with its three rooms, plus kitchen and private bath, all freshly painted. Off the living room, my maple bed and dressing table just fit into the curtained alcove that had been advertised as the bedroom. Dore set up her bed in the central room, which would normally have been used as a dining room. The darkness there, due to another brick building about two feet away outside the only window, was an advantage when Doré slept late on Sundays, but we rarely used the space otherwise.

In the living room, two side-by-side windows overlooking the street let light into a space large enough for the little green piano as well as a davenport and two small arm chairs, with the low brass table in between. Our Chinese rugs redeemed the bare wooden floors and Japanese prints made the walls feel familiar. Furnishings that wouldn't fit were shipped to Pentwater or given to appreciative friends. Many artifacts remained in storage.

While I was in school, Doré walked for exercise, picked out books at a nearby library and lugged small bags of groceries up the steep staircase. Since household help wasn't available "for love or money," as she put it, and Doré felt she should save while she wasn't earning, she was glad the small apartment was easy to keep clean. She felt increasingly well and fully up to the task.

"I'm not happy," she wrote Lurry, "but I can take it, and it will be better when I get to work again. I have too much time on my hands until Judy gets home from school. She is having a swell year—loves being in town among her friends. She had a girlfriend overnight Saturday. I took them for Chinese chow and sent them to a movie, before they giggled and talked into the wee hours. It's good to know that she is content to invite friends here. No false pride in my kid."

...

A gap in Doré's letters to Lurry appears between November 1943 and March 1944. Surely she continued to write. The sisters always exchanged ideas about Christmas presents and described their holidays. As Lurry explained to me years later, "I burned some (*letters*) I would not want any but my eyes to see. I don't feel freed of old sorrows, old happiness, old mistakes—bitterly regretted—but I must not leave records of them for anyone else to have to dispose of."

PART SEVEN

幸运

"*Being a parent means walking around for the rest of your life with your heart outside your body.*"

—Craig Ferguson, host of the CBS Late, Late Show.

AS MOTHER, SO DAUGHTER

On March 15, 1944, Doré wrote Lurry, "I've had one perfect week of work. It's so good to be back in the old department. Nothing is changed. Adelaide is so glad to have me and my boss, Helen Hall, is the same as ever. My schedule is just from 1 to 5, so I don't get tired. After cooking our supper, I can read and loaf in the evening.

"But now, Darling, sit down and take a big breath, for of course *Kind-Dirty* couldn't let things go peacefully for long. Marianna came to see me yesterday and told me that Judy's recent routine x-rays show a minimal TB lesion in her right lung. It's very minor, but it's there. I really caved in... You can imagine how my thoughts have been milling around. If I knew anyone to pray to, how I'd do it. If I could offer myself in her place, I would gladly spare her. I could take it for myself so much better. She's just beginning her life and this will shoot it to hell. But, I know she can handle it, and I must be brave for her. If anyone wrote a novel and gave any two the bad breaks we've had, wouldn't readers be scornful?!"

Marianna Smalley explained to us that there is a difference between being infected with the TB bacillus and having TB disease. To become infected, a person has to be close to someone with TB disease such as a family member or co-worker. Once infected with TB, people carry the TB bacillus in their bodies. Usually their bodies' defenses protect them from this "latent TB" and they are not sick. Only about 10% of them will ever develop TB disease.

Most cases of the disease develop as Doré's did, from activating old infection. In my case, I probably became infected as a child, when my mother was sick but not yet diagnosed. Now I apparently had developed the disease – but not the "active" contagious form. I had no cough or fever or fatigue.

At first, Marianna thought that she could put me on a schedule of pneumothorax treatments– the technique of injecting air into the pleural cavity to collapse a lung. This could let me continue to go to school mornings with bed rest at home in the afternoon. However, the medical specialists overruled her, feeling that only a regimen of complete bed rest could be counted on to arrest my disease and make sure it didn't spread. I had to drop all my classes, without knowing when I'd be able to go back to high school.

In one thing, Marianna did prevail. In response to Dore's anguished pleas, her dear friend arranged for me to stay in Ann Arbor, on the 7th floor of University Hospital. I would not be sent to Dore's hated old hell hole – the Howell Sanatorium.

Doré spent the evening visiting hours of 7 to 8:30 with me almost every night. We still didn't have a car, so she took a city bus, walking to and from a nearby stop. In many ways, my getting sick was harder on her than on me. Any mother hates to see her child suffer, and Doré couldn't quite push away pangs of guilt – or at least deep regret – that I had come down with her disease, tuberculosis. If she hadn't had it, my life wouldn't have been so drastically disrupted. She grieved for me.

At the same time, she was proud of my adjustment to the need to lie completely flat. How could I not adjust? All my life she had modeled stoic acceptance of one's fate. It never occurred to me to weep or to ask, "Why ME??!!"

I never felt "sick," so I passed the time by writing letters, reading, pasting school pictures in a scrap book, listening to the radio and talking with my room mate. It's a good thing that doctors never predict at the outset how long a patient will have to be bedridden. If a person clings to specific dates, those hopes are often crushed. I learned, too, as all patients must, that it is only depressing to dwell on what might have been.

When the university semester ended on June 23rd, Doré wrote Lurry of her frustration at having to stay in the hot city all summer. Much as she yearned to be in Pentwater, she didn't want to leave me. Walter and Rilla Nelson's daughter Pat asked if she could rent our house to friends of hers for a month. She offered to put our private possessions in the study and close off that room. Doré was pleased to do the Nelsons a favor and glad for the money. She wrote Lurry that, much as she loathed the prospect, she was "resigned to staying in this sweaty apartment and be peaceful of heart. I could not go on being wrecked and rebellious."

She was glad to be on hand when doctors decided to start me on "pneumos." Doré knew, all too well, the dangers of the treatment, and felt torn about signing for it. But hoping that collapsing my lung would hasten my recovery and protect me against advanced disease, she agreed.

I didn't mind the procedures, but, it was a hot, boring summer for Dore. She wrote Lurry, "Life seems very empty and dull. I hate living alone and don't do it too well. Too much time for thoughts and a feeling of utter uselessness. But I get through the days and long, long nights, and am ready, if grimly, for the ones to follow."

In August, she finally let me persuade her to get out of the heat and go to Pentwater for a few weeks. The house would be open and running after Nelsons' use, so why not? Since it was my suggestion, she accepted that I would be perfectly fine with Marianna's supervision and visits from Mom Goss.

Just the prospect of change and what she called "coolth" gave Dore a boost. She shopped for two new slacks suits, one red and one two shades of blue, and had her long hair cut and permed. All that and new eyeglasses raised her spirits even further.

Best of all, Lurry arranged her vacation for late August, too, so the sisters could have two weeks together, for loafing and "hashing," as they called it, everything that had happened to each of them in the year apart. Lurry's decision to bring Grandaddy Rowe meant less time for intimacy, but he was so delighted to see Doré restored to health, and to be with his two older daughters, that their hearts were filled with pleasure. They were also able to reassure him that I was being "a good sport" about my enforced hospitalization, and that it would soon result in my complete recovery.

...

Back on campus full time, Doré found the university students "more serious than they were in 1940, with personal problems that include fears that a certain Bill or Bob or Joe won't come back from far places. I comfort them as I can from the wisdom of two partings from beloved men, and they

163

go away with soft smiles and courage. So you see some use comes of every pain, and that I do believe."

Wartime shortages continued to come up in most letters, sometimes with gladness at getting around them. "I beamed for hours this afternoon because my favorite grocery clerk saved me two packages of Tarryton cigs. They came in at ten and he knew there would be none left by the time I left the office. I could have hugged Al for saving them for me."

In November, 1944, Doré asked Lurry how she felt about the election results, adding "I voted for the tired old man, so I was pleased."

On December 13th, Doré arrived at the hospital just in time to hear singers from my high school perform Christmas music at the door of my room. "God it was sweet," she told Lurry. "All those dear young voices filled the halls... When they came to Ben's favorite 'O Come All Ye Faithful,' I could hardly keep the weak tears from spilling, for it was the tenth anniversary of the day that he died...That was no thought to share with Judy, but I did phone Granny March when I got home. She had been waiting and said 'I just knew you would call, Dear.'"

...

By January 1945 my lung had healed enough for doctors to start planning my release. I was allowed to start dangling my legs over the side of the bed, in preparation for "up time." No one could have been more thrilled than Doré, who knew that "dangling" meant the beginning of the end. Because there were 19 stair steps leading up to our apartment, I had to take extra time to master climbing hospital stairs before being allowed to leave – on February 27th.

Doré wrote Lurry: "It is so good to have her home – to have someone to talk to and cook for, to have her here when I come in at night, and, well, just being together. She has full bathroom privileges and dresses and walks to Marianna's office, a block away, for her pneumos twice a week. The first time we walked home the long way so she could look in the windows of the import shops and jewelry stores in the Arcade and get the thrill that comes from all the most usual things after a year in bed."

"I shop on the way home in a small neighborhood store where I don't have to wait in lines and can get most everything we need and even a can of tomatoes once in a while....

"Judy is writing to you about our new companion, a black Cocker Spaniel puppy named Michael. He is a darling and the answer to Judy's heart's desire. I knew it would be a lot of company for her while she is home alone so many hours. And, even tho I did wonder about the bother of a dog in a small second storey apartment, I love him now that we have him. He is trained to use papers and sleeps all night in a box in the kitchen. His big black eyes and long curly ears are entrancing, and he is so affectionate that anyone would adore him, and I have taken it in my stride. If you could see my Pooh's pleasure you would understand."

To keep Michael from destroying our shoes and slippers, Dore's old friend Chaney came to the rescue. A ward helper during Dore's hospitalization, she was now working in an area of unclaimed clothing. Stout, with shiny scrubbed cheeks and stiff grey hair, Chaney had little formal education and no experiences anything like Doré's, so she loved to hear the China tales my mother loved to tell. Doré was a good listener to hospital gossip, too, so Chaney kept our puppy supplied with old shoes to chew.

Dore's job continued to give her great pleasure. She enjoyed the work, and she was able to get time off if she needed to take me to the hospital for a checkup or over to see the high school principal. Twice widowed, she worked because she had to support herself and her child. It's a comfort to me to be reminded, from the letters, how much she loved her job.

ANOTHER SULTRY SUMMER

To start making up some of the school work I had missed, I was allowed to study at home that spring and take exams under supervision. By late May the doctors agreed that I could walk to the high school for one summer school class and study for another on my own, back in bed.

Doré was disappointed by the prospect of again spending June and July in our small apartment over a dry cleaner during Ann Arbor heat. But by going to summer school that year and next, I would be able to make up the semester I had to drop and could graduate just one year behind my original class. Doré told Lurry, "That matters so much to Judy that I feel that I should be graceful about it, and I will be."

One amusing memory from that summer is how embarrassed I felt when my mother sat in her slip by an open front window. When I muttered about people seeing her from the street, she said, "If they've seen it before, they won't care. And if they haven't, it's time they did." I also remember that she sharply and firmly told me, "Don't ever again call me Kiddo."

Having days free of office demands, Dore was able to take more time "to work at the hellish business of finding food." It was, she said, a daily struggle that required going to several places and standing in line. "Meat goes on sale at seven-thirty a.m. Tuesdays and Fridays. So those days I leap up before insulin or breakfast so I can clutch a few lamb chops or a steak." She felt grateful for the extra ration points she received for being diabetic. "The prices are awful," she told Lurry, who must have been experiencing similar wartime shortages in New York, "but I pay, and that is that."

Mom Goss supplemented our meals with homegrown vegetables and gave us a large electric fan that oscillated to create a blessed artificial breeze between Doré's favorite chair and my bed.

Although Chaney loved my mother's cooking, she sometimes brought us "Chicken in the Rough," a commercially "broasted" forerunner of Kentucky Fried. For the two unlikely friends, the meal would be accompanied by several drinks from the government's monthly allotment of whiskey as they talked on through the evening.

In late July, the doctors gave both of us the okay to go to Pentwater as soon as I finished my final exams. Doré didn't tell Lurry how worried she was about her own chest x-rays until the results came back negative. "I feared that the first long year of full time work might have been hard on the old pod, but all is well, so I feel gay and hap. I so want to keep at the job. I just got a notice that I get a raise of $150 next fall, which is really something. I feel very up about that, and I do like being important to my tall, lovely daughter."

On August 3rd, we took a train to Grand Rapids and a Greyhound bus the rest of the way. "Mikey," the cocker spaniel, shipped by crate, was insane with joy to see us in Pentwater. The three of us were cheered to be back in our cool, tree-shaded house, knowing that the sugar sand shores of Lake Michigan lay only a few blocks down the beach road. And what delight it was to sleep under blankets and quilts! Dore was astonished to find all the meat one could afford at Myers Market, so she grilled steaks with soy sauce, garlic and joy.

The longed-for month in the dear familiar setting was made possible because a doctor was available to give me my pneumothorax treatments. Jack Heysett and his wife Jerry were old summer friends who now planned to make Pentwater their year-round home. Jack was on the staff of the hospital in Hart and could arrange to see me there. His familiarity with "pneumos" was personal. He had had TB himself and had even learned to give himself the refills of air into the cavity around a lung.

The one disappointment that summer was that Lurry couldn't come. She decided that she must spend her vacation with Grandaddy Rowe. In his late seventies, he had failed quite a bit in recent months, and she was afraid that she would have little enough time to give their father some attention. Doré wrote, "I hate for you to give up your two tiny precious weeks to cheering Dad, but I do see that you must, even as I had to give up half the summer to my child. It makes me realize how much we are bound to our young and our old. I want you with me in the peace of Pentwater, but we can't have what we want, not often, and we plod the road as it is laid before us, and grin as we plod."

Both sisters were sorry that their father felt fearful about facing death. Doré said, "I have no fear at all of death. Why, with his strong religious faith and his belief in a glorious hereafter, he is so afraid does seem strange to me. Poor sweet lamb. Why can't he see this next step as an exciting journey to far places? He always loved adventuring so much, each new ship and Pullman train. It seems so simple and easy to me. I hope life is over soon for him, that he need not fret and worry and be lonely anymore. For us, he will live always in our hearts, a forever part of our lives.

"Tonight after doing the dishes, Mikey and I went roaming in the back yard. The jack pine that you and Walter cut free from the honeysuckle bushes is gorgeous this year. All the trees prosper and it gives me a feeling of the goodness and meaning of life. I am so glad remembering that these beloved trees live on, after Ben, and will after me, in years beyond knowing."

On August 14th, she wrote Lurry that she had been listening to the radio for hours after learning that World War II was really over. "There will be no more wars for you and me to live through, and how I hope no more for my Judy."

Though not reflected in Dore's letters, I remember August 6th even more sharply. I can picture sitting on the edge of her bed talking earnestly about our country's decision to destroy Japanese cities with something called an atomic bomb.

...

The first order of business after returning to Ann Arbor was getting a fresh batch of x-rays taken to determine if I could go back to high school. YES!! Marianna Smalley allowed me to take a full junior year schedule, and the High School cooperated by arranging all my classes in the morning. I was to take a "rest hour" from one to three and then do my home work for the next day. It was a great relief to Doré to learn that everything would work out as we had hoped.

During wartime, the University of Michigan went on a schedule of three semesters a year. The objective was to shorten the time needed to earn a degree, but it was stressful for students and faculty alike. Fortunately, because of its small staff, the Fine Arts Department did not hold summer classes. So, although I was back in school right after Labor Day, Doré was still off work until November first.

This gave her two months to undergo having all her remaining teeth pulled, and being fitted for new full dentures. She wrote Lurry that she was thrilled to know she would be through with "the pain and wobbling" of her few natural teeth. On October 10th she wrote, "The teeth are all out but the top front four and I am now at the dentist's every day getting fitted for the new models. The last four will be taken just before the attractive new lightweight plates are put in, and I will have time to get used to them before starting back to work. Some of the bone surgery was rather painful, but now I am all healed and am so glad it is all behind me. I had some awful insulin jags while we were getting the amount regulated, but Judy knows how to pour the sugar and orange juice into me. She says that the funniest thing I do is talk to her in Chinese all the time I am out of my head. She says I seem to think she can understand it."

My mother was pleased that her new "store bought" teeth looked and felt perfectly natural and did not "clack" like the old fashioned false teeth she remembered in her parents' generation.

PASSAGE

Another long gap occurs in Doré's letters to Lurry between late October, 1945, and early April, 1946. We stayed in Ann Arbor over the holidays and had Christmas dinner with the Gosses. Lurry must have been in Pennsylvania with their father, who died in March.

He had been failing for so long that both Doré and Lurry felt that his passing was a blessing. Lurry bore the burden of being with him at the end and arranging the funeral, which drew brother Davey and a number of other relatives. Doré wrote supportively to her sister, understanding the strain it had been. "I decided not to send funeral flowers," she said. 'All I wanted to do was pin an orchid on you!

"I am grateful that Daddy went peacefully and unafraid at the end, and that he is safe in whatever the hereafter holds. Perhaps for him it is something he enjoys. Bless his dear childlike heart with its dreaming. For his sake, I hope he finds Mother and the people he knew and loved. Ben's sister Helen wrote that Daddy was a shining part of her memories of China. Remember the summer he was in Peking with Ben and you and me and Helen? How long ago that seems. Please bring his old photo albums with you to Pentwater. I'd love to see them. I'm so glad that he was able to spend time with us here, so that Judy will always remember her sweet, white-headed Granddaddy Rowe."

PROMOTION

In April my mother learned that with the retirement of her boss, Helen Hall, she was to be promoted to the position of Supervisor of Photographs and Slides, with a hefty raise of $350, starting in the fall. She wrote Lurry, "It will be good for me and stimulating and fun, and I look forward to it merrily. Although being the underling hasn't bothered me, and I have been grateful to have the job, still it will be fun to have this advance in rank and all that goes with it."

As it turned out, her new job responsibilities started with the summer session, so she was able to ease into being in charge. The Department of Fine Arts planned to offer four summer classes that year, and knowing that I would be going to summer school again, Doré was pleased to be asked to work during July. The pay of $200, which she called "a fat check," would help with Pentwater expenses. She soon wrote Lurry that "It is heavenly being able to run the Study Room my own way. I have many ideas for doing things more efficiently and can't wait to set them in place."

She also wrote of having to buy summer dresses, accustomed as she was to living in shorts and slacks. In those days, working women also had to wear girdles and stockings, which were usually rayon. Doré told Lurry, "I am lucky that Mom Goss stood in line to get me three pairs of scarce nylons as a birthday gift."

Their brother Davey, his wife Kit and sons Andy and Bobby rented the Pentwater house for June and July. It pleased Doré to have them enjoy her piece of paradise, and it was a treat for her to arrive on August 3rd with her beloved house open and welcoming. Lurry was able to arrange her vacation to begin that same time, so for one weekend the three siblings enjoyed a rare reunion and I got to know my young cousins.

However, Doré was disappointed to discover that the unemotional remoteness Davey had shown in his infrequent letters was the true face of the academic persona he now lived and breathed. She later told Lurry, "I miss my baby brother more than he will ever know, but there is nothing I can do to bring him back out of his stuffy, self-centered existence that is the pattern now." She feared that he was lost to her in any way that mattered.

In a letter written after Lurry returned to New York, Doré said, "What a good two weeks you and I had. I loved every minute. I'll never forget us walking home barefoot in the rain. That's the kind of lovely foolishness I miss so greatly in my usual role of a mama and staff member." Fortunately, the regular crowd of "summer resorters" carried on with their social whirl which always included Doré.

Back at the Ann Arbor apartment, she tore into fall housecleaning. "I had a nice kid here two afternoons washing the kitchen and bathroom walls, ceilings and woodwork," she wrote. "I found red and white checked oilcloth and made curtains for the kitchen and new covers for sink board and shelves, so it looks gay and elegant. Closets are cleaned, summer clothes packed away, and Judy's school clothes out of moth balls. I feel so virtuous it's pitiful! I don't get domestic often, but when I do I'm obsessed"

She was sorry to discover that "Absolutely bare meat shelves met us here. Chicken, eggs and frozen fish are all we can get. Ah, memories of Pentwater butcher counters! I'm glad I was extravagant up there."

When the new university semester started, the department chair decided that the fine arts study room should be kept open one night a week. So Doré went back from 7 to 9:30 p.m. on Wednesdays, but that meant that she had Saturdays off for the first time. Having a full two-day weekend was a welcome trade.

She felt so pleased to be in charge of the big, light room and be able to plan her work in her own way. She had 1200 books in her care and all the art magazines to enjoy. The old system for filing slides made little sense, she found, and the labels were "fearful and wonderful. Some in French, some in German, all in hen track writing. I certainly learn something each day as I dope out where to bed them down.

"I knew nothing of Egyptian art but its highlights. Now I'm getting so smart that when you say, as if you would, 'Benihasen,' I can mutter to myself, 'Yep, wall paintings on the tomb of Khnumhotep.'" Can't say it matters to anyone else, but it's fun to see the details of a painting called 'Feeding the Fawns' and be able to place it. The Fifteenth Century school of Spanish painting is also beginning to make sense now and new names fall into place."

In October I was elected to the Student Council and auditioned into the á cappella choir. This promise of normal high school activities was not fulfilled. In November, my routine chest x-ray showed what the specialists feared was a new TB lesion. Our own doctor, Marianna Smalley, did not agree, but until further tests could say for sure, she asked me to give up all outside activities, come home after classes at 2:30, go to bed and stay there. Doré was "dying six deaths" with worry and weary of waiting on me hand and foot. "Judy is being a lamb about it," she wrote, "but there is no way to make this up to her. She is almost 18. She deserves to be gay and have dates and get tired if she feels like it."

A series of x-rays dragged on for weeks, but finally, in December, the doctors concluded that because Jack Heysett had been giving me more than the usual amount of air with each pneumo during the summer, my lung was collapsed more than necessary. This caused a spot of the pleura between two lobes to stick together and suspiciously alter the look of the films. No harm was done, apparently, but I had to have x-rays every six weeks and was still restricted all winter. I could be up around the apartment, but was not allowed to resume any extracurricular activities.

At least I was able to stay in school, and chances were good that I could graduate and go on to college. Doré said that this news was "the most wonderful Christmas present in the world."

We stayed in Ann Arbor for the holidays again, but this time we had a Christmas tree in our apartment. Doré wrote Lurrry, "The tree came from Hart [near Pentwater], which added to our sentimental attachment, and we even put on lights, the first I have ever bought."

On Christmas Eve, we learned that back in June Kelly Goss had married Verna Frost, a slim, stunning dark-haired divorcee. His sister Do was being what Doré called "an absolute bitch about it, as she selfishly wants to keep him around to take care of her and their mother." Doré rejoiced in the news. "I am so glad Kelly has Verna. She is a real person and a dear and he needs to get away from home and lead a normal life."

As time went on, Verna and her mother-in-law became very close, and Verna's devotion greatly eased Mom Goss's last years.

1947

For my eighteenth birthday, Doré bought me the tabletop "Victrola" I had dreamed over in magazine ads. The radio-phonograph was not only housed in a streamlined wooden cabinet, it featured the technical advance of stacking five or six records that automatically dropped in sequence onto the turntable. "She can put on a whole symphony and forget it while they play," Doré marveled.

Meanwhile, Doré, at almost 49, was struggling with the side effects of menopause. She wasn't much bothered by hot flashes or extreme mood swings, but she felt drained of energy. She told Lurry that it took all the strength she had to haul herself through the work day, cook supper for the two of us, force herself to listen my to current concerns, and, dulled by a couple of stiff drinks, remind herself to get enough sleep to begin it all again in the morning.

Otherwise, our spring was dominated by daily mailbox checks for a letter from Oberlin College. Although I'd grown up feeling connected to the University of Michigan, Doré had always agreed completely that I should get away on my own for college and have the fun of dormitory life.

In her work, Doré tried her best to compensate for the huge size of the university. "I want my room to be a place where the kids can come and talk. I know their names and find out their grades, and they are so full of gratitude just for a pat on the back. One girl said that I was the only reason she was passing her course, if not the reason she decided to stay in school. I see encouraging such kids as the most vital part of my job."

By late spring, the doctors relaxed their grip enough to allow me to go on my senior class trip to Washington, D.C. and New York City, where I spent a glorious afternoon with Lurry. Until I read the letters saved by my aunt, I had no idea that my mother borrowed money from her sister to pay for my travel wardrobe, my first formal, my senior pictures and cap and gown.

The benefit checks I had received from Don Goss's Social Security stopped when I turned 18. But, in asking for the loan, Doré told her sister, "I will be sitting pretty when I have only myself to support in the fall. Judy's college expenses will be paid for from Ben's life insurance proceeds which Daddy March has so carefully invested for twelve years."

While I was on my senior trip my mother had a taste of what it would be like when I left in the fall. "I find myself cherishing each hour of the remaining months, and being happy and grateful," she wrote. "I feel that Ben would be glad to know that Judy has turned out so wonderfully, and that I have not hung onto her or deterred her when she got ready to leave the nest that I have built for her while her wing feathers grew."

Doré was as thrilled and grateful as I was when I was accepted by Oberlin. She also freely admitted to Lurry that, "Although I will miss Judy like hell, in some ways it is a relief to have the day by day job of raising her done. She and I are so close that I suffer with her over a hard assignment, and listen to all the troubles about which boy she will date and what they said and did. It is fun, but wearying. Some evenings I am so tired that all I want to do is rest and eat late and read the paper. It has been a whale of a job getting her to where she is. It has been worth it, but I do look forward to next year with only small Mikey dependent on me."

That vision of "next year" was sharply altered by news that our landlord planned to convert the building's four apartments into offices. The eviction notices said we had to be out by mid June! So, instead of just getting ready for a Pentwater summer, we had to pack all our belongings and put them in

173

storage. A silver lining for Doré was the promise of moving into an attractive large apartment in a residential neighborhood in late August. Meanwhile, the money saved on summer rent paid for movers to pack china and glassware and cart everything away.

Lurry was able to take her vacation in late June, and their brother Davey and family also spent two weeks in Pentwater before he taught Far Eastern Politics at Michigan during summer session. The visit was "dismal" for Doré, because the detachment Davey had shown the previous year was intensified. He talked only of his own interests, puffing himself up, with no concern for his big sister's life and no offer to pick up any of the costs of their stay.

ANOTHER SNAG

Ten days before we planned to leave Pentwater, Doré received a letter saying that the lovely Ann Arbor apartment she had lined up was no longer available. The landlord decided to sell the house and retire to Florida. "I can't quite believe," she wrote Lurry, "that *Kind-Dirty* is doing his worst to me again."

Professor Jim Plumer and his wife Carol invited us to stay with them when we returned to the city. Doré spent her days shopping with me for college clothes and dormitory bedding and her sleepless nights fretting over her homeless plight. The demands of returning veterans made apartments just as scarce as they were when defense factory workers needed homes. And Doré's particular needs – for something affordable within walking distance of campus – narrowed the field. Everyone she knew was trying to find her "a spot for my weary head."

With all my own expectations and apprehensions focused on Oberlin, I went off to college blithely assuming that a perfect apartment would soon materialize. Not so.

Doré never let on to me how frantic she felt. As she told Lurry, "I keep my worries all tucked inside me so Judy won't be bothered." Fortunately, the Plumers allowed Doré and our little black dog to stay on in their home – using the room that belonged to their elder son, who was away at college. Doré expressed her gratitude by making herself as useful as possible to the family – babysitting the younger children when the parents went out, or taking her turn at cooking.

In her letters to Lurry, she described one dead end after another as she followed every possible lead for an apartment. One perfect place would not have her because they wanted a young couple who could take care of the yard and garden all summer. Others were well beyond walking distance to her job, and Doré still felt that she could not afford a car.

A welcome break in the routines of work and anxious house hunting was her "simply perfect" Thanksgiving weekend with me at Oberlin. I got her a room at the Inn near campus, and she cheerfully ate the holiday dinner and other meals with 300 students. On Wednesday evening, she helped me, my room mate Suzie and our dorm mates get dressed up for the first formal dance of the school year, even doing mending and alterations for the other girls. On Friday, she went with me to my Fine Arts class and toured the Allen Art Museum. As the curator began to show us the Chinese collection, Doré said, "Mrs. King, I think you'd be interested to know that Judy's father was Benjamin March." The woman beamed with pleasure as she recalled the time that Ben came to Oberlin to help her set up her first exhibit of Chinese paintings. She had never forgotten him.

What Doré never told me, all that fall semester, was that, although living continued to go smoothly enough for her at the Plumers', Jim was allergic to dog dander, and she had had to board small Michael at a kennel. She naturally assumed that it would only be a matter of weeks before she had an apartment, and she hoped that I would never have to know how miserable the spoiled pup was to be cooped up.

As she told Lurry, "Judy can't do anything about it, and she would only grieve to hear that he spends his days clawing to get out and has stopped eating. So it is my private woe. If Mikey were my dog, I would have Dr. Hannawalt put him away at once and let that end it all. But it must be Judy's decision, if it comes to that."

None of us dreamed that Doré would still be living at Plumers when the holidays brought their son—and me—home from college. Luckily, the secretary of the Fine Arts Department and her husband were going away for Christmas and offered Dore their one-room apartment. With the help of a friend, she got Michael out of the kennel and managed to have him bathed and fattened up a bit before I came home, unaware. While enjoying Christmas dinner at Skylodge with the Goss family, we shut him in their laundry room and pretended to ignore his pitiful whining.

During the two week vacation in a cramped apartment, sharing the bathroom with five other people, Doré grew even more pessimistic about finding a decent place to live.

But, on December 30th, Mom Goss called to say that Kelly had heard of a suitable place and Doré should call immediately. My mother was so excited that she stuttered on the phone. The renters moved out on New Year's Eve and on New Year's Day we saw an attractive studio apartment that promised to be an ideal winter home for Doré. Seven blocks from her office, it was one of two units on the second floor of the landlords' home. With a dining alcove, Pullman kitchen, large dressing room and private tiled bath, it also had built-in bookshelves and generous storage space. The studio couch would open into two beds for the times that I would be back on school vacations.

There was, however, a catch. No dogs – period. The landlord, agreed to hold the apartment for a few hours while Doré talked to me. She was now forced to tell me the truth and to endure my impassioned pleas to spare my precious pup's life.

"Darling," she urged, "It's my feeling that it would be so much kinder to have him put away than to have him go through the hells of kennels again"

"I know, Mommy. But it isn't FAIR to kill him just because of this rule!"

"That's a harsh way of putting it," she said, frowning. "He would be at peace."

"Yeah, I guess so," I sniffled. Then brightening, "But maybe you can find another apartment where he could live with you."

"Judy, be realistic," Doré pleaded, trying to hide her irritation. "Everyone I know has been hunting for months. Finding this place is something of a miracle." Pausing, she decided to appeal on her own behalf. "Darling, I simply must have a bit of a home for myself again. I am so sick of living out of suitcases and cartons in someone else's house."

"Oh, of course you are," I said truthfully. Then, gradually coming to an awareness of this aspect of the situation, I conceded. "I understand, Mommy. This is a grand place for you and I know you really must take it."

"Oh thank you Darling. I knew you would see it that way. I wish I could have Mikey here. I have missed him myself. But we have to face facts…"

"I know," I interrupted tearfully. "It's just that I can't bear the thought of

Mikey being gone." Another long pause and then, "and yet I hate to think of him feeling wild and deserted either."

"You know what I would do, Pooh," said Doré. "But this must be your decision and I'll go along with whatever you say."

Grasping at an unrealistic hope, I launched a final appeal, "Maybe we can find some family to take care of him from now 'til summer when he can be free to roam in Pentwater again."

So that is what Doré agreed to try. Both feeling like heartless villains, we returned Mike to the kennels on my birthday. As the poor pup trembled and whimpered, we wept and the vet promised to try to find him a home.

Some of the families that Dr. Hannawalt approached wanted a puppy, and none wanted to put up with Mike's neurotic fear of being alone. After three more months of continuing to pay the costly kennel fees, Doré finally wrote to me. In what I now see as a clever move, she said that if I would cash in one of my war bonds to help pay for boarding him, she would keep it up and take him to be with me one more summer in Pentwater. Then we must dispose of him somehow.

I knew that it would have taken weeks for the dog to feel secure again during the summer, and then we'd just have to face the tough decision again in the fall. So I wrote back for her to sign the papers and go ahead and have Mike put away and not to tell me about it. David Hamberg, my old classmate who had also become Doré's supportive friend, drove her to the vet's and saw her through the pain of parting from our pet.

Reading about this in my mother's letters, I am chagrined to be reminded of how selfish I was and the, "sad, helpless feelings of private woe" I put her through. But, as she told Lurry, "I wish I had all the money I spent on Mikey's unhappy days at the Vet's, but the decision had to come from Judy. Any other way she would have hated me for urging. So I keep her close and she does not have a yammering mama she could resent."

PART EIGHT

"Life which was defined yesterday is redefined today and tomorrow will find itself subjected to a new definition."

—Aurelia Henry Reinhardt

FLYING SOLO

Doré was "simply thrilled" with her small apartment at 418 N. State Street. From storage, she retrieved her Chinese rugs, small pieces of furniture, familiar pictures, books and artifacts. "I guess, as you get to be almost fifty, the loved things of the years behind become more treasured," she told Lurry. "Not that you lean back or live in the past, but just that you take their spirit-hands as you go ahead into the unknown. I have never, in my entire life, made a home alone before. It is sort of important to do it well, and not be lonely....

"Actually, it is a complete joy to me after the busy days at the office, surrounded by the faculty and the droves of the young, to come home and not have to speak to anyone, and eat when I am rested and ready." It was also a pleasure, after the years over a dry cleaner, to be back in a residential neighborhood, where she enjoyed the deep backyard rimmed with flower beds.

...

Doré's brother Davey was now teaching at Yale University. At his suggestion, the venerable Ivy League school decided to buy all of Ben March's photographs of Oriental art. Doré was so pleased to make the pictures available to scholars after so many years. She was also happy to have Yale's check.

To kick off the summer, my buddy David Hamberg and I planned a celebration of my mother's 50th birthday. Tall, with blond hair that fell over his boyish forehead, David had been one of my closest friends since third

178

grade. During our school years, we talked on the phone almost every night. Although we went to movies and a few dances together, he was a best pal, not a "boyfriend." After I left for college, he often spent time with Doré and went out of his way to help her.

To mark her half century milestone, he and I took her out for Chinese supper, and then, with three other friends, surprised her with dozens of silly gaily wrapped presents plus "likker," sodas, nuts and chips, for a fittingly festive party. She told Lurry that she couldn't have felt more touched and loved. Mom Goss drove us to Pentwater, staying for a few days of well-deserved rest and pampering.

I held my first job that summer, at the Pentwater Dairy Bar. Among the customers came three University of Michigan graduate students. Al, Bob and Bill, who were planning to be architects, became friends of ours, and my mother loved having them over for big home-cooked meals, followed by an assembly line of dish drying. One late night when the boys came up frozen from a beach party, she made them fried egg sandwiches and enjoyed chatting on after midnight. She seduced them as she had my boyfriends. Not that she took them to bed, but by the time she had played up all her Oriental mystery, they might have wished she would. Most memorably, those three students hauled a magnificent piece of driftwood up to adorn her back yard. The four foot high tangle of bleached roots we called "The Inferno" was admired for years.

Doré took up crocheting that summer. Soon every bare end table and shelf, even the top of the toilet tank, was covered with strips of turquoise and coral cotton "Granny squares." When she started in on bright red potholders, she told Lurry, "I have enough to set up a church bazaar." Lurry said she was afraid that shrouds for the dining room chairs would be next. Fortunately, Doré turned her talents back to knitting, which she had enjoyed in her youth, and that winter she made me several sweaters that I wore with pride.

The death of our beloved doctor/friend Marianna Smalley left Doré with "an empty place that that woman always filled, firm and comforting and strong…. Life is so insecure and full of grief," she wrote. "I believe there is a reason beyond my understanding—a pattern bigger than me that must make sense of the uselessness and apparent waste. I will miss her always, but I am glad she is without pain and at peace and maybe finding Ben and

Poppy and telling them how well their two loved girls are doing. Since no one can prove me right or wrong, it is fun to imagine. That would be good, in its way, but whether or not, I can't see an end to living as all that difficult. I am happy now, but I don't want to go on until I am sick and sad. I would so much rather go quickly, except that those left living would have a harder time."

The doctor who gave me my weekly pneumothorax treatments at the Ludington hospital that summer had been a U of M. classmate of Marianna's, so that connection was meaningful to us both.

When we returned to Ann Arbor in September, my x-rays looked so fine that the doctors decided I could stop the pneumos. To give me some protection, a surgeon crushed the phrenic nerve in my neck–the nerve that controls movement of the diaphragm. This procedure was used to rest the lung enough to insure against a relapse of TB as I returned to Oberlin for my sophomore year.

Doré felt full of pep to start the fall semester, and with 600 students enrolled in Fine Arts classes, she would be happily busy. One of her favorites asked her to chaperone a dinner dance at the Theta Delta Chi fraternity house. She later told Lurry, "The other young people were happily surprised to be invited to call me Doré, and I enjoyed the evening more than I expected to."

In December, Eddie McDonald, a Pentwater lad who became a good friend of Doré's while attending U of M dental school, was married at 29 to a Danish nurse, Trudie West. For a wedding gift, Doré outfitted their new kitchen. "I had fun picking pots, pans, red and white canisters, dishpan and drainer, red-handled utensils and cutlery," she told Lurry. "For an extra surprise I made a red and white oilcloth cover for their little kitchen table." She also arranged to loan them some of her own furniture from storage, including the "Hollywood" bed that Don Goss had chosen and a Chinese rug.

When I decided to do a paper for my Oberlin contemporary art class on "The Influence of Japanese Prints on French Impressionists," Doré offered to find illustrations. In her files at work, she found just the right Hokusai prints and Degas paintings and had them copied for me.

On Christmas night, she wrote Lurry that it was wonderful to have me home for the holidays, and fun to hear me and David Hamberg caroling with a group of sixty high school classmates. For my 20th birthday, Doré threw a "kiddies" party for me, with childhood girl friends. As she described it to Lurry, "It was a lovely time—so interesting to hear those college girls talking about their studies and dreams and plans."

In February, she reported, "Saturday I got into a major house cleaning mood, waxing all Chinese furniture, polishing silver, and washing windows. Even the john shines, and my virtue stands tall. Then, longing for spring, I asked my landlady Mrs. Doll if I might cut some stark brown branches of forsythia and force them in my warm room. Today I have a great bouquet of lovely yellow flowers on the maple table and get a thrill out of it every time I look that way."

The Dolls also bought her a new hide-a-bed sofa that pulled open into a comfortable double bed with a "Beautyrest" mattress that could be left made-up when folded back in during the day. She was grateful for the change from the narrow studio couch.

Doré wrote to me every day while I was in college. I can picture her seated at the end of that sofa, taking a drag on her cigarette and sipping a drink as she typed on her little black portable, the "laptop" of her day. When she came to Oberlin for a long weekend in March, my housemother told her she had never heard of a girl who got so many letters from home!

Doré visiting Oberlin College

181

In April 1949, she wrote Lurry, "You won't know your yellow room at Pentwater this year. It is to be furnished with Judy's maple bed and three-mirrored dresser, desk, bedside table and the Peking camphor chest. I suddenly got fed up with large bills for furniture storage and have sold everything I can't use. I put an ad in the paper and David Hamberg offered to hold the sale in his family's garage during his spring vacation from college. The Chinese things were what brought elegant people, and we could have sold the two straight square chairs ten times.

"I also sold old chests of drawers and bookcases Ben made to hold tall children's books. David is driving a trailer load of furniture, books and pictures to Pentwater, and I'm having four barrels of dishes, vases and glass shipped up. It is the most wonderful feeling to have all this stuff off my chest. Come June 15th I will be free of paying storage bills for the first time since 1935."

Apparently Lurry worried about the loss of potentially valuable treasures, because in later letters Doré assured her sister that she kept all the scroll paintings, Japanese prints, Chinese figurines, Oriental rugs, and my favorite piece, the large red lacquer zhougwi ("jo-gwer").

"Please don't worry," she wrote Lurry. "We still have enough brass candlesticks to set up a Mass at St. Thomas's, and lacquer and pottery and pewter and porcelain and glass. Judy is setting aside things she eventually wants, I will let Bren Hueseman have her pick, and I wish I knew what you might want before I put the rest on consignment in the local antique shop. I don't grieve to see those things go. I have no place for everything. I want to turn them into cash and have them off my mind, and I could not bear to leave Judy to face this big job after I am gone. She has no basis on which to make decisions, while I know the stories and dates and values of each bit."

A five-foot-high plum satin wall hanging with elaborately appliquéd figures of a maiden and doe was something Ben had so adored that Doré nicknamed it "First Concubine of the House of March." She knew that David Hamberg loved it, so it became her gift to him for his devotion of time and energy to the sale and moving of her things.

The artifacts she kept were always displayed on her tables and shelves. She believed in using precious things, not keeping them locked away in a vault–which explains why most of the vases and figurines I inherited bear casually glued cracks and chips.

In late May, Doré also sold Ben March's Art Library to the University of Michigan's Department of Fine Arts. Apparently her sale of his photographs to Yale alarmed Michigan enough to make sure that his books would be kept together as a Memorial Library for the Asian Art division. "Enough money will come from that," she wrote, "to see Judy through her master's degree wherever she wants to go, Chicago or Harvard, and then my stint will be done, with a great feeling of accomplishment to crown me. And Ben will be happy to know that I kept my promise to educate his 'little smooch'."

"I know that I am very lucky with my perfect job, the young about me and leaning on me, and the three months off each summer, even if with no pay. I wish you weren't so bogged down with your job, working Saturdays and never time to play at all or get rested. Why do you do it, Lurry? Life can be so good if it is without pressure and there is time to relax and be at peace."

That question is one that we asked of Lurry for many years. Certainly New York was an expensive place to live, but her motivation was more than economic. Because she had no husband or child, I think she relished the approval she got for devoting herself to Huxley House—at an unusually high executive level for women in her day.

On May 30th, Doré wrote, "The way I spent this legal holiday ain't legal at all, for finals are going on just the same and it was a strenuous day. I answered dumb questions from kids who didn't study until the last minute, told phone callers that the library and study hall are open all day and seven to ten tonight. All the same information was given out in each final class period, but they don't hear. And between the phone and questions like, 'Would you define cubism in ten words?' I have been filing away the piles of photographs for the courses whose finals are over. Whew!"

Mom Goss drove Doré to Oberlin to bring me home when my own finals were over, and David Hamberg took us to Pentwater the next day, with the rear end of his dad's car practically dragging on the pavement. It took two days to unpack all the books and "crud and corruption" from storage. David set up bookcases in the study and listened to records on my "vic" as he worked.

Doré with David Hamberg in Pentwater 1949

The following Monday, my college roommate Suzie, her boyfriend Jim Burnett and an Oberlin boyfriend of mine arrived, and Doré "went into high gear" producing all her specialties of beef stroganoff, pan-broiled chicken, curried lamb and chili con carne, a version I call "Pentwater Chili" to this day. All this while my friends and I languished away lazy days on the beach. But we did dispatch the dirty dishes while Doré relaxed with her after-dinner cigarette and drink. Evenings were cool enough for a fire in the fireplace, if we kept all the doors open.

The bliss of those first nine days came to a crashing halt when we picked up our mail after the guests left. It happened to be on Doré's birthday, and I told her that the letter waiting for me was a lousy gift.

LOW BLOW

Dr. Eleanor Smith, who had taken over Marianna Smalley's practice, wrote to say that the routine x-ray I'd had while passing through Ann Arbor showed a suspicious shadow, and that I must return immediately for more tests and a consultation with University Hospital doctors. Although I didn't realize it at the time, the news of a possible relapse of TB was even harder on my mother than it was on me.

Doré wrote Lurry, "I was as near sunk as I have ever been, but we went right home and began to plan. We phoned her girlfriend Lilias, who agreed that Judy could stay at her house until she knew what gave, and we packed her up for a 5 a.m. bus the next morning. Then, with Bren, we managed to gird the loins and dress up purty for my birthday dinner at The Jenny Wren. It is wonderful what you can make yourself do!"

My mother never prayed. *Kind-Dirty* was a personification of Fate who changed lives according to whim and could not be persuaded by words or weeping. But she often spoke as if she believed in the old Chinese custom of lighting incense to influence the outcome of events. "I'll burn some blue smoke," she would assure me, before a final exam or while waiting for news from a doctor, as if confident in its power. She seldom actually lighted the fragrant sticks of incense kept in a zhougwi drawer. Presumably, just holding the thought of burning one could bring desired results. I can see her imagining blue smoke rising while waiting to hear from me.

In Ann Arbor, seven TB specialists conferred over my case, disagreeing about whether I had a new lesion, or they were seeing just a bit of scar tissue. They put me in the hospital for a broncoscopy exam and another phrenic crush operation, such as I had the previous September when they stopped the pneumothorax treatments.

"How I wish they had not stopped the pneumos," Doré wrote. "Judy was protected then. Marianna had thought she should continue them through college, and she was right. But all the higher ups thought otherwise…Until they admitted her to the hospital I held onto a tiny gleam of hope that she would be able to come back to Pentwater. I'm pretty sure she won't, or get to Oberlin this fall. I could beat my head against the nearest wall. I sometimes think *Kind-Dirty* should get tired of trying to bog me down, for I won't bog, but he never gets tired."

"Judy does not mind the surgery and does not want me to come unless they start talking about sending her to Howell for bed rest. If they do she is wiring me and I am tearing down and raising holy hell to prevent that. Otherwise, with my apartment sublet, I am staying here, so please do come for your vacation and stay as long as possible."

An orphaned grey and white kitten adopted Doré later that month.

Because of his little black mustache, she named him "Charlie '49," and cherished his companionship. It was also a blessing that she could keep busy unpacking the barrels and trunks of belongings from storage, with some items still wrapped in 1935 newspapers. In her letters to Lurry, she described just where she hung Chinese scrolls and Ben's portrait by Paul Honoré and mine by John Carroll, as well as where she put the tall blue ginger jars and various lamps and warrior figures.

She also practically adopted a nine-year-old boy named Hank Freeland, grandson of the family whose barn formed the rear boundary of our yard and provided a backdrop for our plantings. He had come around offering to cut the lawn and do other odd jobs. When she invited him in for a coke, he marveled at the "square ices" she put in the glass. She enjoyed the subtle forms of "education" she was able to give him during their chats, sometimes over meals of the nourishing foods he never got at home. When Lurry came for her vacation, she, too, was entranced by the little red-headed guy, and she offered to pay a dentist to examine and treat Hank's painfully decayed teeth.

Doré's other summer project in '49 was to finally start writing a book about her father. The title, "The Moon is Level with the Steps," came from an ancient Chinese poem. She used it "to convey a life of great brightness and at the end shining over my own back terrace." She began it on what would have been Grandaddy Rowe's 80th birthday, but typed only eight pages. I am guessing that she was distracted by batches of house guests and social life with friends, but I so wish that she had kept going. My regret at not having the rest of his story has moved me to finish hers.

. . .

Much to Doré's relief, and mine, I did not have to be moved to Howell, and was able to continue my bed rest on the familiar seventh floor of University Hospital in Ann Arbor. When Doré returned to work in September, it cheered me to be able to talk face-to-face during her almost daily visits. Only too well acquainted with hospital frustrations, she was an empathic listener. And, like a mama bird, she fed me tidbits of town and campus gossip that nourished me until I could fly again and hunt for myself.

She was also creative in bringing actual treats for my room mate and me—such as hot chili one night, or cokes and sugared donuts on a Saturday afternoon when we all listened to the Michigan football game. One Sunday, she and David Hamberg toted lamb curry and all the condiments to share supper with us.

As she told Lurry, "Judy is full of courage, but it has been hard on her knowing that her friends are starting back at Oberlin. I wish I could be mailing letters to her there instead of sitting by her hospital bed, but that can't be this year. All I can do is spoil her silly."

Doré's little Pentwater cat "Charlie" settled blissfully into apartment living, never failing to use his litter pan or keep quiet while Doré was away at work, and curling up beside her in the evening. "Sometimes," she wrote, "he gets frisky in the pitch dark at six a.m. When he does, I just shut him in the bathroom until my alarm goes off." She bought a tiny pet carrier and leash so she could bring him up to the hospital to meet me.

On a November Saturday, Doré wrote: "Judy has had four stabilized x-rays and may start getting up around Christmastime. I miss Marianna so very much. She used to read Judy's x-rays immediately and call me at once with all the details. Now, with doctors scarce and help useless, it is sometimes three weeks after an x-ray before they get to reading them, and I feel so frustrated. But I keep the Rowe chin up. Just once have I really bawled my eyes out. It was pointless, but came of my fury over all this happening to Judy and my helplessness to keep any of it from her."

I picture Doré pausing in her typing to click open a favorite Zippo lighter. Of matte finished chrome it was engraved, per my orders, with her distinctive signature. After a few puffs, she would roll the lighted ash off the end of a half-smoked cigarette so she could save the butt to enjoy later, feeling virtuous at the money saved.

"My days are long," she continues, "with going up to see her most nights. So when I get home I am tired and just fold up and go to bed. I am lucky that a bus comes to my corner every fifteen minutes and takes me to the hospital door in three minutes, and back as quickly. And my job is so satisfying that I look at my watch with amazement to find it is nearly five. I am busy but never pushed, and have a fine sense of mattering and being needed. Here at home, I delight in a lovely vase of bronze baby mums on the brass table beside me."

Concluding, "So, basically, life is good," she fitted the hard, black faux-leather lid back onto her portable typewriter and called it a night.

...

Lurry didn't respond nearly as often as her sister wrote. Doré's letters often open with something like "I was so hoping to hear from you today," or close with, "Please write soon." So when Lurry said that she was coming by train to Ann Arbor for Thanksgiving weekend, the unprecedented visit was "heaven" for both sisters, and for me.

My hospital room mate went home the week before, so my bed was moved over next to the window. I not only loved being able to look out at trees and the night sky, I still had the room to myself when Doré brought Lurry up to see me. It was a blessing to have that privacy for a long catch-up conversation. Lurry needed to witness for herself that I was taking my confinement in good spirits, and she didn't mind sharing Doré's double bed in order to be able to picture her sister's attractive studio apartment.

That December, Doré's friends Eddie and Trudie McDonald welcomed twin sons, Pat and Mike. As the doting godmother, Doré adored making herself useful to the new parents until Eddie's mom could come for the holidays.

A week before Christmas I had my fourth phrenic crush operation. The scar tissue from the other three made it difficult for the surgeon to find the right nerve. Doré told Lurry that, "Judy was in such pain that they finally gave her a hypo and I left her asleep at one-thirty. She was calmed and ready for the ice cream I brought at three-thirty. God, it hurts to see your young one go through something like this!"

As Christmas approached, my mother pinned long red ribbons onto the moveable wheeled privacy screen in my hospital room. To the ribbons she paper-clipped the prettiest of the many greeting cards I received. On the 18th, she and David Hamberg lugged a four-foot-high balsam fir to my room, secured its stand on a purloined table, and covered it with lights, balls and tinsel. Presents began to be piled high on the empty extra bed, and we three celebrated with Chinese "chow" out of paper cartons on Christmas Eve. David and other friends who always went out caroling that night gathered beside the big tree at the 7th floor nursing station. "It was so touching and good to hear them," Doré wrote Lurry. "I thanked them for Judy and said, next year she will be singing with you again. O please, *Kind-Dirty*, may it be so!"

On December 28, my Oberlin room mate Suzie and her sweetheart Jim Burnett were married in Youngstown, Ohio. Because I couldn't be her maid of honor, she and Jim thoughtfully made Ann Arbor the first stop on their honeymoon. I was eager to hear all the wedding details, and, after their hospital visit, Doré had them over to her apartment, with David, for Chinese dinner. In their honor, she spread the opened table with an embroidered Chinese cloth and used her special two-tone green dishes and long red lacquer chopsticks.

For my 21st birthday, my local friends Lilias, Marilyn and Patsy joined Doré and David by my bedside for a festive party, featuring Grandma Goss's traditional devil's food cake. A week later I got the best possible present: news that I could start "dangling," the prelude to sitting in chair, then walking, and eventually going home!

As Doré described it to Lurry, "Judy's x-rays have shown the exact same, stabilized condition for four months, so there was no question about her being ready. I am so happy it hurts! As previously planned, tonight I gave her a shampoo and changed her pillow cases and tightened the sheets, watered the flowers, and then, with her hair wound up in a towel and me sitting by with a cigarette, she dangled her legs over the side of the bed for five minutes. It sounds silly to be so thrilled over that, but it is the longed-for beginning. You probably remember that after six and a half months of complete bed rest, getting up must be a slow process. Instead of taking the bus home, I treated myself to a cab. It was extravagant, but the occasion seemed to call for it."

During the mid-January semester break, Doré was invited to ride with some students to see the Van Gogh Exhibition at the Chicago Art Institute. As she wrote to Lurry, "I hope you saw it in New York. I have never been so thrilled. There were so many of my favorite paintings that I hardly knew which way to look. I bought Judy a reproduction she craved; a bridge at Arles, but not the best known one. It's the one painted from the opposite bank, with a blob of white cloud and two cypresses at the left–more stunning to my way of thinking."

She stayed two nights in South Bend, with the family of Libby Myers, a graduate student who was to become Doré's assistant in the Art History Library starting after the break. At 24, Libby was mature and responsible, with a mellow personality and zany sense of humor. She became a good friend of Doré's – and of mine – but that's getting ahead of the story.

Another winter highlight for my mother was hearing a lecture by Eleanor Roosevelt. Her tenth row ticket was one of my Christmas gifts to her. To Lurry she wrote, "Mrs. R. is quite a person, her hair snow white now, and her dress a deep blue satin. She spoke convincingly about the need for patience toward the United Nations machinery, saying that Americans must learn that it is not easy for representatives of many nations to work together immediately. I came home floating on a cloud."

...

A few days later, I sat in a chair for the first time while admiring a check for $3,500 which the University of Michigan paid Doré for Daddy Ben's books. She knew exactly how the first part of this fortune would be spent: on a car! Not just any car, of course. It had to be a Ford and it had to be blue. David Hamberg took her to the dealership.

As soon as she saw the 1950 two door sedan with sloping silhouette and such astonishing innovations as a radio and a cigarette lighter as well as a heater/defroster, she knew it would be hers. But, with an inscrutable face, she drew on old familiar Chinese bargaining techniques.

While the salesman shifted uneasily from one foot to the other, she and David walked all around, opening doors and the trunk, speculating loudly between themselves about where my Victrola and cartons of records would fit and Charlie's cat carrier and all the boxes of books and suitcases that would be going to Pentwater.

"I like it, but the price is a little steep for me," Doré told the salesman. "Would it make a difference to you if I paid in cash?"

"Oh, well.....in that case," he stammered with a big grin, "we could actually offer you a ten percent discount."

"Ten percent, hmm?" she mused thoughtfully. "Well.....that would help...a little."

"And of course that discount would apply to the cost of undercoating and the license plate," he added hurriedly. Still, Doré pretended she wasn't sure.

Finally, she sensed that the delaying tactics had made the gent nervous enough to be accommodating. She turned to him, saying, "I think it will do… if you can allow me one more thing. I want the title to be in my daughter's name as well as my own and I will have to take the papers up to her hospital room for her signature."

Doré had been so grateful to Ben for his having put everything in both their names for ease of inheritance when he died. She made sure that her Pentwater house and all other belongings would pass easily to me when, in the Chinese expression she always used, she "went to join her ancestors."

The salesman, eager to close this sale, became positively obsequious and perfectly willing to wait for her to bring the documents back an hour later.

David agreed to keep her new car at his house until she could get her driver's license renewed, and he was happy to break it in slowly driving to his classes at Eastern Michigan University in Ypsilanti. On the way home from arranging for auto insurance, they drove up to the hospital, parked in a taxi stand right under my window and flashed head lights at me so I could see it! Doré called her car "The Blue Bug," long before Volkswagens acquired that nickname in this country.

As she wrote to Lurry, "Though I haven't driven since 1941, I long to get back at the wheel, and the Blue Bug will be coming to Grand Rapids to pick you up from the train this summer. Judy had another clear x-ray yesterday, so what can old *Kind-Dirty* do to stop us now?"

In February she wrote, "Judy sent me a Valentine corsage of two gorgeous pink camellias! I wore them on a grey suit to the hospital, then all day at work, and I now have them, still lovely, in a glass bowl on the brass table."

Although it appeared certain that I would be released in late spring and be allowed to resume college in the fall, I would only be allowed to take two courses. This meant facing reality. As Doré explained it to Lurry, "It is insane to pay Oberlin's high tuition for a limited schedule, and dormitory life there would not allow Judy to get the rest she will need or to be as 'different' as she will have to be if she is to prevent another relapse. So I know she should stay here and go to the university, but I have been dreading the thought of giving up my beloved small studio apartment in order to make a home for her again.

"My darling landlords came up with the perfect solution. They offered a large, first floor apartment in another house they own, just two doors down the block from mine! It will become vacant in late August, and Judy and her former hospital roommate Stella Smith are going to split the rent and live together there next fall. It will give them independence and, for me, you can imagine what it will mean to continue to live by myself, unimpeded by her schedules and needs.

"She qualifies for vocational rehabilitation funded by The American Lung Association. That will pay for tuition, books and fees, plus a small amount toward room. And I will take money from her college funds to cover the rest of the rent. You know that I treasure my daughter above all else in this life, but I need to be free, Lurry, and not have to listen to her phone calls or talk nightly about her studies or her friends. I am so pleased I could purr like Charlie."

Doré's sweet small cat Charlie died that winter, of an epidemic that felled many local pets. "It seems too stinky of *Kind-Dirty* to take Charlie away," she wrote Lurry. "What does heaven need of a little bit of grey fur and a laughing mustache when I have no one to greet me at the end of my day and curl up lovingly beside me?" As always when facing her losses, she speculated, "Maybe there is a need greater than my loneliness and a pattern I cannot see."

Happily, a week before my homecoming on May 19th, Doré was offered a four-month-old coal black kitten she named "Sambo." He was already housebroken, but prone to mischief, so I was able to curb his ways and enjoy his frisky company during the days I spent alone in the cramped apartment until the university semester ended.

WHO WILL LIVE WHERE?
In early June, all the plans made with Stella Smith "fell with a sickening thud," as Doré put it. Stella's lesion had cleared up so quickly that she believed she had never had TB. When she was released, she overdid and suffered a relapse. It was not only a disheartening setback for her; it meant

that she would not be able to share an apartment with me in the fall.

Doré's assistant, Libby Myers, was planning to sublet my mother's apartment for the summer, so our first thought was that she could just stay on there, and my mother and I would take the large apartment. For two weeks, we tried to accept that solution, but neither of us really relished the prospect. Doré clearly wanted to maintain her quiet solitary refuge; and, although we were about as close as any mother and daughter could be, I felt that living together at that stage in our lives would really jeopardize that closeness. In contrast to what she described to Lurry, I saw my mother as overly preoccupied with my life, resenting if I didn't share every letter I got and putting in a word or two during my every phone conversation.

Doré always felt that it was her job to make me happy. Most of the time, it was endearing. The downside was that if she felt irritated or annoyed, she would sulk, giving me the "silent treatment" so familiar from my childhood. She also had a way of offering to do things and then acting the martyr afterwards. She would create her specialty meals for me and my friends, but then sigh heavily about how much work it was. She would take on a sewing project – such as making over an old evening dress of hers into a formal skirt for me – and then let it be known what a chore it had been. What she required was to be thanked repeatedly and profusely, so she would feel needed and appreciated. Probably she deserved more gratitude from me that she received. I could be picky, demanding and impatient about imperfect results. The restrictions imposed by my illness kept me uniquely dependent on her.

When I solved our living dilemma by arranging to share the large apartment with an old school friend, Doré threw a fit. Unlike my other friends, Lilias had never been impressed by my mother's worldly sophistication. Proud of her own solid Germanic heritage, she never begged to hear stories about China nor sought Dore's advice as the art history students did. Adulation was terribly important to Doré. I understood her hostility to my plans.

When none of her objections swayed me, desperation drove her to ask Libby Myers if she would consider sharing the large apartment with me. Libby was willing to consider it, and after she and I spent time getting to know each other, we agreed to move in together in the fall. Since she and

193

Doré were already fond of each other, and Libby had the maturity my mother felt was needed to adapt to my limited lifestyle, it turned out to be an excellent arrangement. But Doré's interference created a turning point in our mother-daughter relationship.

Apparently Lurry suggested to Doré that she back off from directing my daily doings, now that I was 21, because my mother later acknowledged to her that, "in my sorrowing, I overdid being loving and trying to make her happy, and then I did hit the roof when she made her own plans. You are right in reminding me that I have never been able to get openly mad at anyone I loved. I fear that I take after our mother in being for peace at all costs. She did martyr badly and I hated it, as Judy does in me. I don't mean to do it, but when I feel hurt, I get sick and quiet, and no one likes that."

I don't remember her trying to control me ever again. In fact, she went to the opposite extreme. Had she probed more deeply about a critical decision I made the following year, I might have made a different choice.

Lurry took her vacation in June that year. She badly needed "to absorb the peace and quiet of Pentwater," and the sisters cherished every minute of their two weeks together.

Lurry and Doré at Pentwater 1950

In July, Doré's little redheaded Pentwater protégé Hank Freeland turned ten. She served him a steak dinner followed by ice cream and cake. Afterwards, I treated him to a movie and popcorn. We were right on time as he proudly consulted his gift – a real wrist watch. He repaid my mother's kindness and earned spending money all summer by washing the painted floors and stair steps, getting in firewood, running errands and lapping up all the wisdom of the world she poured into him.

My own days dragged, as I was still limited to only a few hours of "up time" and otherwise restricted to lying on the built-in daybed called the jazz couch.

"It is so hard," Doré wrote, "to have Judy saying she wishes this summer were ended and she could be back in school. I understand it, certainly, she being lonesome for friends and looking forward to beginning an independent life. But it crushes the loved days here for me."

"The cream of Oceana County"

Life looked up a bit in August when I met a young man named Jim Gamble at a Yacht Club dinner and he invited me to be his date for the Commodore's Ball. Doré reported to Lurry that, "He is a nice guy and considerate of Judy. He understands that she can't dance much and he doesn't care. For her it was a thrill to be able to go at all."

Jim's attentions raised my spirits, which in turn, of course, raised Doré's. He had grown up on a farm in the nearby town of Hart, served in the Navy and was now living in Pentwater to care for his maternal grandmother. She was one of the grand doyens of the resort village who had retired there from Detroit some years earlier. Five years older than me, Jim had a cheerful open face and a steady maturity that appealed to me in comparison with "boys" I loved in college.

I was also grateful to be admired by someone who didn't expect me to go roller skating or square dancing or stay out late. The irony that I was unaware of at the time is that Jim was putting in such long, exhausting days running the widow Brooker's fruit farm that he was grateful to find a nice girl who didn't expect him to take her dancing or roller skating or stay out late.

In early September, Libby Myers, Doré's Art History Department assistant who was to live with me in Ann Arbor, came to Pentwater for a few days. The two of us had fun deciding which of the dishes, glasses, vases and pictures that Doré offered us would be useful or attractive in our apartment. On our return, Doré drove us shopping for other necessities, but she didn't hover, and retreated to her own apartment when we got home.

The Dean of Women gave me permission to live off campus and arranged all my classes in the mornings, so I could nap and study in bed in the afternoon, just as I had in high school. Libby was enrolled in grad school as well as working part time with Doré, so our schedules neatly meshed. We divided up the household chores and she taught me to cook. My mother loved to cook but never showed me how to scramble an egg – just as she loved to garden but never encouraged me to plant a single petunia.

Libby and I invited Doré to our apartment for dinner, and she had us over for Chinese chow. When she wrote about it to Lurry, she said, "You would be proud of what a good job I am doing leaving them alone. Judy calls me often and one evening when Libby went to a meeting of her sorority, she asked me to stop by after work. She had a drink ready for me and a little green Pentwater dish of peanuts. We had fun talking for half an hour before I came home to get out of office clothes. So you can see life goes smoothly."

Doré found that Libby's help made her job much easier. At a staff meeting, she felt "important" when the department chair George Forsyth told new members of the faculty, "You will discover that Doré is the ground wire from which all of us learn student reaction to courses and their worth."

Jim Gamble and I were writing frequent letters to each other that fall, and he came from Pentwater many weekends. He drove overnight to sell fruit at Detroit's Saturday morning farmers market. Then he would come out to Ann Arbor in the afternoon. When Libby and I planned what dinner to serve him the first time, she joked to Doré that she should probably bake a chocolate cake "for the Cream of Oceana County."

That moniker had been attached by Walter Nelson, our old family friend whose summer home was across the side road from us in Pentwater. At the time, it caused me to swell with pride. It wasn't until years later that it dawned on me that the boundaries of Oceana County did not exactly reach to far horizons nor did it offer a world of choices. Still, Walter had also said, "You could go much farther and find none finer than Jim Gamble."

It really never occurred to me to look. As Doré told Lurry "Jim is a kind,

196

gentle guy, practical and capable, with his feet on the ground and complete understanding of Judy's physical limitations. I have never seen her so content."

When Jim and I decided to get married, Doré asked me once, "Are you sure?" I swiftly responded, "Of course I'm sure." End of discussion. She knew that I would manage to finish college, but she didn't encourage me to postpone marriage, to pursue a graduate degree or a career or to travel as she had so loved doing in her youth. She respected my right to make my own choices. And, at that time she couldn't envision my having a full return to health. Although my body did not bear the disfiguring scars that her's did, she knew that I must live under the threat of another relapse of TB. Jim seemed willing to risk that, so, if he made me happy, she was happy.

Grandaddy March sent Doré the money for two plane tickets to Chicago so we could celebrate Thanksgiving with the family in Glen Ellyn. An enormous traditional turkey dinner for eleven was festive fun and my engagement was properly celebrated, but when Doré told Lurry about the weekend, the excitement she shared was over our first air travel. "It is the most marvelous sensation, and only 53 minutes by air for what would take four hours by train!" she wrote. "If I had the dough, I would travel that way often. Gosh, Lurry, do it sometime coming to Michigan. If I can do it with one lung, you can easily. It is a thrill!"

As Christmas approached, Doré proudly reported that she had written sixty personal messages on decorative holiday note paper to relatives and friends. Although she sighed about how much time it took, she always found this ritual much more meaningful than merely signing printed cards.

Lurry's gift to Dore that year was a stunning red crepe dress, which she wore to Skylodge for Christmas dinner with the Goss family's other guests, and to a New Year's Eve cocktail party given by the Fine Arts Department. In between those two occasions, she also took it to Youngstown, Ohio, when Jim drove us to visit my Oberlin room mate, Suzie Burnett, and her family, which now included a three-month-old son. At a dinner party one of the guests was a woman who was born in Lurry's birthplace, Wuhu, China. Three years older than my mother, she remembered her as a little girl during summers in Kuling. "Gladys has been a high school librarian in Youngstown for 20 years," Doré told Lurry. "Small world, isn't it?"

197

That winter, Jim took some pictures of our Pentwater house and yard deep in snow. Doré sent duplicates to Lurry, saying, "Snow up there is so clean and white and unsooted or trampled, isn't it? The inches along the branches of leafless trees in front of the shuttered eyes of the house are beautiful. I have never seen the maples bare."

When Jim and I set our wedding date for the 18th of August, Grandaddy March and my Uncle Don predicted that I would drop out of school. They clearly underestimated my conditioning. Ben March's daughter couldn't imagine not graduating from college. I signed up for one class in summer school and my doctor gave me permission to take three the fall semester. Doré told Lurry that "Every time Judy goes for a check-up, I find myself holding my breath all that day and getting pale at each ring of the phone, but so far, the x-rays have been perfect."

My mother spent her spring vacation in Springfield that April, with her old friend Brenzelle Hueseman and Bren's sister Dee. As she described it to Lurry, "What a wonderful week it was. They have a genius for pampering people and I lapped it up."

MOTHER OF THE BRIDE

For the next six months, Doré's letters are dominated by descriptions of wedding plans. It was heartwarming for her that I chose to have a seamstress make my dress, using an inset of lace from Doré's own gown, and that I wanted to wear her veil that was held in place by a band of the matching lace.

She was also pleased that we asked Harold P. Marley to perform the marriage. A Unitarian minister, "H.P." had been a close friend of my father's since they were students together at Union Theological School in New York City. After he moved to Ann Arbor in 1933, the two men often talked philosophy and religion far into the night, and he conducted Ben's memorial service.

We were all thrilled that my uncle Don March, my Daddy Ben's brother, agreed to give the bride away, saying "Her mother and I do," when asked.

Best of all for Doré was that Lurry was able to get three weeks off that summer, to spend time in Pentwater before and after the wedding. She also helped her sister bear with my surrender to the dictates of etiquette authorities, including conventions about what a mother of the bride should wear.

When I look at the photographs taken that day, I cringe with remorse over forcing my mother to wear a grey lace dress that was totally unlike any garment she would ever have chosen for herself. An irony I learned from her letters is that she had actually sworn, in advance, that she would not wear just such a gown. I had completely forgotten that she and Libby and I went into Detroit one spring day for a Bridal Show at Hudson's department store.

Uncle Don March, Doré, Judy and Jim at Skylodge wedding reception

"I vowed to be the gentle, unbothered mother-of-the-bride all afternoon," she wrote Lurry, "and I did it with grace. The auditorium was jam packed to watch an endless stream of models showing costumes to be worn by brides, bridesmaids – and mothers. I let out with a yip saying I refused to wear pale grey lace, even with a mink stole or a rose chiffon mantilla!"

How could I have forgotten? Especially since I gave Suzie Burnett complete latitude in what she wore as my only attendant. Of course Doré grimly accepted my choice for her costume, complete with a matching veiled hat and wobbly high-heeled shoes. She never wore any of them again.

What made my wedding unique was that Mom Goss generously offered to host the reception at Skylodge. Guests savored seeing the beautiful mansion, spilling over into its formal gardens and gazing down across the wide lawn. I have no memory of what finger foods were spread out upon the dining room table, but I know that Mom Goss and Kelly's wife Verna worked many hours filling and refilling platters, trays and punch bowls. I wonder if the self-absorbed young bride said enough to thank them. I'm sure that my mother did.

PART NINE

幸运

"A mother is not a person to lean on, but a person to make leaning unnecessary."
—Dorothy Canfield Fisher in <u>Her Son's Wife</u>

"AFTER THE BALL"

There is no description of my wedding day in Doré's letters because she and Lurry lived through it together. They were pleased that their brother Davey and his family came for the occasion and spent a few days with them in Pentwater afterwards. It was a gesture of family solidarity that helped Doré feel a little closer to him again.

For my mother, the let down after everyone went home was far more intense than she expected. "Your room looks so empty and neat," she wrote Lurry. "I miss you more this year than ever before, for now I am completely alone in life."

Jim and I made a point of seeing her often when we returned from our honeymoon, but she found it difficult to shake the sadness she felt, and apparently her sister wrote to encourage Doré to accept the change in her life.

"You are right Lurry," Doré answered, "in your words to the mommy now severed from her young, I am not pining. That is pointless. But it has taken a bit of doing to adjust to being more alone than I have been for thirty years. Judy is untouched by this and is so fulfilled. That is what matters most if you plan for making the leaving of a young one good for her. But, for the first time in all the years I am looking forward to leaving Pentwater and getting back to work."

It helped that Hank Freeland's family let him stay with her until school started. Doré hated the thought of taking him back to his crowded family home, where he would certainly not be indulged. She wrote Lurry that "Oh how I wish he would have a quiet place to study this winter."

Meanwhile, in Ann Arbor, Libby Myers moved in with another friend of hers, leaving the apartment we had shared to Mr. and Mrs. James D. Gamble. Initially, when I returned to the university, Jim continued to manage Mrs.

Brooker's farm in Hart and could only spend weekends with me; but, from November 'til March he worked in Ann Arbor, installing television antennas, and as an agent for the Farm Bureau.

This is the way Doré described our life to Lurry: "They manage their money, but with not much over.... They do the housework together and he does the dishes while she studies. They include me in much of their lives. The night she baked her first apple pie, they brought it over to my apartment – with their sterling silver forks and a pot of coffee!"

She also wrote that, "Jim has been so helpful to me. It is nice having a man in our family. He took my car to have anti-freeze put in when he thought the weather was getting cold, put the new license on when needed and fixed my little radio."

So, despite Doré's initial fears, the old saying applies: she didn't lose a daughter, she gained a son. And for the rest of her life she appreciated Jim for his steady, reliable ways and his "merry grin" as he undertook many large and small tasks for her.

That winter, a Dutch publisher offered to pay Doré $100 for the rights to print her book <u>The Begging Deer</u> in the Indonesian language. The recognition was a gratifying surprise and the money most welcome. In her letter to Lurry, she enclosed a check for seventy dollars against a loan her sister had apparently made to help pay for my wedding. This little transaction was kept secret from me. I was glad to learn from her letters that Doré admitted being relieved to have her entire paycheck to herself with no further responsibility for my expenses.

Starting in March, Jim moved back up north, to work full time on the Brooker farm. In May, when I considered going to Pentwater for Jim's family reunion in honor of his Grandmother Gamble, I hesitated to leave Doré alone on Mothers' Day. But she said that was silly, and told Lurry, "I don't care what weekend they label as my day. Judy and Jim love me the year around and I am so grateful!"

Lurry's Pentwater vacation came early that year, and by July 15th, Doré was missing her deeply. Fortunately, the Freelands let their young son Hank live with his benefactor again for the summer, which not only offered her companionship, but gave her someone to feed and fuss over.

Hank Freeland with Doré in Pentwater

MOTHERING A FARMER'S WIFE

Doré's letters do not describe the large abandoned farmhouse on the Brooker farm that Jim and I were allowed to live in that summer. Apparently Lurry had seen for herself how we did dishes by sitting on a milking stool at an astonishingly low kitchen sink. Frank Brooker had been of the old school that put whatever money he had into farm machinery and a modern barn before considering improvements to the house. We learned that the kitchen sink was no higher because that's as far as available pipe would reach the day it was installed.

At least we had electricity to run the old wringer washing machine and a cook stove. There were no cabinets or countertops in the kitchen, but I prepared meals on a central table and learned to can fruit. If our primitive set-up dismayed Doré, she was never less than encouraging to my face. I think she was both amused and proud to see my determination to be a good farmer's wife.

To our surprise, Doré agreed to help with a big fund-raiser at the Pentwater Yacht Club. Although she usually hated the thought of anything resembling "committee work," she joined others in putting on a Gay Nineties Review. As she wrote Lurry, "My job was to prompt and push the two boys to open and close the curtains and to help with make up and back stage emergencies. It was a rat race but I really enjoyed it and we cleared nearly $400 for the club."

Jim's Grandmother Diner was a founding member of the Pentwater Garden Club. For the annual two-day flower show there in August, she asked Doré to create an "Oriental" table. As much to please me as Grandma, I think, Doré agreed. To her astonishment, her unusual arrangement of three tiger lilies in a tall blue vase beside a place setting of Chinese dishes and a seated Buddha, all on a gold brocade cloth, was awarded first prize! She sent Lurry the newspaper article from the Muskegon Chronicle, and the blue ribbon, which Hank Freeland coveted but relinquished for Lurry's sake.

Her letters were full of descriptions of how far Hank could swim, and how much he ate, and how well he cleaned her house and weeded flower beds to earn money for the end-of-summer County Fair. Once again, she dreaded leaving the boy for the winter, when no one in his large family would dote on him the way she did or even notice his accomplishments.

Amid packing up for the trip back to Ann Arbor, Doré wrote, "There is a full moon this week and it is so lovely over the cedar hedge and the blue spruce and the yard seems bathed in daylight. The final lemon lily bloomed in beauty last week and I loved it all day long. Why I make a fuss over those flowers I don't know, but they please me so and their timing is so subtle.

"It is something to see how early it gets dark. The sun sets shortly before seven and by seven thirty the world is really black. It seems so funny, but I shouldn't yip after three lovely months here. The white birch logs are piled high by the fireplace, and Jim and Hank will bring in the big driftwood 'Inferno" to spend the winter in the study....

"I hate packing away my small treasures and rolling up the rugs and defrosting the fridge. Most of all I hate taking Hank's prized possessions back to that dismal basement where he must sleep with four other boys. I got him a garment bag to protect his clothes, but it breaks my heart when he says 'no more clean sheets and quilts after you go.' I've fattened him up to 77 pounds, which may help prevent colds or ear aches. Right now, that is all I can hope for."

She daydreamed that after another healthful summer, she could gain his family's approval to take him back with her to attend junior high in Ann Arbor. But, by late October, when Doré was once again cherishing her quiet solitude after long, demanding days at work, she began to question whether she wanted "the strain on my relaxed evening and morning schedules and charting him through his homework and such."

"I know it would be a lifesaving thing for our boy," she wrote Lurry, "so I am still thinking about it. Hank is thinking about it, too, and admits that he is scared about a new school. We have not spoken about it to his family yet."

By January, she had decided to take him on, and had even lined up a larger apartment they could live in together if he came. So, when Hank wrote to say, "I really don't want to go to Ann Arbor," it was a blow, but not unexpected. She had heard that he had been skipping school and not doing well. As she told Lurry, "He probably hates the idea of anyone in control that tells him he has to do his homework before he does anything else."

Over the winter, while I carried five courses, Jim worked for the University's Psychology Department, helping to set up experiments. His most interesting task was constructing a light-tight "vision cube" in which scientists tested colors for school buses. Doré liked to brag that he played a part in influencing the government to switch from red, white and blue vehicles to the safer bright yellow.

JUNIPER ORCHARDS

Meanwhile, Jim and his brother Joe formed a partnership to buy a farm in West Golden Township, near Mears, less than a mile from Juniper Beach on Lake Michigan and just ten miles south of Pentwater. Of the 420 acres, more than half of it was set in fruit – vast orchards of cherries, apples, peaches, plums and pears. It was a dream come true for "the boys" to have a farm of their own, and I wanted to move there, too, but we were worried.

It was against University policy for students to spend the final semester off campus. We hoped that my good academic record would persuade them to make an exception. Much as Doré hated to have us leave Ann Arbor, she was thrilled for me when the dean said that he would not like to see me drop out of school so near to graduating and agreed to let me take my remaining three credits by correspondence.

So, in early March, Jim and I moved into the main house at "Juniper Orchards." Joe, still a bachelor, continued to live with Grandma Diner in Pentwater. Our house was dark and drab, with worn linoleum floors, long out-dated appliances and no work counters in the kitchen. But the west windows looked out across open fields toward lovely piney woods and I threw myself into sketching the improvements we could make when possible.

It amuses me to read Doré's letter to Lurry after she spent her April spring vacation with us. "The setting is beautiful," she wrote, "with huge shade trees in front and gorgeous views. And the house has so many possibilities."

It never occurred to me at the time, but thinking about it now, I'm reminded that Doré was an old hand at remodeling and redecorating. Her Pentwater house, with its white brick fireplaces, built-in bunks and closets, rosy pink woodwork and deep blue floors all testified to her creative imagination and eye for potential changes. I took all that for granted, growing up. But she was the one who planned and supervised that transformation.

Doré' wanted to see Hank Freeland – to discuss his future face-to-face. "He will be 13 in July and is feeling very big and stubborn and mighty," she wrote Lurry. "He is now determined to drift along until he is 16 and can leave school. Poor little guy, with no one but me caring if he graduates or not. I could see that there was no point in urging him to come to Ann Arbor. I should have brought him down before now. So ends a dream. It makes me very sad."

Soon, Doré would cope with another disappointment. Lurry wrote to tell her that their nephews, Andy and Bobby Rowe, had begged her to spend her summer vacation with them on the Connecticut shore. Their dad, Davey, was too self-absorbed to pay any attention to them, she told Doré. And she knew that if she went, she would be welcome company for their mother, Kit, too.

Doré admitted that she "bawled like a fool over the thought of you not coming to Pentwater, Lurry. Those three weeks are the high spot of the summer for me. But I do see how you feel about the boys and their rapture over having you share their lives. You have to do what you feel must be done, and I do understand, Darling."

As it happened, that year Doré had her longest summer vacation ever. She finished at the University on June 4th and didn't have to be back until September 21st.

Doré's first letter from Pentwater described the familiar thrill of being back: "I have just lighted the first white birch log in the fireplace. Of course the front door is wide open, but I wanted a fire for the fun of it. The house is utterly beautiful – vases of cedar clippings on all the stair steps, a huge blue bowl of pine on the low red lacquer chest, a yellow bowl of blue and yellow iris on the k'ang table to my left, and lilies of the valley from my own beds on the end table by my chair. The Numdah rugs are down, the kitchen in order and all cartons unpacked. My yard looks its very best – the grass very green from all the rains we have had, and the cedars with lovely pale green tips."

In late June, Doré wrote about her 55th birthday. "Judy and Jim asked me and Joe and Grandma Diner over to the farm for dinner. Judy made place cards for all of us with a tiny balloon tied to each. She served a delicious veal and rice casserole and molded aspic salad and my birthday cake was a two-layer strawberry shortcake massed with fruit and swirled with whipped cream...."

Such detailed descriptions are typical of what Doré wrote, at length, to Lurry. Her letters always included menus of the meals I served, or that she cooked for friends. In this summer of 1953, she also slipped in a line saying, "The upstairs is very empty at night, but Sambo keeps me company on my bed."

Although Hank Freeland didn't choose to live with her again, he was happy to make money by taking over lawn mowing and other yard maintenance for her that summer, and he picked cherries on our farm, alongside the Mexican families who migrated up from Texas every summer. He trusted Doré to keep his earnings for him.

Our vegetable garden seemed as big as a football field when I had to weed it and harvest the tomatoes, green beans, peppers, Swiss chard, cucumbers, cabbages, carrots, potatoes, corn, squash and melons. Doré often came over to help me freeze the beans and can the tomatoes, as well as the peaches, pears and plums from the orchards. I was very grateful, not only for having her share the work, but for laughing along with me when our glasses fogged up and slipped down our noses with the sweat from our brows as we pulled another rack of steaming jars out of the big speckled blue enamel canning kettle.

A late summer storm drew Doré to Pentwater beach several times in a day to watch the powerful drama flung out on the watery stage. She told Lurry, "The breakers looked like they started a mile out in the Big Lake. They were so huge they broke right over the road in front of the bath house, and it is a miracle there is any cement left there." In later years the road was moved far inland.

Doré's return to Ann Arbor was eased by finding that her apartment was left in spotless condition by the best summer renters she'd ever had and word from the University that she was to have a $200 raise. The Art History Department added a professor of Islamic Art, so, with 17 courses being offered first semester, Doré worked at what she called "break neck speed." But that made her days tear by, which she appreciated.

In November, Jim and I met my mother at the Chicago train station before the three of us drove out to Glen Ellyn for a weekend with my grandparents March and other family members. In the car, I shared some news.

As Doré described it to Lurry, "Judy said she wanted to tell me rather than write, so she waited for this trip. The Gambles' first young'un is expected the middle of June! They think they have timed it very neatly to have me for a built-in baby sitter next summer when they want to go to Yacht Club dances. O Lurry, you must come to Pentwater then to see my grandchild. Please!"

In November, a magazine called _Tween-Age Digest_ called to ask Doré if they could publish one of the stories from her book Traveling Shops. She gulped when the magazine's offer for the rights was about three times as much as she'd received in the past. Later, she surprised Jim and me by donating the check to our remodeling fund.

Reporting on her Christmas vacation with us on the farm, she told Lurry,

"I started knitting a tiny peach wool sweater for my grandchild, and I have mended coat linings, hems and pockets, and took over the cooking. This gives Judy time to keep up with her English Lit course, which she will finish on January 15th and be eligible for graduation. She is feeling fine. How wonderful it is to *want* a baby the way Jim and Judy do."

Following a family gathering at Grandmother Gamble's home in Hart, Doré wrote, "They are such dear people. Judy is lucky to have, at last, a big nearby family."

"Every afternoon," she continued, "I don galoshes, coat and hat and go for a walk with Tess (*the collie*) beside me, down the road to a footpath that goes thru the woods, or down to the road that turns north to Pentwater, just for some air and exercise. The stark black fruit trees against the snow are a stunning picture, and the pines and white birch make patterns against the leafless orchards. This farm is so beautiful and I do love it all."

I feel sure that she really meant that. Having me settled in the region she loved, only ten miles from Pentwater, offered her a feeling of security that she might not have felt if I had married someone I met at the university and moved to Oregon or Maine. And if she had never imagined a fruit farmer as my husband, she continued to appreciate Jim's strong character, loving nature and capacity for hard work to build a solid future for me and our family to be.

In addition to updates on my pregnancy, Doré's winter and spring letters were filled with her excitement over the new kitchen that was being installed at the farm. I had made a major contribution toward our remodeling goals by winning a "Plan Your Dream Kitchen" contest sponsored by the Crosley Appliance Company. We received all the sparkling new appliances and cabinets that I had indicated on my design for the room.

As Doré told Lurry, "You can imagine what a wonderful break this is for the kids! Judy has been told that it was her precise measurements and attention to detail that made her a winner. She's certainly Ben's daughter in that, and wouldn't he be proud?!"

When <u>Redbook</u> magazine profiled me with "before" and "after" pictures, they posed me in a gathered apron designed to conceal that I was in my seventh month of expectant motherhood. Our daughter Jennifer was born June 10, 1954.

Becoming "Grammy"

My mother had wanted to hear every detail of my pregnancy. Toward the end, she not only shopped for baby clothes and crib sheets but read every word of the popular guide to up-to-date child care by Dr. Benjamin Spock. For a few weeks after "Jenny-Roo' and I came home from the hospital, Doré drove over to the farm almost every afternoon, to help with household chores and to beam at her granddaughter.

Doré was glad that I could breast feed and she completely approved of the practice of assuaging a baby's hunger "on demand." She told me in remembered horror of the rigid schedules that "modern" medical experts imposed on intimidated young mothers in her day. It was pure agony, she said, to feel forced to listen to me cry while watching the clock until exactly four hours had elapsed since the last feeding. She even had to weigh the, by then, kicking-and-screaming infant before nursing her and again afterwards, to make sure I had received enough milk. Never mind if I had contentedly fallen asleep. I might be deprived.

Diapers were still made of cloth when I became a mother, and Jim and I didn't have an electric dryer yet, so the clean necessities had to be pinned up on clothes lines in the yard. Doré claimed that she enjoyed hanging the latest pastel, polka-dot and rosebud print "dydies."

She also marveled at a mechanical wonder in my new kitchen. As she wrote Lurry, "I am completely sold on the electric dishwasher. After breakfast you rinse the dishes and tuck them away in the machine, out of sight – same with lunch dishes and silverware and pots and pans, and dinner dishes, and then you start the machine going for the whole day's worth. It is completely automatic – washes, rinses and dries with hot air! Glorious!"

In July, Doré reported that she helped to make 37 pints of cherry jam and freeze 16 quarts of fruit for winter pies. "When Judy stopped to nurse Jennifer, I could take a cigarette break," she wrote Lurry, "but then it was back on our feet to keep stirring. I was tired at the end of the day, but it was so satisfying to see how pretty the ruby jars looked, with their paraffin hats, lined up on a new kitchen counter."

During the summer, Jim and I often left the baby with Doré for a few hours while we went to a Yacht Club dance or a beach party. It warmed her heart to be trusted with that responsibility. As she told Lurry, "Jennifer is so good here, when full of milk, and I adore having her at Grammy's house."

My own grandmother – Granny March – died that summer, after emergency gall bladder surgery. Doré told Lurry, "Judy and I both wept buckets as we grieved that her dear, gentle presence was gone from our lives and that Jennifer would never know her."

Lurry scheduled her three weeks vacation for the end of August and into September that year– ideal timing to be smitten by her infant grand-niece when Jenny had begun to smile and babble. One more "Pentwater present" was added to the generous stack she pulled from the enticing depths of her suitcase.

In New York, Lurry hardly ever cooked, but in Pentwater she enjoyed giving Doré a break by concocting what my mother called "ventions." Lurry's favorite lunch was a liverwurst and cucumber sandwich, which she munched with a cold beer on the back terrace.

Another memory: Lurry used fine cloth handkerchiefs rather than the Kleenex my mother kept around the house. Not because she was environmentally conscious then, but simply in preference.

Dominating the sisters' conversations that summer was Pearl S. Buck's memoir <u>My Several Worlds</u>. As Doré said, "The story of her early life is our life too. Her descriptions of Kuling and Nanking made me so homesick for the China of our youth."

The Rowe sisters could certainly identify with these passages from the book:

"I grew up in a double world, the small white clean Presbyterian American world of my parents and the big loving merry not-too-clean Chinese world... When I was in the Chinese world I spoke Chinese and behaved as a Chinese and ate as the Chinese did and I shared their thoughts and feelings. When I was in the American world, I shut the door between.

"I loved the ineffable peace of the temples [on Purple Mountain], and although I did not worship the gods there or anywhere, I liked to sit in the quiet of their presence or perhaps only in the presence of lost prayers, still lingering in the fragrance of the incense that burned unceasingly before the images, a symbol of yearning human hope."

Needed on the Job

In September, Doré wrote, "It is right nice to be so genuinely welcomed back by all our staff and having them lean on me when they like, and expecting me to take care of them. My students are an everlasting joy – their problems, minute to one of my age, are faced as best I can, trying to remember what it felt like to be 19 or 20. They are so grateful and dear.

"Today there was a mid-semester exam on Leonardo, and one boy came in afterwards and asked to see the photos once more. He said one slide shown was a detail of a landscape he didn't recognize. I asked if it was a drawing, of which they had had three that I knew of. No, it was an oil, he was sure, and said 'I won't be able to sleep tonight unless I find out what it was. There was a sort of flowing river...' I said, 'Maybe the landscape to the left of the Mona Lisa?' And that it was, and I felt good, but he felt mad at himself for not remembering it and growled. So I said, 'But now, Barney, you can sleep tonight.' And he finally grinned.

"The second study hall is going very smoothly this year and I am getting compliments on how well Jerry is managing. So I am at peace about it – a peace you can understand, knowing how I have yipped in other years over do-less help.

"You and I are so alike in giving our all for our jobs," she told Lurry. "You are right in saying that it is a sign of our ages that we are more fussy and meticulous about wanting things to go just right. But that makes each of us happy in our own way doesn't it? It actually saves me time to do the filing myself, even if I can't finish any day's work. A mis-filed photograph in our huge metal cabinets is just like a book filed incorrectly in a library. It is lost until inventory checks through sixty thousand photos. I get weary more easily now but I try to keep things in proportion, and find that I am able to make myself walk slowly home from unfinished business. It always waits patiently for tomorrow."

Doré had come to believe that, in her job, grey hair was an advantage. As a girl, her dark brown, almost black hair was stick straight. In the late 1920's she'd had her long locks cut into the popular bobbed look. When styles changed again, she got permanent waves, which were often too tightly curled, but they probably helped her feel in step with the times. She started to go grey in her late forties. Once, when she was fifty-something, a vain friend told her she should dye her hair, "for professional reasons, and for social success, too." But hair coloring was far less subtle then, and, as she told Lurry, "I think that some of the students who come to me with their troubles, knowing I am a grandmother, might not if I colored my hair and pretended."

In November she wrote, "Darling Jim brought me a huge bunch of bronze chrysanthemums from the farmers' market. They have delighted me all week. Having a flower about the home, or a little branch of pine and a few red leaves is so very satisfying to me. A dear old gal in a fancy flower shop here saves me little broken-stemmed bits that fall off her formal arrangements, and I collect them on Saturdays – for nothing. She likes doing it because I am so grateful and love having two short red roses in a tiny vase for my weekends. Perhaps I love them more than if I had the price of a dozen American Beauties! Bet I do."

A SPRING SPREE

In April 1955, Doré flew to New York to spend her spring vacation with Lurry. Choosing to stay in the friendly, familiar Shelton Hotel this time, rather than having her sister give up her room, she went museum-hopping on her own while Lurry was working and walked nostalgically around Washington Square. She acknowledged that she no longer wished she could live in Manhattan, but for a six-day jaunt it had endless charm. In the evenings, they went to out-of-the-way restaurants for the best Chinese food, saw two hit plays, and fulfilled their mutual need for long face-to-face conversations.

"Darling, every minute of my wonderful spree delighted me," she wrote when she got home. "I am grateful beyond saying that you treated me to our dinners out in style and the extravagant play tickets… I hope you are rested up from having a visitor 'from the provinces'."

Apparently Lurry had mentioned being depressed, because, in a later letter, Doré suggested that it might be caused by the approach of her "change of life." She told her sister that her own had left her feeling "almost entirely spiritually do-less."

When I was a girl, my mother taught me about "the curse" along with other facts-of-life, which my friends were astonished to learn and I was forbidden to describe to my cousins. But she never explained about menopause. Her letters to Lurry affirm what I witnessed at the time without understanding the cause.

"I had no interest in what I wore or how I looked and could not make myself buy clothes or wash the ones I owned," she wrote. "I was very low in the mind for no findable reason."

Doré urged Lurry to "Keep telling me how you feel and don't try to hide it or laugh it off. I really think what would do you the most good would be a vacation long enough to forget your work harness entirely. I know that I can take anything and giggle inside through the madhouse of each day with temperamental professors because I know that I have my summers in Pentwater."

Lurry's vacation included another invited guest, her apartment-mate Paula Simmons. Paula had lived with the Rowe family in Nanking in the early 1920's. Doré had enjoyed reconnecting with their cousin during her spring vacation and thought it was "high time she knew what a blissful place Pentwater is." Although an invalid in her later years, Paula was, during the 1950's, an interesting, successful career woman, and the Yacht Club crowd enjoyed her immensely. But with the increased social whirl, the vacation couldn't have offered the solid rest that Lurry needed.

A SURPRISING HOBBY

In the fall of 1955, Doré surprised us all by enrolling in a "Jewelry Craft" class held every Tuesday evening at the high school, just four blocks away. Initially motivated by wanting something different to do with her time, she enjoyed the new creative outlet more than she expected to.

"The teacher and I hit it off at once," she wrote Lurry. "I now have a fascinating array of tools – duck billed scissors, all manner of files, three weights of solder, a bar of sterling silver and a foot of silver cord. My designs were approved, but I won't tell you my plans, lest I melt them into a shining heap."

Nearer to Christmas she wrote, "This week's class was simply marvelous. Your pin is finished. I love it and hope you will. I will give it another shine with the huge rouge wheel next Tuesday and then mail it to you. I got so much done this time that I am beginning to realize how much I know. Judy's earrings came out beautifully, and I finished a silver bracelet that pleases me."

She wore that bracelet the rest of her life, and I think it would please her to see it on her eldest great-granddaughter's wrist today. I can picture the twisted silver cords slipping down onto my mother's hand as she reached for another cigarette or a cup of cooled coffee. She often made coffee at night and drank it without reheating it the next day.

In addition to crafting jewelry of her own design, she made creative use of other items. "I am sure you remember Ben's silver watch fob that was my wedding gift to him," she wrote. "It has a lovely piece of dark green jade in the center and carved on each side is a dragon and a phoenix. I put a sterling pin with a safely clasp on the back of it so I can wear it on suits instead of having it just sit around in my jewelry box." She also made earrings out of some 18th century Chinese buttons.

"Lord, how much I have learned about this hobby," she wrote during second semester. "I now go and heft every piece of Jensen jewelry I can find in a store. I know the gauge the silver is, and can understand the ways he uses it. My name doesn't count like his of course, but we have a stamp to press on the back of our work, with a mighty whack of a wooden mallet, so the tiny word 'sterling' appears."

She enjoyed the class and classmates so much that she continued it a second year, even when she had to drive three miles across town to the new high school in dark snowy weather. In April she wrote, "The parking lot is a swamp of unlandscaped mud, but the class means more to me than anyone knows. Last night I made a pair of sterling cuff links for David Hamberg.... Then I was moved to use a foot of shining copper wire which I just wound eight times around the ring mandrel to my finger size. I bent the end up over across the rolls, soldered it tight, filed the rough ends smooth and wore it home, beaming, while driving in the dark in city traffic which I hate."

The following December, she wrote about Christmas presents she loved making, including "a perfectly foolish modern fish pin I designed for Judy." Despite the nighttime winter driving, she planned to enroll again second semester. "I know it is good for me to do this creative work once a week and I have plenty of ideas and materials for doing it in my little metal work box."

A FRIGHTENING YEAR

One of the reasons that night driving was frightening to Doré is that the sight in her left eye began to fail. She knew that diabetes is one of the leading causes of vision loss, and, thinking the condition to be permanent, she was afraid of going blind. Not surprisingly, she carried that as a private burden.

Doré never feared pain or death. What she feared was dependence. As her eyesight became seriously impaired, she worried that if she were unable to work, she might have to live with Mom Goss, which would have hurt her pride, or with us, which would have been even less to her liking.

It was a huge relief to learn that it was a cataract causing her vision loss and that it could be removed. She scheduled the surgery for early June, at the end of the school year. But she dreaded going back into University Hospital. Cataract removal was much more complicated in those days. Unlike today's out-patient procedures, Doré had to lie completely flat for 48 hours and was in the hospital for seven days.

A fringe benefit of what Doré called her "captivity," was that diabetes specialists monitored her carefully as they converted her to a new form of insulin that gave her much better control over her blood sugar levels in the months ahead.

I went to Ann Arbor by bus to drive her north for the summer, as she had to wear a "tea strainer" over her left eye. Eager as she was to get to Pentwater, she agreed that spending three days with us at the farm was smart. "It is hard to go slowly and not get tired," she told Lurry, "and to NEVER bend my head."

In Muskegon she got a temporary left lens for her glasses. Unlike today, when a surgeon can replace the old clouded cornea with a clear artificial one, just the cataract itself was peeled off. It took several months for the eye to adjust and vision to settle into its new pattern. Then only thick-lensed eyeglasses compensated for the change.

She wrote Lurry, "Judy insisted on driving me to Muskegon and back. She wouldn't hear of me going by bus. You get so much by not asking. Judy is good to me mainly because I never demand anything or moan, and she respects my ability to accept what has to be taken with grace."

It was all worth it. "I can't tell you how brilliant everything looks to the new eye," she wrote Lurry. "Colors are fabulously bright. And what a delight it was to see the new white coat of paint that Jim gave the whole outside of my house, and brilliant Doré Blue enamel on all the downstairs floors and staircase."

It was a mellow summer, with house guests and cocktail parties, dinners and dances. Once again David Hamberg stopped in Pentwater en route to his family's cottage further north. My mother was deeply touched by his annual visits. David and I also exchanged letters for many years. I guessed at the reason that he never married, but he could not then be open about being gay.

...

In August we all went by car ferry from Ludington to Wisconsin to visit Granddaddy March, now living with his daughter Helen and her family. Doré was so happy to see "that dear old man that I have loved so long and who has been so helpful to me all these years." Jim and I enjoyed showing off our daughter to my aunt, uncle and cousins.

But there was disappointment when Doré returned to Ann Arbor.

On October 1st, she wrote Lurry, "I hate to tell you the news about my eye... With my heavy new lens I can see well and read if my right eye is covered, or with my right eye if the left is covered, but I could not use the two eyes together. The condition is called "hypophoria" – which means that the axis of vision for one eye is lower than that of the other eye. Reading, I saw a line of print here and an inch above it the same line! Whew! I was never so glad as to get those glasses off!"

That doctor said nothing could be done about it. Despite the shock and letdown, Doré managed better with no correction for the left eye. The slight blurring caused headaches, but at least she didn't have double vision.

Eventually, the doctor supervising Doré's insulin intake suggested that she have both her eyes tested again by a far more capable vision specialist. His opinion that surely something more could be done gave her new confidence. "I now know I am not losing my mind," she wrote. A strong lens was prescribed for her left eye and a frosted lens over the right one. This created a new problem: impaired depth perception. Walking outdoors was the hardest, she said, as she was so afraid of falling.

"Isn't it amazing," she asked Lurry, "what you can do when you are determined and willing to get through the miseries connected with a complete change like that? You would laugh at how much I listen to the radio instead of reading. It rests my eyes after the long days at work."

She told no one at her office. "Everyone has his own problems," she said, "and at times I do get a big kick out of the howling that some people do over things that are so minor and unimportant. The old sense of humor holds, Lurry."

Still, she was clearly depressed. "Do you ever get a feeling that you have had it, and life has been very good, but you would so like to be done with it?" she asked Lurry. "I doubt that you do, but there are times when I feel that, except for making Judy unhappy. I won't do anything desperate, Lurry, I promise, but I am a bit tired of the struggle and wonder what the point is for going on with it. To me there is so little unfinished business left."

"I will go to the farm for Christmas. I won't stay long, and Judy and Jim are aware of my state and will help me all they can. There won't be too many Christmases left for me, I hope, and I want Jenni to remember me, Lurry, for she is such a sweet loving little girl."

"I never thought until your letter came of going to New York to live with you there. Being with you would be wonderful, but I am still hoping I can go on being independent and self-supporting. If the old right eye holds out, I will do it.

"Yes, I have walked a very lonely way for years, but that has been in the cards for me, and I do find it hard to talk about myself to anyone. Knowing that you and Judy are so lovingly concerned helps so much. I do hate making both of you worry about me, but please cheer up, for I know I can handle this and I will. How I would love to be done working, but what would I do with myself then? It will be very odd to be sixty in June, but I forget it by plugging away and being useful."

...

One consequence of Lurry's concern about her big sister was that she chose not to burden Doré with medical news of her own. She had been diagnosed with breast cancer. It wasn't until after having a total mastectomy that she asked her brother Davey to telephone their sister.

"It was a horror to learn what you have gone through without ever letting me know anything about it." Doré wrote. "I am so very sorry, hating you to be having pain and surgery and all those things I well know are not fun. But I am glad that the doctors think they got the growth in time. How good that Davey and Kit and Paula were with you. HOW I wish I could see you, too, and be of some use other than just loving you so very much from a distance. You have yipped at me for not telling you things, but you have gone me one better this time!"

The following week she wrote, "I think about you all the time and last night I dreamed that both of us were happily walking north on the Pentwater beach, feeling so carefree and beautifully do-less and unworried about anything!"

Lurry's annual trip to Michigan was out of the question that year. She spent her convalescence during May 1958 at the home of two women friends, and planned to go to Davey and Kit's cottage on the Connecticut shore for her July vacation. In a rare burst of generosity, Davey sent Doré plane tickets to fly east to be with them all. Jim and I gave her a set of blue suitcases for her milestone 60th birthday, and the three weeks with her siblings were "wonderfully good."

The mastectomy had a profound influence on Lurry's life. For many years, she and her dear friend "Steck" postponed marriage. He was one of those men who could be described as "tied to his mothers' apron strings." I don't know whether Mama Stoeckler asked her son not to marry, but as I remember it she did not want him to move out. He and Lurry were treated as a couple by his family, who loved her as much as we did, but by the time his mother died, Lurry said that she felt too set in her ways to marry. I know that, like her sister, she saw her body as deformed by surgery. I believe that was the primary reason that she and Steck continued to live apart.

...

When another cataract formed on Doré's right eye, she lived with the impairment for months, erroneously believing that it could not be removed until she could see no light at all. When she finally admitted her condition, we urged her to be examined by a different specialist. This noted surgeon said that he would have operated on the right eye soon after the left one, which would have spared Doré all the pain of split-level vision and another year of poor eyesight.

Fortunately, the second surgery went smoothly. In a penciled letter, the next day, she described the operation: "Dr. Fralick explained everything for admiring students and told me to ask anything I wanted to. Snip, stitch, snip, stich. Suddenly I SAW his head in profile over my face! He did a stitch and I saw the scissors coming from the right. It was so thrilling! I mentioned same and they all said 'Good!'

"They suck out all the fluid just before slicing off the little round thing that looks like cooked abalone the size of a corn kernel, and when they put the fluid back, even before sewing the top down, you have vision! I was complimented on being 'extremely cooperative,' and told that if I could sit up in bed, quite high, absolutely motionless for four hours, I wouldn't need any sand bags. Of course I did that. A cute young nurse lit a cigarette and put it in my mouth, and did that ever taste good."

After an outpatient check up, she wrote, "After three years of using only one eye or the other, I walked out to find a cab with my head up and eyes ahead. I have depth vision again and things are rounded again instead of flat. I was late to the office, but jumped into the work with such relief from the load of uncertainty that has yoked me for so long."

For the rest of her life, Doré had to wear glasses with thick unflattering lenses, but at least she had normal vision. Work went well and she was able to resume her chosen activities.

CREATIVE STORY TELLING

Doré's four books for children went out of print in the 1950's, when China was viewed as an enemy. For most Americans, Communism under Mao erased any nostalgia for quaint tales of an ancient culture. Later, in the wake of the civil rights movement, ethnic heritage became a prerequisite for authenticity in literature. Just as it was no longer politically correct for a white person to write about the black experience, even Pearl Buck was no longer considered a reliable voice on things Chinese.

My mother left behind rafts of early unpublished stories about China. Poor health and sorrow may explain why she never wrote about her life in

America, but I never asked. She took notes for stories about hospital life and she started writing about her father, but apparently she just never had the physical or emotional energy to do more. With family and friends, however, my mother continued to spin tales out of the most quotidian happenings.

"The gorgeous spring weather enchants me," she wrote to Lurry. "I saw my first big fat robin on the way home across campus and spoke to him to his surprise, but he only politely tipped his head and looked at me. There is one tiny squirrel on campus that knows me and my handouts. He comes along to me, if I have five minutes to stand still and wait, and will take a treat from my hand. But he makes with fearful scoldings if I say good morning but have not brought a scrap of toast for him."

In another letter is this late August description: "Yesterday I brought home the first cartons from the grocery store to pack the crud and corruption that has to go back to Ann Arbor. I did the big desk drawers, then things in the pantry that I won't be using again here. Finally I decided to play games with myself, hating packing up as I always do, so drove down to the Beach. Even there it was hard to pretend, for the dune grass is high and feathered, and after a night of rain no humans were about. The sea gulls whirled low, and the little sand pipers made the delicate pattern of their small foot prints and seemed to say, 'Wow, how nice to have no more humans walking this sand and the place belonging to us once more.' I sat on a driftwood log and watched them parade."

My mother also told what could be called "tall tales." Her accounts of current encounters were almost always embellished with colorful details that probably didn't really happen that way, and lively quotations that other people probably didn't really say that way.

Some of her embellishments are funny, in retrospect. The plant growing so abundantly around the back terrace in Pentwater, which Doré called "bamboo," was really the noxious weed kudzu. Having lived many years in China, she surely knew what bamboo looked like. But I was an adult before I realized that real bamboo grows as tall, thin, graceful trees with small narrow leaves, not as enormous elephant-eared bushes. I guess she just enjoyed using the evocative word.

Some fifteen years after my mother's death (when I could no longer question her motives) one of her tall tales caused me considerable embarrassment. An art appraiser informed me that the delicately decorated white vessel that Doré always called "The Ming Vase" was simply a pretty 19th century porcelain. I regret never taking a college course in Asian Art. Had I not turned my back on my heritage while focusing on becoming a farmer's wife, I would have learned about Ming blue.

My mother also seasoned everyday speech with swear words. They would be considered tame compared to today's ubiquitous use of the F-word, but she believed that, "A well-placed damn or hell never hurt anybody." She also swore in Chinese.

I can't spell the expressions accurately, but what I heard as a child sounded like "Mollykochobee" and "Shahdeegomybee." Every time I asked her what they meant, she'd say that I would have to wait until I was 21 to find out. The meaning was unfit for tender ears. As I grew, it became a joke between us, but she continued to maintain that I must wait until the age of majority.

When that significant milestone finally arrived, I wasted no time. "Tell me!" I insisted. How we both laughed when she revealed that the expressions meant something like "A curse upon your ancestors!" – the worst thing one Chinese could say to another.

幸运 # PART TEN

"While she waits by her bedside, Helen finishes another sketch.... Once she had thought that she might discover some key to her mother if only she could get her likeness right, but she has since learned that the mysteries of another person only deepen, the longer one looks."

— Debra Dean – in <u>The Madonnas of Leningrad</u>
(HarperCollins/William Morrow 2006)

IN A PARALLEL UNIVERSE

The jewelry class she had so enjoyed was in a way symbolic of a new reality in our relationship. Doré and I were living quite different lives. When I had been in Ann Arbor, spending my days on campus just as she did, we remained deeply enmeshed. But, after I moved to the farm and was busy with an expanding family of my own, our interests significantly diverged.

During each academic year, her job became increasingly demanding. By 1955, the department head, George Forsyth, had agreed that a graduate student was needed to supervise the second study hall. Doré was gratified when, with only a soft suggestion from her, he hired a smart young woman whose efficiency matched her own. By 1956, she also had three young male assistants who took over the filing of photographs and slides.

"The boy babysitters, who have only studied all their lives, are not as good at the housekeeping aspects of the job," she wrote, "but with an enrollment of 1194 students in sixteen art history courses, I am grateful for their help."

As busy as she was, when her day at the office ended, Doré missed daily contact with me. She realized that she needed to widen her circle and pursue her own interests – such as that jewelry class. She went to movies with new friends and lapped up a long weekend near Detroit at the elegant home of friends made when Ben worked at the Art Institute.

Meanwhile, I had entered what I call my "civic matron years," and my mother couldn't understand what made Judy run. She had always derided "causey women." Never did she join any sort of organized group and she despaired of understanding why I participated in civic organizations that she considered pointless pursuits.

An exception was her approval of the time and energy Jim and I put into the Pentwater Yacht Club. When he was elected Commodore, we joked that I was the "Mommodore." I spent countless hours planning, cooking and decorating for dinners and dances, and Doré pitched in to create floral arrangements for those events.

...

My mother was totally supportive through my second pregnancy, and was as thrilled as we were when we had a son, Christopher James Gamble, on February 26, 1956. Doré regretted that she couldn't help me that winter, but she more than made up for it by babysitting both Jenni and Chris often during the summer. Keeping them, in her quiet way, at her own house, was taxing but satisfying. Being at *our* house was less fun for her as the children grew.

After our small son's first Christmas, Doré told Lurry, "I adored being with them, but I did not rest much. I was tired beyond words and close to tears often, being unaccustomed to the everlasting noise and activity levels of two small ones. But so what? You are right in saying that I could do with a little care myself, and I would love it, but I get a huge kick out of giving of me for my four Gamble darlings. Perhaps the rewards of being wanted and needed are greater than any kind of depending or leaning on another could be. To me it is deeply satisfying. I am also amazed by the way Judy handles it all."

It further amazed her when McCall's Magazine invited me as one of a hundred delegates to a Women's Congress on Better Living in Washington, D.C. Much as Doré bragged, it still astonished her that a child of hers could focus her life around homemaking.

Nevertheless, being part of my family continued to be deeply satisfying to her. Letters in the 1950's were filled with detailed accounts of every cute thing that Jenni said or how beautifully she sang. When Chris first sat alone or stood up and then walked, it was a cause célebre.

Looking forward to Christmas one year, she wrote, "I will have a week with the dear family at Juniper Orchards. Jim's brothers, Joe and Jack and his wife Nancy will share the day with us and it is good to be a part of such a big and loving family. With the threat of nuclear annihilation hanging over the world, I find in that spot a shining loveliness that is what the world needs but does not have. Daily news broadcasts are so depressing."

She also worried about us when bitter weather and spring frosts damaged our fruit crops. "I am fully aware that I am a clucking hen about Judy, my 'all of my eggs in one basket,' and cringe at anything that hurts her or makes her fret. Being a mother is one of the most marvelous things in living, but it opens you wide to pain, as it always does to love deeply."

"Judy tries every way she can to earn money—such as catering a wedding reception and taking the school census. But, I am accustomed to a check in the bank the first of every month and could not live with such financial uncertainty. The story going around is about someone asking a farmer about his cherries, and his answer is that he hopes, if they are careful, to get enough for a pie! Part of my fury at *Kind-Dirty* is something that Judy may understand when the fates deal badly with Jennifer or Chris. But now, I carefully do not utter curses, but rejoice for what is saved. I do try! Time will tell."

When Jim was offered a job as sales representative for agricultural chemicals, he was both relieved and troubled. It would mean moving.

Joe had already left the farm to earn a doctorate at Purdue University. So the brothers hired a manager, and in late 1959 Jim and I moved our family north to Traverse City. Our first year there, Jim spent every weekend at the farm, but eventually, he and Joe made the painful decision to sell Juniper Orchards. Although I had truly loved our farm home, I looked forward to the benefits of living in a larger community, with more cultural and educational advantages for us and our children.

Laid out along the shore of Grand Traverse Bay, Traverse City abuts the base of Leelanau County, which Michiganders call the little finger of the mitten. Long a popular tourist destination, the city was also year-round home to an assortment of artists and professionals. Schools were good, a community college had been established, and the National Music Camp (which later grew into the Interlochen Arts Academy) was just 20 miles away.

Doré told Lurry that she was sure we were doing the right thing, adding, "Judy is going to miss her wonderful kitchen, for sure, but will be happy not to have to cope with the big vegetable garden and so much canning ever again." In truth, Doré was as glad about that as I was.

Our first Christmas in Traverse City was quiet. We had moved on December 12th, so there had been no time to make friends before the holidays. Doré wrote Lurry, "It was a blissfully peaceful vacation without rafts of people around. Judy was rested and happy, too. On New Year's Eve, she and Jim went to a movie and came home in time to have a drink and some herring and cheese and crackers with me to see the New Year in, something we have not shared for many years."

I felt chagrined to read that letter, realizing how often we had used her as a babysitter on New Year's Eve, believing her assertion that she didn't mind being alone.

SLOWING DOWN

Apparently Lurry had been concerned about her sister when Doré said she didn't have pep enough to come to New York for spring vacation 1960.

"Don't worry about me. I have been fine, not a cold for more than a year, no insulin reactions. I just don't feel moved to travel and go around to shows and museums and the like. The thing I face is accepting that I am nearly 62 and I get tired more quickly now than in the good old days… I am not shutting you out about anything. I simply have little news because I do nothing but do my job and don't have much pep to write at night. On the weekends I read a lot and have the radio playing softly. I slept until eleven this Sunday morning, and am all ready for the fray come tomorrow."

During her annual Pentwater visit, Lurry felt that Doré was more than usually "withdrawn." Doré wrote that she had simply been "trying hard not to get 'djoa-dji' (*upset*) about all the confusion when Judy and the kids and their friends were there. You and I only had one tiny little week alone before things became so hectic"

I don't know whether that answer satisfied Lurry, but reading it caused me to regret the assumptions I made about how much uproar my mother could take. She said she was willing to have our out-of-town guests stay at her house, and I seldom considered her further before making plans. As my own years have hurried by, I have come to understand much better why my mother cherished her "peace and quiet."

In July 1961, Doré suffered a serious bout of double pneumonia. She was hospitalized in Hart, but we took her home to Traverse City with us to recover completely. She told Lurry, "I have never been closer to the Pearly Gates, and was goofy for about five days, hearing voices and dreaming dreams, but suddenly I came out of it and felt so fine the doctor could hardly believe it. It did help to have another week of convalescence at the Gambles' before being alone again."

It was deeply disappointing to Doré when Lurry was unable to come to Pentwater that summer. Cousin Paula had broken her hip and couldn't function without Lurry. Doré wrote, "I do understand it all, of course, but it breaks my heart because YOU need a little loving care and tenderness yourself, and that I have for you, as always the long years through."

FINAL YEARS ON CAMPUS

In September 1960, Doré told Lurry, "I never quite anticipate the first feeling of claustrophobia I have when I get back to my small one-room studio apartment after the joy of a huge house and yard and the lovely outdoors, but I can't imagine winter days without my job, for which I am so grateful. Twenty-five years just now since I began it – and I do love the work"

Her load was lightened that fall when her study hall was moved into what she called "a stunning new building."

"It is air conditioned, with modern light and a spiffy lounge and rest rooms" she told Lurry. "I have 912 students who use my room and I am learning their names. Some wild mistakes are being made by the grad students who are pulling photos for the other study hall, but I don't say anything, and when the profs roar, it is not my grief anymore, and Oh, how good that is! The people running the old place now are very slow, and I keep remembering how I had all the pictures out and hung the same day a class was held. They keep calling me to ask such questions as 'WHERE do we find the interior views of the Catacombs?' And I can answer 372-ZX-3 and that amazes them all. You don't put so much of your life into a department and then forget such things.

"The marvelous change is that I am no longer dead tired when I come home in the evenings, and how I do enjoy that. I am a lucky gal, and to have time to get to know the students is rewarding."

The passion for order that Doré felt about Art History Department files was also seen at home. I can't remember anything that could even remotely be described as a mess. Doré never left junk mail or "to be read" or "to be sorted" piles around, and her magazines were neatly arrayed on a low table beside her favorite chair. Orderly surroundings, to her, promoted serenity of mind.

Although she was compulsively neat, my mother still didn't care much whether the house was clean. She could let that go for weeks. I remember noticing once that a precise row of bobby pins had etched their silhouettes in a layer of dust on her dressing table, where she had carefully laid them down the night before.

...

Meanwhile, after renting for nearly a year, Jim and I bought an old house on the west side of Traverse City, set among enormous trees on a lot bisected by "Kids Creek." We moved in two months before our much-wanted third child was born.

All during that pregnancy, I felt estranged from my mother.

Doré was always proud of never letting her face or voice betray pain or fear. But, I could usually read her displeasure or disapproval. What I couldn't fathom was the reason that she was so cold and withdrawn, never sharing my happiness over expecting another baby. I guessed that she didn't approve, but I never asked her about it. Nor did I say how much it hurt. We wrote and talked about everything else, as we always did, but she didn't knit or sew for the baby and changed the subject if I brought up any plans to accommodate an addition to the family.

Once Cynthia was born, on February 13, 1961, Doré was completely enchanted. She was an eager babysitter during her vacations, and the estrangement I felt during my pregnancy evaporated. She and I were close again, and nothing was said about it. Our family was complete, and I was happily fulfilled.

...

There are few letters saved from 1962. I can only wonder what moved Lurry to burn the others. In April Doré wrote, "I feel so good and am never really beat with the easy, pleasing job I have now. *Kind Dirty* has sure been good to me as I near my 64th birthday. And YOU will soon be sixty! Quite a milestone."

Summer was 'heavenly," with Lurry in Pentwater for three whole weeks. As always, Doré delighted in "the same dear place," but by September she was glad to be back on the job.

"After sleeping in late all summer, I woke the first morning just before the alarm went off. It was fun to walk the familiar Ann Arbor streets to work again. We have a huge enrollment this semester, and more than a thousand students are to use my room. Many old friends came in to say hello the first few days and seemed glad I was back at the old stand again."

In January 1963, she reported on a busy week. The study hall was jammed to the rafters with kids facing final exams. "I am so glad that I don't have to file the hundreds of photos. The grad students say they expect to spend all the time between semesters putting them away. My Gawd! They have no system. I always had my assistants bring the photos to me with the white filing labels all on the right side, and the numbers in each category together. Boy, how fast I could file! But how very good it is not to have that gigantic job any longer mine."

RETIREMENT

The academic year of 1962-63 would be my mother's last on campus. The University of Michigan's retirement age was 65, but Doré considered begging for an exception to work at least another year. Then another life-threatening bout with pneumonia changed her mind. I went to Ann Arbor to care for her for two weeks following her release from the hospital, but desperation about such an illness frightened her into realizing that it was time to live closer to me.

"I have never been as really scared as I was the morning I couldn't get my breath," she wrote Lurry. "My first morning back to work my boss came over to see me. I told him I am going to retire this June, when I reach 65. I know this is the right thing to do, strange as it will seem after living in Ann Arbor for thirty years…

"I will stay here spring vacation to get all the pension paper work done at the university and see about Social Security. The university will continue to carry my Blue Cross at the group rate. Packing looks like a huge job to me, but that may be because I'm not as peppy as usual yet. Judy says it will be a cinch. She and Jim are coming May 31st and will hire a U-Haul trailer to take my furniture, books and dishes to their garage until we find me a studio apartment in Traverse City. How utterly lucky I am to have their loving care!"

Surprisingly, there is no description of a retirement party in Doré's letters to Lurry. Probably she told her every detail over the phone. I remember hearing how warmly the whole departmental staff wished her well. Rather than a gold watch, they gave her a uniquely glazed flower bowl created by an acclaimed Michigan potter.

"After Jim brought me to Pentwater," she wrote, "Jenni stayed on to keep me company for a week. At nine, she is such a help and loves taking care of Grammy. The little village is the same beautiful place....."

Jenni and Chris knew she was mourning the death of her black cat Sambo, who had succumbed to a brief illness. For her birthday, they surprised her with a new kitten. Small grey and white "Tippy" settled in at once and was curled on Doré's lap while her long slim fingers typed on her new lightweight Hermes Rocket machine.

She cared for her fingernails and creamed her hands, but they revealed one nervous habit. With the nail on her middle finger, she would absently pick at the skin on the inner side of her thumb nail, creating a tough callus.

To Doré's delight, Lurry came for the entire month of July that year, and their sister Caroline (whom they still nicknamed "Barbie") and her husband and youngest daughter joined them for a week-long reunion. When Lurry's first letter after her vacation described waking to an alarm clock again, Doré empathized, adding, "I know it will seem strange to me not to hear that this fall. But I am relishing the utterly do-less days here and, when the weather grows too cold to stay, I will continue to enjoy the leisure in my small apartment in Traverse City."

PART ELEVEN

幸运

"*Intermittency... How can one learn to live through the ebb-tides of one's existence?... It is easier to understand on the beach... So beautiful is the still hour of the sea's withdrawal, as beautiful as the sea's return. ...Perhaps this is the most important thing for me to take back...simply the memory that each cycle of the tide is valid; each cycle of the wave is valid, each cycle of a relationship is valid.*"
— Anne Morrow Lindbergh in <u>Gift from the Sea</u> (Pantheon Books, Inc. 1955)

TRAVERSE CITY

Her new studio apartment was just four blocks from our house, so we could easily spend planned and unplanned time together. Doré could maintain her cherished peace and quiet, tolerating family gatherings but preferring to have me drop over alone or to entertain one grandchild at a time in her own space.

As she told Lurry, "It is completely right for me. There are two huge windows and a small kitchen with all appliances and lots of cupboards, divided from the living space by a high bar. The new studio couch makes a comfortable bed. My chairs and brass table and Oriental rugs, plus the little zhou-gi and old bijoux shelf that Ben made make me feel right at home. The john, just by my door, is shared with two women in the other upstairs apartments. My landlady and her daughter live on the first floor. A neighborhood supermarket is only half a block away, and I found a home bakery almost as good as Suchey's in Pentwater.

"I simply love it all. I walk easily to the Gambles' or north to Grand Traverse Bay, sparkling blue and lovely. Not a problem in my world! I feel proud of being able to work all those years and now to be financially secure at sixty-five."

To Doré's delight, the first lecture in Traverse City's new Contemporary Art Gallery was given by U of M Professor Marvin Eisenberg, her last boss and a teacher I also admired. She sold tickets and later wrote Lurry, "People in the overflow crowd were rather impressed to see Marv give me a big hug and kiss! He said sweetly that they all missed me greatly. We went with him and a few of the town's bigwigs to the gallery owner's house for drinks afterwards. Much fun all the way for me."

Doré in her Traverse City apartment

Her letters to Lurry continued to be full of descriptions of what I was doing and how her grandchildren were growing and every cute thing they said or did. Now that she was near us in the winter, she saw one or more of them often and enjoyed having them pop up to her apartment after school.

In February, she talked to Jenny's Girl Scout troop, plus a group of Brownies, about her days in China, and ended by reading one of her stories from <u>The Rabbit Lantern.</u> "The forty kids sat quiet and interested," she told Lurry. "Jenny was so proud and later most enthusiastic in telling Judy how 'well organized' I was."

Apart from art-related activities, Doré continued to find most of my community endeavors preposterous, but she usually kept her incredulity to herself. That is until Jim and I became founders of a Unitarian Universalist Fellowship.

Religion always seemed "unintelligent" to my mother, and she raised me outside of any faith tradition. Yet she lived her life according to the "Golden Rule" and taught me by example that all people have inherent worth and dignity, with an equal claim to liberty and justice; that revelation is on-going for the open mind; that human beings are only a part of an interdependent web of all existence; and that love must be the motive force in human relationships.

She had known that, from the time I was in high school, I found comparative religion intellectually compelling. She neither encouraged nor discouraged my interest. I only regret that she never told me how like my father I was in that regard.

While Ben was teaching in China in 1924, he realized he no longer believed the Christian dogma. Tired of having no answer when people asked about his faith, he arranged to join the San Francisco Unitarian Church by proxy. He pursued independent study. And when he returned to China for six months in 1931 he was secretly introduced to a revered ancient doctrine that he believed might have been a primordial reservoir for all later religions. I didn't know any of this until I read his journals and a scholarly paper after Doré died. Surely aware of Ben's fears about misuse of that doctrine, she had apparently destroyed his detailed notes.

When I had joined church choirs my mother understood that it was for the joy of singing. But using musical talent was quite different, in her view, from putting so much time into planning, organizing and running a congregation. So, in 1964, she risked questioning our motives.

"I get it that you want your kids to have some education about religion," she told me. "I know you wish you had gotten that when you were young. But you picked it up when it mattered to you, didn't you? I hate the idea of indoctrinating young children."

"You know that Unitarianism is different," I retorted. "There is no creed or dogma that is crammed down anyone's throat. It has liberal principles that fit with our beliefs, and we think that it will help the kids to have a grounding to make their own decisions later in life."

"Well, we shall see," she sighed. "But I think you may regret it. And don't expect me to attend."

True to her word, she came to a Fellowship service only when one of her grandchildren had a part in some special program or holiday pageant.

Pentwater summers continued to be the high point of every year. The grandchildren were old enough to be more help than burden when they spent time with her there, and she paid the July and August rent on the Traverse City apartment so she could return to that "perfect place" in September. "I love knowing it is waiting for me," she told Lurry. "I am living so easily on my pension and Social Security checks and am not stinting in any way."

The year after she retired, the University of Michigan converted to a trimester system. Watching the last of a summer shower drip off the maple leaves, she wrote "how good it is not to be going back, now that August 31st is the opening day."

I can picture her with a cigarette and cold coffee, sitting in her favorite round wicker chair. She positioned it where she could look out through the front door to watch passing bikes and cars and welcome anyone who came up the path of red cement paving squares to her small porch.

Most days, she read short stories in _The Ladies Home Journal_ and _The Women's Home Companion_ and looked forward to _Redbook,_ which published work that she considered more akin to literature. She also lugged home armloads of books from the Pentwater Public Library, enjoying biographies and current novels, but never the mysteries that her sister loved. Lurry called detective fiction her "bloods" and used them for "pure escapism."

BEING ON CALL

That winter, my mother volunteered for two hours on Fridays at the elementary school library. "I let forty-some second graders take out books and sign for them with care and marvelous scrawls," she told Lurry. "I enjoy doing it and Jenny and Chris are both so proud of their Grammy."

Doré loved it when Jenny rode her bike over to her apartment after school, or when I put Cyndi down for her nap on "Gammy's" bed. When, at my urging, Chris visited her, it was a treat to be served 7-up and olives. Doré always preferred to dote on one child at a time, but she didn't mind if he brought along a friend for moral support, and she often agreed to stay at our house with all three kids.

As she told Lurry, "With Jim out of town, I babysat for eight hours Wednesday, and last night I was there for supper and the evening. Tonight I am grateful to be on my own again with nothing to do but shuffle through huge snow drifts to the grocery store just a block away.

"Sometimes I don't want to baby-sit, but I am always glad that I do it, for I feel useful to Judy, and I don't ever want to say no to her if I can help it. I don't mean to sound noble. I simply want to give, to be subordinate and selfless. Out of that, by a secret alchemy, my own happiness is made. It's a purpose, a reason somehow."

I like to believe she meant it. But judging from the occasional defensive tone in Doré's letters, I can guess that Lurry was encouraging her to pursue her own interests apart from serving me and my family.

Meanwhile, I dreaded telling her that, despite birth control, I was pregnant again. It was a shock and disappointment, but, in those days, abortions were illegal in this country. When I considered seeking one in Mexico, I felt uncharacteristically superstitious and couldn't bring myself to do it. My doctor, Bill Fishbeck said, "Don't worry about it, Judy. This is the child who will grow up to be President of the United States." Easy for you to say, I thought bitterly.

Because I was unhappy enough anyway, I didn't tell Doré until I began to "show" and would need maternity clothes. Remembering how estranged we were when I had been expecting Cyndi, I didn't want to live with her disapproval again. But I was in for a surprise – and welcome clarification.

She was sitting at my kitchen table, smoking, while I peeled Northern Spies for apple crisp. Drawing a deep breath, I plunged in. "Mommy, I'm pregnant…" Seeing her shock, I hurried on. "We didn't plan to have more children. Our diaphragm failed us."

"Oh Darling, I'm so sorry!" she said, with immediate understanding. "I know you didn't want this. Are you feeling all right?"

"Yes, I'm fine physically, but it's a real blow. My life is so busy now, with three kids, that I dread the idea of having another."

"Of course you do," Doré said, sympathetically. "It will make a big change in your life." She thought about that for a moment before adding, "But I know you can handle it. I wish I had known sooner…."

"I didn't tell you because I assumed it would upset you, the way it did when we decided to have Cyndi. You were so cold to me during that pregnancy. I dreaded going through it again…."

235

"Oh Darling, I didn't realize that my feelings showed that much."

"Oh, I can read you pretty well, Mommy. I guessed that you were against our having another child, but I could never figure out <u>why</u>!"

"Well, Judy," she said, pausing for the right words, "I simply could not understand why you <u>wanted </u>another child. You already had one of each – a boy and a girl – and that seemed to me to be a complete family."

Noting my surprise, she continued, "It's just that Jenni and Chris were getting so independent by then, and I hated to think of you facing diapers and night time feedings, and being tied down by infant care again."

Pausing to think, and then slowly revealing an underlying feeling, she added, "Truthfully, Darling, I guess I had always envisioned more for <u>your</u> life than coping with snotty noses and stinky bottoms."

Stunned, I huffed, "Is that all you think there is to having children?"

"Of course not, Judy," she said, annoyed. "I'm sorry. But I guess I thought that once Chris was in school all day, you would have time to <u>yourself </u>at last – to maybe find a job where you could use your abilities or be free to express your talents in other ways…."

Tears of relief filled my eyes as she spoke. It was so good to have this issue out in the open between us. It helped me to understand the basis for her earlier behavior. She simply wanted more for me. As we continued to talk, she could see that, for that time in my life, childrearing and mothering were deeply satisfying to me despite the work load and times of frustration.

Doré acknowledged that Cyndi had been a joy for the whole family and had helped Jenni and Chris to mature. At the same time, she confided another aspect of her feelings to Lurry: "I do miss being able to have Judy to myself. Three kids are something to cope with, and she does a marvelous job of it. It's just that life revolves totally around them. Sometimes they leave me limp. It's hard to imagine having another one, but I am taking it with grace."

And, because Doré knew that my fourth pregnancy was an "accident" that I regretted but couldn't help, she was nothing but supportive throughout.

I had always believed that my parents' decision to have but one child was based on their sorrowful assumption that Ben's heart condition would bring him an early death. They anticipated that Doré would be forced to raise any offspring alone. This was so, but not the whole truth.

From her letters, I discovered that Doré never really wanted another child after me. She resented the demands that an infant placed on her time, and those limitations on her own life would have reduced the pleasure she might have felt in another baby. I learned from her letters that she only enjoyed my company when I grew to be nine or ten years old and only appreciated me as a person when I was about 14 – the summer I took care of her after she was released from a TB ward.

...

But Doré was a good sport about grandmothering, and it did mean a lot to her that my children loved Pentwater as much as she did. In addition to the times that I asked her to keep the kids, Jenny and Chris and Cyndi were invited, as special treats, to spend separate weeks alone with their grandmother. The older two were each allowed to bring a friend. Doré really enjoyed those times. Lurry sent a croquet set, which our kids and their friends used hour after hour.

Before Jim brought Doré to Pentwater the summer of '64, he and his brother Jack installed a new ceiling in the living room and Jim and I painted the kitchen. It surprised her that we wouldn't allow her to pay for any of the materials. She gratefully accepted the gift after Jim reminded her of all the babysitting she did for us.

As we anticipated our fourth child's arrival, Doré expected to take care of the other three while I was in the hospital. After some thought, she told me frankly that she would rather keep them in Pentwater than to stay in our Traverse City house where there were so many other kids in and out all day. "Also," she told me, "your children are better behaved when I have them to myself and what I say has to be it."

As it turned out, Lurry was also in Pentwater that hot, humid August. So, together, she and Doré, with practiced help from ten-year-old Jenny, managed until Scott Benjamin Gamble made his appearance on the 14th – two weeks late. Having another boy seemed to balance our family so neatly that everyone rejoiced in his birth. The "accident" of his conception was never a barrier to our adoration of that little guy.

In early 1965, deep snows kept Doré housebound much of the winter. When she did venture through the drifts or along icy sidewalks, she told

Lurry that she felt "scared to death that I will fall with a dozen eggs in my bag." She also had several bad chest colds.

At my urging, she made an appointment for a complete checkup with Dr. Bernard "Bud" Sweeney, who was mature enough to please her. She had always dismissed very young physicians as being "still wet behind the ears."

He assured her that she (and I) had nothing to worry about. As she said in a letter to Lurry, "We know that any cold I get goes into the bronchial tubes, but what little coughing I do otherwise is from smoking, and he said nothing about stopping that, for which I am grateful."

How little medical science knew then about the effect of cigarettes on health. Today it seems astonishing that a woman who spent two years in TB wards and gave up one lung to "The Cure" continued to smoke throughout those ordeals and for the rest of her life. I can't help wondering: what if she had gotten cancer in her remaining lung?!

In a letter of May, 1966, Doré described budding trees, warm breezes and Grand Traverse Bay bright blue in the sunlight. "The Gambles are fine," she wrote. "Young Scott is growing up so fast and is the dearest little guy. He loves to have me baby-sit, which I have done for 25 hours already this month."

She also told Lurry about Jenny spending a Friday night with her in the guest room that any of the tenants in her building could reserve. "She is such a darling, so intelligent and fun to talk to, so grown up at almost twelve. We had cocktails and dinner together and then she watched TV with my landlady until nine. I showed her where I keep dry cereal and bowl and milk for morning so she could help herself when she woke up. She came in quiet as a mouse, took her breakfast back to her own room where she worked on a project for school. When she finished it we had lunch and I kept watching her sweet face."

I didn't know until recent years that Jenny saw her grandmother as "cold and austere." I was accustomed to Doré's grim, tight-lipped demeanor while doing her duty. It never occurred to me that it bothered my kids. It seemed to me that she was fairly lenient and doting. She certainly loved my children, even while preferring to be with one or two at a time.

The summer of '66 all four of the kids and I spent most of July in Pentwater. Every day, as we hosed off the sand following an afternoon at the beach, I would inhale the rich aroma of chili con carne or Creole pork chops with never a thought to the hours that Doré had been standing in the kitchen to prepare those meals. She said she was happy to have dinner waiting for us, and I chose to believe her. As usual, she gave Lurry a more complete picture: "I have been a stinker about writing but the quiet moment does not come often. I am surrounded by Gambles, and busy cooking for six or seven of us. I do enjoy it but find that I cave in early in the evenings with no pep for letters."

Years later, a workshop leader asked participants to answer, off the top of our heads, "What did your mother always say?" My response: "Don't slam the screen door." My children and I had a good chuckle remembering that.

When Jim came to Pentwater on weekends, he and I freshly papered and painted Lurry's bedroom – yellow of course. It was a way of repaying my mother, and the results were much appreciated when our beloved aunt came for her vacation.

DIABETIC CRISIS

In March of 1967, Doré nearly died in a diabetic coma. Dr. Sweeney initially thought that she might be better off in Ann Arbor, where "experts" could monitor her recovery and set insulin doses. She dreaded the prospect and was vastly relieved when the plan was discarded, but Dr. Sweeney was disappointed when the University Hospital doctors told him they could do nothing more than he was already doing. The leading endocrinologist could give no cause for her collapse, saying, "When an occasional elderly diabetic suddenly goes haywire like this, it's terribly dangerous. Of course it means you lose some of them, but there just isn't a lot you can do."

That dispassionate expert did suggest dividing her insulin into two doses, taking one just before her evening meal. Dr. Sweeney agreed to try this and told Doré, "We're going to keep you in the hospital one more week and we'll either cure you or kill you." She knew he was joking, but she told him that there had been moments when she would have elected the kill.

This recommendation appeared to be the solution. Although she weighed only 106 pounds by the time she was released, she recovered, and her health improved steadily as the months went by. She wrote Lurry that it was good to be back in her own apartment after two weeks at the Gambles.

"Judy and Jim were so good to me and the kids were all darling. I miss them, but not the noise, and I am not afraid alone any more. It takes time to cook my three big meals, but it's a pleasure, too. I walk a little bit every day and sleep around the clock."

By June, Dr. Sweeney gave her permission to go to Pentwater and said he didn't want to see her until the end of September. I asked the Todd family across the street to watch Doré's bedroom window in the mornings and to come over to check on her if her shades weren't raised by noon. It put my mind at ease, and Doré told Lurry that she felt "protected and cared for."

Lurry retired that year, so the highlight of Doré's 37th summer in her beloved resort village was having her sister there for the entire month of August. They had a "perfect" time together, but the extended visit also gave Lurry a chance to see just how much Doré was drinking.

PART TWELVE

幸运

*"(In September) the fact of Dave's retirement hit him in the face all over again...
(The students) had worn him out. But now he found himself missing their voices
and their cataclysmic emotional crises... It was like walking down a red carpet
and then turning to find the attendants rolling it up behind you. He was gone. It
shook his whole view of himself to discover how much he minded."*
—Anne Tyler in <u>Digging To America</u> (Alfred A. Knopf 2006)

HOW MUCH IS TOO MUCH?

Doré saw religion as a "crutch for the weak." Her own crutch was whiskey.

For cosmopolitan young people during "The Roaring Twenties," drinking was a way of life. Everyone in her Detroit crowd had a drink or two before dinner. The cocktail hour was as much a part of one's day as breakfast in the morning. On weekends, when friends gathered, the drinking went on through the evening. They came of age believing that hard liquor was a perfectly acceptable stress reliever.

As long as she had to get up and go to work, my mother controlled her drinking during the winters, and never missed a day on the job. Though she had a drink or two during a lonely evening, that never kept her from rising with the alarm clock for another day of interaction with students and colleagues. Saturdays were housework and errands days, but in the evening she could allow herself a couple of stiffer drinks, because she could sleep in on Sundays.

In the summer, the weekend routine became a daily one. She made her first drink of the day at five p.m. This time corresponded to the cocktail hour traditionally observed by British expatriates in India who waited until someone declared, "The sun is over the yard arm."

During my childhood, Doré got together with one or more friends almost every night, and most of her crowd drank quite heavily. I don't remember her ever serving wine. Some of her friends drank beer. But she drank only rye whiskey and sometimes brandy, such as applejack, in the early years. A favorite drink with her crowd was a combination of applejack and grape juice. They called the potent concoction a "So Now to Bed."

I remember Doré being a little high or "tight" every evening, but she was never repulsively sloshed or belligerent. When she felt "pleasantly looped," she went upstairs and slept until noon the next day. During the later years when she was more often alone, she just kept sipping at a whiskey and water all evening.

Doré was not yet 44 when Don Goss died. She was a woman who craved passion, yet never again experienced physical intimacy. I recently read the following comment about a bereaved woman: "She could force herself to be cheerful, but she would never be happy again." It reminded me of my widowed mother. She enjoyed times of pleasure and satisfaction, times of contentment even, but never again those "flashing moments" of surpassing happiness. I don't offer that as an excuse for her drinking too much, but, given that she felt no social stigma against alcohol, it's not really surprising that she pacified herself with whiskey.

Lurry had apparently become concerned about her sister's drinking years earlier. In a 1954 letter Doré rationalized, "I am sorry to have upset you this summer. I guess I drink mostly just for something to do, as I smoke cigs and as I drink coffee during the day time. There are times, such as after driving at night, when I need something to relax me and I really want a drink. But since I came back to Ann Arbor I have changed over to tea most of the time and that goes all right, so I hope you are pleased. Social drinking is rare for me here because I am weary at five and just want to get home."

This was about the time that her eyesight began to fail. Because she didn't realize that the change in her vision was due to cataracts that could be removed, Doré believed that she was going blind. At some point, while she kept her fears to herself, she switched back from tea to whiskey.

After she retired and was spending her winters in Traverse City, the summer pattern went on all year. Without any focus for her days she drew more and more into herself and drank more. As she had dreaded, she missed having meaningful work that gave a structure to her days and made her feel needed and appreciated.

Although she knew that I needed her, and she wanted to help me all she could, her energy level was not what it used to be. Moreover, watching over small children was not rewarding in the same way that her professional career had been. She felt that she had "outlived her usefulness."

In addition, she might finally have been acknowledging layers of loss long buried under obligations of work and mothering and her need to keep strong for me. Now perhaps, whiskey-soaked, her losses worked their way to the surface. She rarely gave in to self-pity, but I wonder: as she faced old age did unfinished grieving haunt those long solitary evenings?

I knew nothing about alcoholism at that time. It didn't occur to me that she could be what is called a functioning alcoholic, because she never drank during the daytime and never seemed drunk. Although Doré limited her intake when in charge of my children, Jenny noticed that Grammy slurred her words later in the evening.

Lurry became increasingly concerned and asked me to help keep an eye on my mother's drinking. Lurry was no teetotaler. She enjoyed a social drink with friends. But she was also acutely aware of its dangers. In New York she suffered through the frequent binges and blackouts of her apartment-mate Cousin Paula.

Doré promised us all that she would cut down, and we believed that she had, but we found extra whiskey bottles hidden on high shelves behind cereal boxes and under the sink behind dishwashing detergent.

In retrospect, it's clear that a diabetic should not have been consuming the amount of sugar found in hard liquor. She compensated for it by cutting back on carbohydrates in foods, which certainly wasn't a healthy solution. Dr. Sweeney would surely not have approved, but he had no clue about her drinking, and I was then too ignorant of its dangers to mention it. In October he was pleased to find her blood sugar levels the lowest they had been since she had been so sick.

"I have walked a lot these lovely fall days," she wrote. "The trees are turning now and the two huge ones outside my windows are bright yellow, with masses of leaves on the ground. I'm so glad you could visit me here before you flew home. I love knowing that you can picture me going to the store and visualize each detail of my small, loved apartment. I simply could not go to the airport to see you off. I would have bawled and the kids would have been upset. I knew you would understand..."

LETTERS END

That letter of October 17, 1967 is the last among those that were left to me. It may be that later letters were saved in another box which Lurry inadvertently discarded. Whatever the answer, from here on I must tug out my own memories from the tangle of succeeding years.

Because my mother and I shared most of the large and small details of our lives, I had the illusion of knowing her. I understood that she didn't want to appear "weak and wobbly." But I didn't know until I read her letters that Doré didn't show me the depths of her grief, her fears or her pain.

Nor did I reveal all that was on my mind or in my heart. Had I known then what I later learned about her extramarital affair in Detroit, I might have disclosed more about my own unhappiness. I like to think that she would have understood and, perhaps, helped me through the next few years. But, maybe not. Whenever I said anything that sounded as if I might seek a divorce, she quickly doused the idea with all the cold water she could hurl.

"How on earth could you raise four children by yourself, Judy?" she asked, creases deepening between her eyebrows and her tone arch. "You don't even know how to support yourself! You've never held a real job!" True – then.

We often invited Doré to attend community events with us, but rarely did she agree to go to a lecture, and never to a symphony concert. She turned down invitations from the mothers of my contemporaries – assuming that she would have nothing in common with those "old biddies." Before long, they stopped asking. Yes, she was a widow, but so were some of the most active, interesting women I knew. Yes, she was somewhat frail, but still relatively fit, with fewer current health issues than some.

I felt that she missed so much by not having a caring community of supportive, like-minded friends. Still, it was her life, after all, and eventually I accepted that she was determined to be a recluse. In a rare poem from those years she wrote:

The tall magnolia tree
When its spring splendor ends,
Drops round its feet
A wide pink circle of fallen flowers.
This image speaks
To every understanding heart.
"Step not too near.
Ask of me no more blooms this year.
Grant now this little privacy,
Protected by a magic ring,
To a very tired tree."

When I was living on the east coast long after Doré's death, I met an old Detroit friend of hers. As I described my mother's last years, Hope's response had me gasping with regret.

"Why didn't you connect her with some college students?" she asked. "Doré spent all her working years with young people. That might have lifted her out of her depression."

How I wished I had thought of that. One of our faculty friends at the local community college could have invited her to volunteer in some capacity on campus. Today I can think of several ways that she might have been useful and might have established relationships with compatible students, the way she had in Ann Arbor.

Doré might not have made the effort. But, at the time, preoccupied with my own pursuits, I never thought to suggest it. Nor did I think of steering her to a therapist. I didn't know anything about clinical depression then. Today, a professional might say that she "self medicated" with alcohol.

We never knew just how <u>much </u>liquor she was consuming until mid January, 1969, when she was hospitalized with devastating injuries caused by a freak accident.

THE ACCIDENT

That month the Grand Traverse region received record breaking snowfall. During nearly a week of blizzards, repetitive onslaughts of snow closed schools and offices. Doré was housebound. For her safety, I urged her not to attempt to walk in deep snow or, even if shoveled, on lumpy slippery sidewalks.

"Okay, I won't go out," she assured me in our daily phone conversations. "I have plenty of food here in the apartment and I'll be fine."

When the skies finally cleared and the sun shone again, she assumed that the streets were passable enough for her to venture across and down the block to gather fresh milk and eggs from the neighborhood grocery store. The streets <u>had</u> been plowed – enough for cars to pass – but Doré didn't realize that the plows had simply piled the enormous quantities of snow high along the sides of the pavements to await removal.

That sparkling morning, she reveled in the crisp fresh air as she stepped carefully off the curb to peer around the towering snowdrifts for oncoming traffic. We later reconstructed what happened next. Apparently she believed that she was stepping into the parking lane. The driver of a pickup truck had no time or space to avoid hitting her.

"She stepped right in front of me," he told me in horror and regret while we waited for an ambulance.

A crushed pelvis, broken hip, broken ribs and multiple contusions not only required hospitalization; she was strapped on a board within a six-foot tall wheel-like contraption called a Stryker Frame. It allowed the nurses and aides to turn her broken body to prevent bed sores, while avoiding further injury. Fortunately, she was sedated during two weeks on that rack, while the initial healing took place.

When she was able to lie in a regular hospital bed, I wept with relief. I had been so afraid that she would die. Jim happened to be in the midst of redecorating our living and dining rooms. Gently, he kept urging me to decide on paint colors. While in a haze of exhaustion and a kind of psychic stasis, I had barely been able to decide what clothes to put on to go back to the hospital each harrowing day, much less such a long-range decision as that! So, he used his own good judgment and we enjoyed off-white walls the rest of our years in that house.

Once we knew that my mother would live, we expected an upward trajectory toward recovery. But an unforeseen development astonished all of us, including her doctor, "Bud" Sweeney.

Doré began to have chills and sweats and frightening hallucinations. She would cry out to me to shoo the cats off her bed. She saw shadowy figures not visible to anyone else and complained of strange noises no one else could hear. Amusing to hospital staff, these apparitions were clearly terrifying to her. Soon Dr. Sweeney realized that she was having "delirium tremens," the consequence of withdrawal from alcohol. His diagnosis was confirmed by a discovery I made.

"When I checked her mail for bills that needed paying," I told him, "I found out that she has a standing account with a nearby liquor store."

"Oh, no wonder," he sighed. "But, I thought that was illegal."

"Me too. I called them and they said that while it is against the law to charge alcohol, it is not illegal to establish an account and pay in advance."

During the worst winter blizzards, the store had been delivering all the liquor Doré wanted. I was shopping for groceries and household products, but she never wrote whiskey on the list. I would have known how much she was drinking.

She must have been starting to drink as soon as "the sun was over the yard arm" (somewhere in the world at least) and never stopping until she was just short of 'blotto" – still able to open the hide-a-bed and crawl between the sheets. Blotto was her word for drunk. It was appropriate, because her aim undoubtedly was to blot out all thought and slide blissfully into nothingness until about noon the next day.

The miseries we witnessed during her withdrawal were a wake up call for us, and for her doctor. While she believed our descriptions of what she had been through, she had no memory of it and said nothing when he suggested that maybe she should quit drinking.

At least she survived, and began to recover from her injuries. After about a month in bed, she was allowed to get up and sit briefly in a chair. As soon as she was helped to walk very slowly along the hospital corridor, we began planning for her homecoming. She clearly would not be able to return to her second floor apartment any time soon.

"Oh Mommy, it will be no problem for us to convert Jim's office into a bedroom for you," I said cheerfully. The office was right off the living room

"Heck yes," Jim echoed jovially. "I can easily move my desk and files down to the rec room."

"We can set up a bedside commode until you can use a walker to get to the bathroom," I went on.

247

While Doré could surely appreciate the love behind our plans, her grim, tight-jawed expression told me how much she dreaded inconveniencing us, being so reliant on us and having to live within our active, noisy household of ringing phones, four children, their friends and several pets. Perhaps, also, she assumed we would ration her drinks.

Without confiding her fears to me, she became increasingly frantic about having to be so dependent. Years earlier, she had written Lurry that she dreaded the idea of my having to take care of her in her old age. So, even as she acknowledged the need to accept our help until she recovered enough to climb stairs or until we found her a ground floor apartment, she was silently "stewing" about it.

Her expression for worrying was particularly apt. She stewed herself into bleeding ulcers. They were beyond any medicinal relief, and her condition was grave.

AN OVERWHELMING CHOICE

One morning her doctor, "Bud" Sweeney, motioned me into the hospital corridor to tell me, "The only way to stop the internal bleeding is to operate to repair the damage. Truthfully, Judy, in her severely weakened state, I really don't think she can survive the surgery."

In the six years of her life that she had been his patient, this compassionate man had come to know Doré well enough to understand that her having worried herself into stomach ulcers was, in a way, a death wish.

"It is your decision, Judy," Dr. Sweeney told me, "but I seriously doubt if she will make it through a long operation. I really wonder whether we should put her through it..."

"But, if you don't operate," I asked, "what then?"

"If we don't stop the loss of blood, she will probably die."

"You mean soon?"

"Yes, fairly soon, I would say – within the week.

Seeing my shock, Bud encouraged me to follow him to a corner lounge where we sat down while he gently urged me to be realistic.

"I have suspected for some time that Doré is not a happy woman," he said, his dark eyes shadowed with sadness. "I think you know that, too, but it's harder for you to admit it."

"Yeah," I sighed. "You may be right.... But I don't know if she wants to <u>die</u>."

"I think she does," he said softly. "I don't think that she has found life much worth living for a quite a while – and now that we know how much she has been drowning her troubles..." he trailed off.

After hearing his assurance that he would give Doré morphine as the end approached, so she would feel no pain, I agreed to think about it overnight, talk to Jim, and let the doctor know in the morning.

After agonizing for hours, I had to admit that my mother's life had been a burden to her for some time. She pulled herself together for family gatherings or when she stayed with the children, but other long days dragged by. With no hope of more "flashing moments," she was using whiskey to blot out reality.

I had to face it. It would really be a kindness to let her go. She was drifting in and out of consciousness by then, but if I had been able to ask her what she wanted, I feel sure that she would have agreed.

In the past, when the illness of a friend weighed on her spirit, Doré wrote to Lurry, "How entirely I agree with you about wishing we could know when our days are numbered, and being frankly told by someone. I don't think that would be very hard to take, really, I am definitely without any yen to live on for decades. I have spent a mighty amount of me in making my days happy and a bit useful. I never give in to being sorry for myself, and I do extend my dreams into the lives of my small family and my loved students, and so loneliness sits just beyond the days, with a silly frown, because I won't let it in. But living to be ninety is not my idea of happiness or an achievement!"

In the morning, I made the decision, and told Dr. Sweeney not to operate.

I can't remember if death came in three days or five, but I sat by her bedside almost constantly as the end approached. I couldn't always tell whether she could hear me or understand, but I held her hand and talked.

"Oh Mommy, I'm <u>so</u> sorry you have to go through all this! I so wish that there had been some way you could have been spared so much pain and fear." Faltering as I dabbed at stinging eyes, I struggled past the tightness in my throat to say things I failed to say often enough before.

"I just want you to know that we all love you SO much," I stammered. "You've been a wonderful mother to me...I hope you know how much I appreciate all that you have given me and everything you do for me….and for the kids…You're a wonderful grandmother to the kids…. I love you…. I love you…."

Finally, one afternoon, her eyes flew open and she asked, quite audibly, "This is it, isn't it?"

"Yes, I think so. I hope so, Mommy, so you have no more suffers."

Nodding, with a soft smile, she closed her eyes. Her breathing slowed to what seemed like minutes between breaths and, a little later stopped altogether.

A close friend thought that my saying "I hope so" was cruel. But I know that if Doré heard me, she understood it the way I meant it – that she had struggled long enough and was free to go.

I don't regret my words, but I do wish I had put my arms around her. We hardly ever hugged. I think she followed the modeling of her generation, which I saw among the Marches and the Gosses as well. Years later, when Lurry told me how good my hugs felt to her aged body, I wished that I had hugged my mother.

Doré died on March 16th, two months after the accident, and just about three months short of her 71st birthday. Her death was a devastating blow to her beloved sister.

"She was too young to die," Lurry sobbed over the telephone. "Oh, too soon, too soon," she kept repeating.

At 40, I did not think of 71 as young. I saw my mother as a resigned old woman, whose step was slow, whose interests were narrow, and who preferred her solitary routines to seeking any new connections. Although I couldn't begin to imagine my own life without my mother, I was willing to let her go because I believed that she had lived a long time – long enough, I thought. What I mourned was not just my loss but hers. I grieved for whatever it was that had kept her from engaging in life after retirement.

In a 1922 letter, she wrote of reading <u>Gitanjali and Fruit-gathering</u> by Rabindranath Tagore. "The words I love best," she said, "begin, 'When I go from hence let this be my parting word, that what I have seen has been unsurpassable'."

Knowing that she could no longer envision surpassing scenes for herself and had long been ready to be through with living, I was at peace with my decision.

How others saw her

For every life, there is more than one truth. If a woman has two or more children, each son or daughter will remember her differently–often quite differently. Friends' memories of a woman can be starkly unlike the way her children saw her. As an only child, I couldn't compare my impressions with a sibling.

Thus the letters that Doré's friends wrote to me after her death meant more to me than routine condolences. It was touching to read that she told others how much she treasured me as a daughter and valued me as a woman. Several mentioned that she often told them how lucky she felt to have me – and later "all six Gambles."

It was also heartwarming to be reminded of Doré's light-hearted and unconventional early years and of all the quirky, creative, cosmopolitan characters who were drawn to her and who certainly enriched my child-hood. I learned that she kept in contact with a wide circle of friends – from an ambassador to a char woman.

I heard from friends she met with Ben in Detroit who shared memories of "those beautiful Chinese costumes she always wore" and "her wonderful stories about growing up in the Orient."

"Pentwater weekends were the highlight of our summers," wrote one man. "She was such a marvelous cook and hostess. I'll always remember those intense conversations far into the evening. And those chili suppers down on the beach were so completely different from anything in our city lives."

Chaney, the orderly from University Hospital, said she would never forget their heart-to-heart talks over take-out chicken or Chinese chow in our small apartment over a dry cleaner. That following summer "the boys" in the Pentwater post office let me know how much they missed her friendly banter, as did scads of other villagers.

It was also meaningful to hear from a half dozen Fine Arts Department colleagues who wrote of her "dedication to running a tight ship" and her "unfailing willingness to try to get us whatever we needed and solve any problems she could."

"When she retired," another wrote, "we really learned how much she had done silently, beyond our notice."

I loved learning about the insights she passed along to a generation of grad students. "She always told me to believe in myself," one said. "Without her encouragement, I don't know if I could have made it through some of those tough courses."

"She always remembered our names and asked us to call her Doré," wrote another. "Her desk was an oasis. When I would come into the study hall on a Monday, she always greeted me and remembered something I'd told her – like asking how my parents' visit had gone. She made me feel like a person, not just another faceless student."

HER "FINAL JOURNEY"

It had always been my mother's wish that no funeral or memorial service be held after her death. She found such occasions gruesomely depressing and she did not want her relatives or friends to feel obligated to travel "to pay their respects." Despite a few raised eyebrows, I made no arrangements for a gathering.

I finessed the issue by writing, at the end of her obituary, "There will be no local services." Since this was published in The Ann Arbor News as well as the Traverse City Record-Eagle, people who read it in each city could assume that something proper was being done in the other location.

It wasn't until a few years later that I realized that a memorial service is not for the person who has died. It is for the living. It is a way to bring, by sharing memories in community, some healing and closure to those who mourn their loss. But Doré had been utterly firm about her wishes. Without even understanding, much less considering, my own needs or those of my family, I honored her memory by honoring her desire.

And one decision that I made on my own would have delighted her.

I knew how much she hated what she called "the ghoulish ritual" of embalming, dressing and painting a dead body for "viewing." She particularly found that custom "barbaric" when a body was "to be sent on its way in flames."

As she once told Lurry, "I am sure that Judy and Jim will spare my aged bones that indignity, regardless of what people may say. It can be resisted, and it is the business only of those who are close to the spirit of the one who has died."

We made Doré's wishes very clear to the funeral home that picked up her body from the hospital. So I was unprepared when the director phoned to ask me to bring over an outfit of clothes for them to dress her in.

"What?" I gasped, "I told you she wanted to be cremated! She is not to be embalmed!"

"Oh yes," whispered the well-meaning Mr. Martinson, "We are carrying out your directives. But we will be transporting her to the crematory in Grand Rapids…"

"Okay – so don't you just wrap the body in a sheet or something? Why would you need clothes?"

The poor man's anguish was palpable over the phone line.

"Don't you want Mother to look her best for her final journey?" he tried.

"Who on earth is going to see her?" I blurted as he stammered on… "Oh, all right," I gave in. "We will bring over some clothes."

As Jim and I shared our amazement at this unexpected request, we came up with a sneakily perverse idea — an idea that we knew Doré would love. Jim went over to her apartment and selected a bright red slacks suit that had been one of her favorite outfits and dutifully delivered it to the funeral home. If those unctuous men who received it were horrified, they were well trained not to show it.

The slacks suit was decorated with small brass studs along a yoke, front and back. I wished that my mother could have worn it again on some thrilling, exotic final journey. But imagining those bright round rivets scattered among her ashes gave me a vitally needed chuckle. And I like to imagine that Doré was chortling with glee.

幸运 # EPILOGUE

> *"Life is not a given, but a priceless gift. One day something will steal it from us, a seizure in the night or a driver in the morning, but that doesn't diminish its value. On the contrary, fragility and impermanence ensure life's preciousness. We can truly love only that which one day we must lose."*
> — F. Forrester Church in <u>Everyday Miracles</u> (Harper & Row 1988)

"ACCEPT WITH GRACE"

I was once asked whether, had it been possible in my childhood, I would have traded my exotic cultured mother, for whom I was something of a burden, for a simple homebody who would have just spent time with me. I said I couldn't choose, because I'd want it all.

Today, I could choose to remember only her reclusive years of drinking herself into nightly oblivion. But there was so much more to my Doré than that. I am so thankful for her sensitivity to beauty, her creativity, her love of learning, her lack of bitterness and her sense of whimsy.

I remain profoundly grateful for her lifelong commitment to me. As a girl I took it for granted, because that was her intent. But from her letters to Lurry I learned that my mother had private, inner yearnings that I never recognized nor appreciated. I wish that she had been able to follow her own heart and experience those far flung adventures she dreamed about. I have sometimes wondered what our lives would have been like if she had "tucked me under her arm" and taken me "home" to China. Yet I am certainly thankful that she didn't "toot off" around the world <u>alone</u> and leave me to be raised by others.

I am grateful for her fatalistic Chinese outlook on life. "Accept with grace," she would say, as if that was all there was to it – all that was needed to cope with shattering illness and loss. But, when her letters moved me to think again about her life, I realized that acceptance was only the first step. She drew on some inner reservoir of strength and courage and took the next step – resistance. Don Goss said it perfectly: "That's my braver."

I now believe that Don's death was the single greatest tragedy in Dore's life. Her diabetes, her two years on TB wards with disfiguring surgery and a paralyzed arm were undeniable hardships. The loss of my father was overwhelming because he left her to raise his child alone. But Don's death was the last straw. It was more devastating, I think, not only because it came at a time when she was so dependent on his love, but because he loved her differently.

Don's job was just a means of earning a living. He was not absorbed in his work the way Ben March was in his career. Ben had an all-consuming passion for his scholarly and creative pursuits. He surely loved Doré in his way, but not with the depth of adoration she craved.

When she and Ben met, Doré admired his intelligence and character and, doubtless, his good looks. That he had fallen in love with China, her adored homeland, must surely have been a large part of his appeal and the bond between them. But she didn't anticipate his growing ambition. To her credit, she never tried to change him, even when his time-consuming interests threatened his life.

For Don Goss, on the other hand, Doré was central to his being. Not only was she adored, she was needed – in a way she hadn't known before. The feeling of being deeply cherished and vitally needed is a potent combination for any woman. For Doré, it was the breath of life.

Although Doré and Don lived together for only three months, and hospital visits were like chaperoned dates, Don's devotion did not wane. Some say that intense passion rarely lasts in any relationship. But devotion does. Don also demonstrated his commitment to Doré in the way he rose to the challenge of parenting her 12-year-old daughter.

In her later years, Doré rarely spoke of Don. As she explained it to Lurry: "Don loved me as few women have been adored, and I could have gone on giving him the peace and security he needed, but with Ben's daughter close, it is him I reach back towards and miss the most. There are few men as great as Ben."

True. But, despite the folly of such speculation, I believe that, had Don lived to companion my mother for the rest of her life, her story would have ended much differently.

Lurry and I buried Doré's ashes under the blue spruce she planted in her Pentwater back yard in 1932. The magnificent tree towered over us as we said goodbye. I had hoped to keep her beloved house in the family, but when forced to sell it, I was glad that it went to a kindred soul. The buyer was a lifelong summer resorter who felt the same way that my mother and I did about Pentwater.

We let most of the furniture go with the house, but we moved treasured Chinese pieces to our home in Traverse City. Jim took over the use of my father's enormous desk. After our divorce, I used it for many years, and then passed it along to my daughter Jenny, who shares it with her husband.

The large red lacquer zhou-gwi that was always my favorite piece continues to be a touchstone. As a child, I imagined hiding inside that armoire-like cabinet, not to escape harm, but to save it in case anyone tried to steal it. Today, I still love and protect it in my home, where it stands as a symbol of a unique heritage.

In common with millions of bereaved daughters, it took me many months before I stopped reaching for the telephone to tell my mother some bit of news. Much as I yearned to talk to her, I'm glad that she didn't have to hear that our sweet son Scott Ben drowned when he was not quite nine. It was one heartbreak she was spared. Yet, as I met that tragedy, Doré's voice was always in my ears. "Life goes on."

Of later milestones that I do wish she could have witnessed, two stand out. She would have been proud to see me go to work. And she would have rejoiced in the happiness I found, after age 50, with my second husband, Ethan Davis. Lucky for me, Lurry was still part of my life.

My aunt adored Ethan and was proud of my career. My move from Michigan to New Jersey put us an hour's drive apart for the last six years of her life. She spent many holidays at our home, and we often joined her in Manhattan for plays, museums, lunches and dinners. Lurry said that she thought of me as "the daughter she never had," and she offered me an understanding that transcended the difference in our ages and life choices. Her death at 84, from congestive heart disease, left me with another unfillable void.

...

My mother and I long held the hope that we could travel to China together. By the time I graduated from college, the Communists had closed her homeland, Doré's health had deteriorated, and neither of us had any discretionary income. Although our dream never came true, I think she'd be pleased to know that I was finally able to go.

In my imagination, I see Doré sitting on the back terrace at Pentwater, releasing wisps of a cigarette's smoke and listening. It's nearly twilight but her prized lemon lilies are still open along the low brick wall.

"I'm so thrilled that you and Ethan got to Peking," she says, tears pooling in her eyes.

"I felt you with me," I tell her. "And Daddy Ben too. To walk where you walked, along those old hutong alleys you told me about – somehow, it filled in an emptiness I'd always felt."

"Oh Pooh, I'm so glad..."

"And there's more," I rush on. "I learned that the Freer-Sackler Galleries wanted what they call the collected papers of Benjamin March."

"All those cartons you hung onto for years?"

"Yes! The archivists tell me that scholars quickly found his journals and photographs useful in their study of Westerners in China during the twenties..."

"Wonderful!" She pauses, musing. Then suddenly, "But will your grandchildren get to see them?"

"After putting on white gloves," I say grinning.

"Imagine that!" she laughs. Taking another drag on her cigarette, she asks, "So – what's this about a book you've written?"

"It's <u>your</u> story, Mommy."

There's a silence while she rolls the glowing end off her cigarette into the ashtray. Rising, she says, "Well – that calls for a drink."

I stay where I am – a little anxious but hopeful.

Returning from the kitchen with two libations, she says, "I'm so proud of you."

After lifting her favorite cobalt glass in a toast, Doré opens her copy, smiles across at me and starts to read of the first time she sailed to China.

幸运

A FEW MORE POEMS
BY DOROTHY ROWE

<u>Rain</u>

I like to sit behind the oilcloth curtain
Of a rickshaw when it rains.
I see nothing but the light
Of the rickshaw lantern
Like dabs of gold sealing wax
On the wet wheels that go on and on.
I cannot look over the top of the curtain
Unless I stretch my neck.
So I sit low and hidden.
Where am I?
All the familiar road, unseen,
Is suddenly quite strange.
I like it so.
I listen to the slap of wet sandals in mud,
And the swish of the straw cape
The rickshaw runner wears.
—1923

<u>Needle Pagoda</u>

"Heaven above, Hangchow below,"
The ancients said, and they should know.
They left a pagoda standing there,
Like a needle piercing the upper air.
And it joins Hangchow by its magic art
To the moon and the stars and the sunset's heart.
—29 July 1925

Moon Gold

The Three Pools of the Moon's Reflection
Caught the gold the fifth month's moon,
Full rounded, tossed to them.

The spirits knew this,
They who lurked in goldless depths.
A poet knew this,
Su, who put the stone pagodas there.
We knew this,
We who laughed as gold dripped from our hands.

Who would not come from half the world away
To catch the gold the fifth month's full moon
Tosses into the Three Pools of the Moon's Reflection?
—West Lake – 9 July 1925

An Old Wooden Buddha

The patience of willow trees waiting to leaf,
And the pity of rain for a field that is parched
Rest on the face of the Buddha.
His uncovered breast
Is as polished old amber,
It is soothing and thrilling to touch.
And his garments rest gently
In folds of ineffable peace.
Both the slender brown hands
Are quiet before him.
He sits "a jewel in the heart of the lotus,"
Bringing calm and great glory
To those who silently watch his face.
—Peking 1925

Desire

In a little roadside shrine
Where sit two gods
With fearful, grinning faces
Black with beards and eyebrows
Of real hair,
I saw a girl child
Walk as if each step
Were burning torture
For her new bound feet.
I saw her dark eyes
Wet with tears.

She put a pair of satin shoes
Three inches long,
Before the fiercer, blacker god.
I saw her lips beseech the god
But in her eyes was fear.
And thus the most devout
Must ask for tiny feet,
For golden lilies.
Thus they show the gods
The smallness of the shoes
That they would wear,
And are afraid
Of that they most desire.
—Nanking 1923

 # ACKNOWLEDGMENTS

I am profoundly grateful:

- To Karen Anderson, deft writer and content editor, for reading the first "finished" draft of this book and continuing to give generously of her time and talent to suggest ways of improving it;

- To Abelard Montague, copy doctor, for meticulous attention that gave a whole new meaning to line editing;

- To Tristine Rainer, whose book <u>Your Life As Story</u> was as good as a college course;

- To Nan Davis for painstakingly scanning fragile family photographs, and to Edi Taylor-Richards for expertly cropping and uploading them to the publisher;

- To Ruth Steinberg, Terry Church, Nancy Owen Nelson and Nancy Turich for their inspiration and professional encouragement;

- To Edie Shepherd, Jill Bush and other 'Write On" authors; Linda Goonewardene, Kitty McConkie and many other Unitarian Universalists; "Uncommon Women," "Goddesses," "Old Broads," "Gaia Sisters," "Book Talkers," family members - and Carlos Parra – for years of supportive cheerleading.

- To the editors and designers at Langdon Street Press for professional publishing services that exceeded my expectations;

- Finally, to my beloved children: Christopher James Gamble and his wife Dorothy, and Gretchen (née Cyndi Gamble) Hopkins and her husband Peter, who always knew I could do it

- And most of all to my cherished husband Ethan Davis, who patiently listened, read, offered honest opinions, read more, listened repeatedly, read again with a "fine tooth comb" and loved me throughout.

Judith March Davis
2009

幸运

ABOUT THE AUTHOR

As the only child of Dorothy Rowe and Benjamin March, Judith March Davis is uniquely qualified to tell this story. She grew up surrounded by the treasured artifacts brought by her parents from China to America, and she was profoundly influenced by the Asian outlook that shaped her mother's life. After two years at Oberlin College, Judy earned a BA degree, *magna cum laude*, in Art History from the University of Michigan and became the mother of four children. Her professional writing began in Traverse City, Michigan, where she was a reporter and section editor for the regional daily newspaper, a civic leader and later executive director of the city Arts Council. After moving to the east coast, she was a senior staff writer for the News Service at Rutgers, the State University of New Jersey, and later director of public relations on the Rutgers-Newark Campus. Following early retirement, she wrote freelance magazine features until 1996, when she moved with her husband Ethan Davis to Prescott, Arizona. Lay leadership in Unitarian Universalist congregations has also been central to her adult life.

If you enjoyed this book, please encourage other readers to visit the website at
www.pagodadreamer.com.